MW00563812

RUSSIA'S ROAD TO WAR WITH UKRAINE

SAMIR PURI

RUSSIA'S ROAD TO WAR WITH UKRAINE

INVASION AMIDST THE ASHES OF EMPIRES

Biteback Publishing

First published in Great Britain in 2022 by
Biteback Publishing Ltd, London
Copyright © Samir Puri 2022

ISBN 978-1-78590-770-8

10 9 8 7 6 5 4 3 2 1

A CIP catalogue record for this book is available from the British Library.

Set in Minion Pro and Trade Gothic

Printed and bound in Great Britain by
CPI Group (UK) Ltd, Croydon CR0 4YY

CONTENTS

INTRODUCTION

PUTIN AND ZELENSKY

'Just putting ourselves in coffins and waiting for foreign soldiers to come is not something we are prepared to do.' President Volodymyr Zelensky of Ukraine was in full oratorical flight in Munich as he addressed Western dignitaries. It was 19 February 2022, an audacious date for Zelensky to have stepped out of his capital city, Kyiv, since war clouds were thickening over Ukraine and the storm could break at any moment. 'We will defend our beautiful land, with or without the support of partners.' Support is precisely what he was there to ask for, and why he had risked the trip: 'This is your contribution to the security of Europe and the world. Where Ukraine has been a reliable shield for eight years.'[1]

Eight years was the time during which Ukraine had battled Russia's proxy forces in the eastern Donbas region, but this time things looked truly bleak. To the north, east and south of Ukraine, Russia's legions were poised to invade. The American and British governments now broadcast regular warnings about an imminent major Russian attack, but these countries also ruled out sending their own soldiers to fight alongside the Ukrainians. While Ukraine had friends aplenty, it had no treaty allies whose armies were obliged to defend it. Ukraine's bid to join the North Atlantic Treaty Organization military alliance had stalled many years beforehand, leaving it bereft of NATO's collective defence guarantee.

Sitting at his desk some 850 kilometres from Kyiv in the Kremlin, President Vladimir Putin finally revealed his hand in a televised evening address on 21 February. Having denied for months that Russia would commit to battle the troops it had amassed around Ukraine, he now said the opposite. Flanked by a flag depicting Russia's imperial motif of a two-headed eagle, he claimed that 'the situation in Donbas has reached a critical, acute stage', wilfully ignoring the fact that Russia had transformed the Donbas into a war zone in the first place in 2014.

Putin continued, 'I consider it necessary to take a long overdue decision and to immediately recognise the independence and sovereignty of the Donetsk People's Republic and the Luhansk People's Republic,' naming the Donbas proxy statelets propped up by Russia. But there were far bigger issues at stake: 'I would like to emphasise again that Ukraine is not just a neighbouring country for us. It is an inalienable part of our own history, culture and spiritual space.'[2] The temerity, Putin conveyed – how could these Ukrainians, whom he called 'comrades' and 'relatives', ever have contemplated forging their own independent path away from Russia?

The tale of these Presidents, Zelensky and Putin, encapsulates some of the deeper matters at hand. 'Volodymyr' is the Ukrainian equivalent of the Russian name 'Vladimir', and both names mean 'ruler of the world' (as derived from *volodity myrom*). While the Ukrainian and Russian languages are separate east Slavic languages, they are in part mutually intelligible (only in part, however: one should say *dyakuyu* to thank Ukrainians and *spasibo* to thank

Russians, for instance, and pronounce the softer *Kyiv* in Ukrainian rather than the harder *Kiev* in Russian).[3] Just as the Ukrainian and Russian languages share a lineage but are distinct in their evolution, Zelensky and Putin were both born in the Soviet Union but could not be further apart in what they now represent.

The almost seventy-year-old Putin seemed enraptured by an apocalyptic nostalgia for the Soviet and the Tsarist incarnations of Russian empire. His prior career as a KGB intelligence officer was deeply scarred by the end of the Soviet Union. Now entering his third decade of dominating Russian politics, Putin retained an iron grip at home and a fixation on restoring Russia's old spheres of influence abroad.

Conversely, Zelensky was just eleven years old when the Berlin Wall fell in 1989. The now 44-year-old Zelensky had transcended his past career as a light-hearted television actor to become a modernising national leader, fully intent on speeding up his country's own transcendence from its Soviet past.

For several tense days in February 2022, prior to Russia's all-out invasion of Ukraine, Zelensky and Putin duelled with words.

In response to Putin's televised address, Zelensky appealed to the people of Russia. 'We are separated by more than 2,000 kilometres of mutual borders, along which 200,000 of your soldiers and 1,000 armoured vehicles are standing,' he said, before imploring, 'You are told we hate Russian culture. How can one hate a culture? Neighbours always enrich each other culturally; however, that doesn't make them a single whole, it doesn't dissolve us into you. We are different, but that is not a reason to be enemies.'[4] Alas, the Putin regime's strict media controls meant there was scant chance of ordinary Russians hearing Zelensky's plea.

In an early morning televised address on 24 February – a day that will live on in infamy – Putin announced a 'special military operation' was now under way to 'demilitarise' Ukraine. 'We have been left no other option to protect Russia and our people, but for the one that we will be forced to use today.' This was Putin's pretext for Russia to attack Ukraine: 'The situation requires us to take decisive and immediate action. The People's Republics of Donbas turned to Russia with a request for help.'[5] Although there were some people in the Donetsk and Luhansk People's Republics who wanted to join Russia, others in areas of the Donbas still under Ukrainian government control did not. It was an entirely self-generated reason created by Putin to explain his invasion.

The spectacle that now unfolded, of tens of thousands of Russian troops shooting their way into a neighbouring country that had done nothing to provoke them, shocked the world. Within just two days, a spearhead of Russia's advance forces had reached Kyiv's outskirts, using Belarusian territory to shorten their advance to Ukraine's capital. At this moment, Zelensky may have been forgiven for buckling under the pressure, fleeing perhaps, but his was the opposite reaction, holding his nerve during the chaos and bloodshed, and inspiring Ukraine not to capitulate. Zelensky's next messages were recorded in a dimly lit Kyiv street, rallying his nation: 'Glory to our defenders! Glory to Ukraine! Glory to heroes!'

And so, battle was joined, not just around Kyiv but across much of Ukraine. Russian forces had stormed into Ukraine from multiple directions, not only the Donbas, with the initial aim of deposing Kyiv's government. An astonishing Ukrainian defensive effort brought the Russian military advance on Kyiv to a standstill a month later. This left the war to settle into a slower grind in which Russia shifted its focus to conquering swathes of southern and eastern Ukraine, instead of its capital.

* * *

While it is too soon to judge the consequences of this war, it is never too early to pose questions around how and why the war happened in the first place. Some narratives have, at the time of writing, already gained currency, valorising plucky Ukraine for its defence against the odds, while condemning Russia for launching a callous war of imperial aggrandisement, but there are many more facets to reflect on than this.

Russia's invasion has undoubtedly brought tragedy to Ukraine, killing and injuring tens of thousands of people and forcing millions to flee the maelstrom by becoming refugees. The butcher's bill of the war is immense and continues to rise. Before triumphalism kicks in around romanticised notions of a smaller democracy fighting off a bullying autocratic behemoth, we would do well to pause and recall the words of soldier-poet Edmund Blunden, who said of the Battle of the Somme that took place in 1916: neither side 'had won, nor could win, the War. The War had won.'[6]

This is the story of a tragedy. Of how Russia's relations with Ukraine moved from the constricting embrace of empire to the arm's length handshake of peaceful independence to Russia resorting to the flailing fists of war.

There was no inevitability in this journey of thirty years, which began with the Soviet Union's final demise in December 1991, and which need not have culminated in Russia's all-out invasion in February 2022. Posing such a hypothetical may seem pointless once the invasion was upon Ukraine; but doing so implores us to ask deeper questions about the war's origins, to delve beyond obvious headline narratives, and to consider what the recent past tells us about how Ukraine can plot a path to a more stable future.

INVASION: HOW HAD IT COME TO THIS?

On the surface, the Russia–Ukraine war seems to be a straightforward parable of good versus evil, reducible in its barest essentials to Putin's malevolent imperial ambition and to Ukraine's prior failure to join NATO. Nothing absolves Putin of launching the invasion and, frankly, he did not come across as a man who wanted to avoid responsibility. In the weeks leading up to the invasion, Putin appeared to be looking for any excuse to invade, subjugate, partition or conquer Ukraine. Moreover, Putin enjoyed total command and control over the Russian armed forces, so there is no puzzle as to who gave the order to invade. But, while Putin's malevolence is an essential part of explaining the war, it is far from sufficient for unpicking the multifarious reasons behind why such a precarious situation arose in the first place between neighbouring Ukraine and Russia.

Here are some of the questions that an enquiring mind ought to pose to examine different facets of this war. What were its wider causes? Was Russia and Ukraine's cataclysmic falling out inevitable and what were the missed chances to avert Russia's invasion? More controversially, what was the West's role in the story regarding the support (or lack of) offered to Ukraine prior to the invasion? And more profoundly, would it have ever been possible to build a free and protected Ukraine that was not menaced by Russia, given the permanence of their adjacency in the wake of an imperial collapse? Consequently, what lessons does the past hold when it comes to considering the future viability of a sovereign and safe Ukraine? These are the themes that are addressed in this book.

If there is a core message, it is that Ukraine has been terribly let down in the years preceding the invasion – albeit in *very* different ways – by Russia but also by leading Western countries. Russia is undoubtedly the malefactor, bringing bloodshed and suffering to Ukraine at the behest of Putin's vision of a greater Russia. The aim is not to offer a *justification* for Russia's military offensive; only to offer a deeper *explanation* as to how Ukraine became so imperilled. For their part, some Western countries in NATO and the European Union had, over many years, unrealistically raised Ukraine's expectations of joining these bodies, leaving Ukraine without formal allies but badly exposed to Russian aggression.

Despite spirited attempts to join NATO in the late 2000s in particular, Ukraine never reached the shelter of NATO's nuclear umbrella in time to protect itself from the torrent of Russian bombs. When the invasion came, several NATO states dispatched copious military supplies, and provided intelligence to Ukraine, while vocalising moral opposition to Russia's aggression; but ultimately, they watched from the side-lines as they invasion began. The United States warned Russia that its military would 'defend every inch of NATO territory'[7] but was resolute that US soldiers and pilots would not fight to defend Ukraine, lest they provoke a direct NATO–Russia war, which could lead to nuclear annihilation.

The NATO nations helped in other ways: military training given to Ukraine's armed forces since 2015 by the USA, UK, Canada and others was essential to boost its ability to fight the Russians. And when the time came to do so, NATO nations offered vital arm's length assistance to Ukraine's war effort. Despite this, Ukraine was ultimately let down by NATO in the decade and a half before the invasion, and this is a question worth revisiting in light of present events. Was it fair for the USA in particular to have raised Ukraine's hope of joining NATO when the alliance was never likely to deliver this?

Complex situations such as the Russia–Ukraine war tend to have multiple drivers and causes. Some are slow burning while others are more proximate. Those who prefer a simplified polemical moral case, based on highlighting only the most obvious causes while ignoring others, need to look elsewhere.

As the American novelist F. Scott Fitzgerald wrote, 'The test of a first-rate intelligence is the ability to hold two opposing ideas in mind at the same time and still retain the ability to function.' It is perfectly possible to see the blood on Putin's hands for this war *while also* understanding how NATO expansion, and how it was handled by the USA from the 1990s onwards, exacerbated what has now become a terminal rupture in Russia–Ukraine relations. All of these factors and many more besides are dissected in the pages that follow.

*   *   *

This is the story of Russia's road to war with Ukraine, and the making of a tragedy that will define so many things for a long time to come, from the grandest geopolitical debates to the humblest personal stories of Ukrainians. No matter what the war's ultimate aftermath entails, understanding the backstory to Russia's invasion of Ukraine in February 2022 will remain an essential undertaking.

Eight years before Russia's all-out invasion, in 2014, Crimea had been annexed while Russia waged 'hybrid war' in the Donbas (meaning that it outsourced some of the fighting to its proxy forces, superficially hiding its involvement). Ten years before that, in 2004, a surge of democratic optimism overtook parts of Ukraine in the Orange Revolution, which accelerated Putin's paranoia that Russia was losing influence in Ukraine. I worked in Ukraine in response to both events, and throughout this narrative I draw on my personal experiences to recount what happened. Each crisis progressively outdid the last in terms of its gravity and, looking back, it is akin to a slow-moving train heading to calamity. The protagonists did not experience it like that, of course, which is vital to keep in mind.

It is also important to contend with the legacies of imperial dominance and atrocity that stretch back in time, linking Russia and Ukraine in a historical melodrama that influences the present. To tackle these matters, I draw on my work on how all empires have an afterlife that haunts modern relations between former empires and their past subjects. Too often, this 'anti-colonial' framing has been more liberally applied to certain historical empires over others, with Russia's landed empire ignored in favour of the British, French or other sea-faring colonial empires. Redressing this imbalance is a foundational step in explaining Russia's war in Ukraine, and it is where this book begins.

CHAPTER 1

ASHES OF EMPIRES

A REFLECTION ON LIVING WITH THE PAST

PUTIN'S HISTORICAL HALLUCINATION

Perhaps the coronavirus pandemic had left Putin with far too much time on his hands to catch up on his historical reading, sequestered in an echo chamber of views that revelled in tales of Ukraine's past fealty to Russia. Or perhaps, as Putin awaited his seventieth birthday in October 2022, he was thinking about how his legacy as Russia's latest Tsar in all but name would stack up against the conquests of his predecessors. Whatever his motivations for choosing this moment to unleash wanton slaughter, Putin's view of history contains vital clues to both his framing of the situation and his state of mind at the time.

In the estimation of the CIA director Bill Burns, Putin was of late exhibiting a 'very combustible combination of grievance and ambition and insecurity'.[1] Grievance certainly inflected a rambling essay that was published under Putin's name on the Kremlin's website in July 2021, entitled 'On the Historical Unity of Russians and

Ukrainians'. It is worth revisiting this essay, since it was a bright red flag warning that something wicked was coming Ukraine's way.

The essay proclaimed that Russians and Ukrainians are 'one people – a single whole' because they inhabit 'essentially the same historical and spiritual space'. Why was Putin so confident in holding this view? His interpretation of history. 'Certainly, it is impossible to cover all the developments that have taken place over more than a thousand years,' he admitted, 'but I will focus on the key, pivotal moments that are important for us to remember, both in Russia and Ukraine.'[2] Having afforded himself a 7,000-word allowance, Putin delivered nothing short of a manifesto for Russia's renewed imperial dominion over Ukraine.

Certain lines in his essay amounted to an annihilation of this history and an outright denial of Ukraine's sovereign identity. 'In essence, Ukraine's ruling circles decided to justify their country's independence through the denial of its past', because

> they began to mythologise and rewrite history, edit out everything that united us, and refer to the period when Ukraine was part of the Russian Empire and the Soviet Union as an occupation. The common tragedy of collectivisation and famine of the early 1930s was portrayed as the genocide of the Ukrainian people.

It is difficult to imagine a more one-sided interpretation of how the Holodomor, the Great Famine of 1932–33 that killed millions of Ukrainians when they were part of the Soviet Union, had subsequently shaped Ukrainian aspirations of independence from Russia.

That Putin cared about preserving Russia's influence in Ukraine was no secret, but until this essay appeared, the wider world may not have realised just how maniacally obsessed he had now become.

Of the many guises Putin had adopted in his career, from a KGB officer to becoming a free marketeer, a macho survivalist, a defender of the state, a latter-day Tsar and a self-proclaimed Russian history professor, it was this final avatar that he adopted to announce his invasion of Ukraine.[3]

Imperial history provided a spine to the script of Putin's first pre-invasion televised address, with 'empire' mentioned repeatedly in his rationale for taking military action. 'They [independent Ukraine] spent and embezzled the legacy inherited not only from the Soviet era, but also from the Russian Empire.' He singled out examples. 'In 2021, the Black Sea Shipyard in Nikolayev went out of business. Its first docks date back to Catherine the Great.' Putin neglected to mention that Nikolayev (Mykolaiv for Ukrainians) was where much of the Soviet Union's navy was built, and perhaps modern Ukraine was not overly bothered if the shipyard passed into history.

'Antanov,' Putin then expounded, 'the famous manufacturer, has not made a single commercial aircraft since 2016,' which was an odd complaint since his invading forces would soon destroy a symbol of Ukrainian pride, and the largest aircraft in the world, the Antonov AN-225 *Mriya*, on the tarmac of Hostomel Airport. Putin's crocodile tears continued. 'While Yuzhmash, a factory specialising in missile and space equipment, is nearly bankrupt, the Kremenchug Steel Plant is in a similar situation. This sad list goes on and on.' Sadder still was Russia's periodic attacks on Ukraine's economy, for instance by holding hostage Ukraine's dependency on Russian-supplied energy, and severing Russian cooperation in the Yuzhmash factory unless Kyiv adopted pro-Moscow policies. Amidst Ukraine's repeated requests for large financial bailouts by the International Monetary Fund (IMF), building space equipment may not have been a priority.

To denounce the Kyiv authorities, Putin asked rhetorically,

'Why was it necessary to appease the nationalists, to satisfy the ceaselessly growing nationalist ambitions on the outskirts of the former empire?' And he discerned unbroken traditions between the old empire of the Tsars and the Soviet Union, saying, 'I would like to repeat that the Soviet Union was established in the place of the former Russian Empire in 1922. But practice showed immediately that it was impossible to preserve or govern such a vast and complex territory on the amorphous principles that amounted to confederation.' Putin's reality began and ended with what he called 'the historical tradition' of Russian empire. For him, independent Ukraine was nothing more than an errant province.

What's more, Ukrainians who wanted an independent state were 'Nazis', according to Putin. 'It is not surprising that Ukrainian society was faced with the rise of far-right nationalism, which rapidly developed into aggressive Russophobia and neo-Nazism.' The emotional resonance of the Red Army's epic defeat of Nazi Germany in the Second World War was being cynically manipulated to tar modern Russia's neighbour for its disobedience.

History is ever vulnerable to misuse to justify all manner of nationalistic and militaristic policies. For all the importance placed by professional historians on gathering primary source material and analysing its contents with rigour and balance, the amateur equivalent of the discipline of history places its emphasis on selectivity and storytelling that confirms existing biases. To some extent, history always inhabits a realm of subjectivity and interpretation, but in its misuse, this subjectivity becomes egregious, warping facts beyond recognition. Putin was incapable of acknowledging how aspirations for Ukrainian sovereign independence had arisen partly from the suffering meted out by past Russian empires, examples of which are detailed in this chapter. Indeed, this denial was his inspiration.

Putin had surrounded himself with others who echoed his views of history. An example was Vladimir Medinsky, a relatively minor official who served as Culture Minister between 2012 and 2020, and who was given a major role by Putin at the start of the invasion. Medinsky led a team of Russian negotiators to meet Ukrainian officials in Belarus in the opening days of the invasion, presumably with the intention of imposing a victor's peace on Ukraine.

Medinsky also happened to be an amateur historian, authoring a book in 2011 entitled *Myths About Russia*, in which he referred to lands from the Tsarist era 'in what is now Ukraine', while recounting with pride that 'Russia in the seventeenth century continued to conquer the vast spaces of eastern Europe and Siberia', and that 'the 1654 union of Ukraine and Russia dates from this era' (an interpretation that requires far more context to be properly understood, as explained below).*4

One can readily imagine the tenor of the conversation when Putin dispatched Medinsky to Belarus to meet the Ukrainian officials: in the Putin and Medinsky view of history, the grandeur of their ancestral empires had left Ukraine in Russia's permanent debt.

Which implores us to ask: how had such a jaundiced and anachronistic view of history gripped the minds of Russia's elites?

HALF-LIVES OF COLLAPSED EMPIRES

At the Chernobyl nuclear plant, the site of the 1986 nuclear disaster that took place when Ukraine still belonged to the Soviet Union, the half-life of the leaked radioactive material varies. The half-life of caesium-137, one of the most harmful nuclear atoms released in

---

* Medinsky presents his work as 'historical journalism', adding, 'In this book I have relied on famous works by Russian historians as well as the testimony of foreign observers, but the facts described in these sources have been chosen according to a certain sequence and from a certain point of view.'

the accident, was thirty years, whereas for plutonium-239, carried by winds across Europe, it was 24,000 years.[5]

A half-life indicates the rate of decay and dissipation of harmful materials, and it also serves as a suitable metaphor for depicting the time it takes for harmful imperial legacies to dissipate into innocent nothingness. Empires, with their attendant histories of hierarchy, conquest and exploitation, involving humiliation for some and glory for others, deposit their influence on later generations in complex and ever-evolving ways.

Even this is not as straightforward as it appears: rather than a simple matter of ancestral hatred, we must reckon with the fact that empires in their different guises were entirely normal for much of human history, right up until the last century.[6] As Andrew Wilson observes, 'Many Ukrainians were quite willing citizens of the Polish Commonwealth and the Habsburg, Romanov and Soviet empires, and this should not be wished away.' Wilson had in mind attempts to foist contemporary notions of nationalism and identity onto past eras, because 'nationalists tend to see their nation as eternal, as a historical entity since ancient times'.[7] History does not comprise a continuous and linear struggle of freedom against imperial tyranny – far from it, since the evolving Ukrainian nation must be understood as having its complex origins (as we all ultimately do) in a world of empires.

It is this complexity that has given modern Ukraine–Russia relations much of their tone. The relationship bears the hallmarks of a bitter post-imperial interplay between an ex-empire and the former dominion it once called 'little Rus'. To explain how the weight of

---

* Wilson discusses 'both Ukrainian nationalists' flight of fancy and Russian and other rival nationalities' attempts to belittle or deny Ukraine', adding that 'the Ukrainians may now be becoming a nation before our very eyes, but this does not mean that they were ... always destined to become such'.

imperial history bears down on both Russia and Ukraine, it is important to understand *the processes by which* imperial legacies deposit their imprint on the minds of later generations and on modern relations of states.

'Empire is a relationship, formal or informal, in which one state controls the effective political sovereignty of another political society,' explained the academic Michael Doyle, and 'it can be achieved by force, by political collaboration, by economic, social or cultural dependence'. Regarding governing terminology, 'imperialism is simply the process or policy of establishing or maintaining an empire'.[8] Another academic, Alexander Motyl, sees 'empire as a hierarchically organised political system with a hub-like structure – a rimless wheel – within which a core elite dominate peripheral elites and societies'.[9] In the language of empires, Russia was the 'core' and Ukraine a 'periphery'.

Successor states to the core and the periphery of old empires face diametrically different post-imperial legacies. In Russia's case, its imperial essence continually animates its latter-day statecraft, and while the power of empire still pulsates in the Kremlin's corridors, Ukrainian nationalists conversely aspire to a legacy of resisting this dominion.

This is far from being a specific malady in Russian–Ukrainian relations, and post-imperial lineages of this kind influence so many contemporary global relations (whether the British in relation to Ireland, India, Kenya or countless other countries once in the British Empire, or those that the French once colonised in northern and western Africa and in Indo-China, or the Turks and the former dominions of the Ottoman Empire and so on).

Each of these relationships is unique and in constant evolution, and we can apply four basic criteria to understand their specific

7

natures: identifying the *tangible physical legacies* of empire; identifying the accompanying *attitudinal legacies*; measuring *proximity in history* to imperial times; and measuring *geographic proximity* between the ex-empire and the ex-colony. As we work through this list, it becomes clear just how much of a powder keg contemporary Russian–Ukrainian relations have been.

The *tangible* legacies arising from the end of empires amount to the material, demographic and other properties bequeathed by empires to states that comes in their wake; for instance in how borders are redrawn, rearranging populations and awarding or stripping countries of their access to resources. Ukraine inherited a great deal from the USSR, including the borders assigned while it was a member, and a large Russian-speaking minority, including those who had settled in the Donbas during the Russian Empire's industrial revolution, and much more besides, as examined below.

Other imperial legacies are *attitudinal*, meaning they influence emotional reference points for successive generations, creating mixed feelings of unrequited pride, shame, jealousy, enmity and kinship, as pertaining to the relations that now cross the old boundaries of empires. Again, Ukraine and Russia were highly exposed to these influences. As Vladimir Balakhonov wrote in 1989, 'Among Russians the imperial instinct is tremendously strong, and we cannot as yet imagine any form of existence other than our current empire, stretching from Brest to Vladivostok.'[10] The borders may have changed (Brest is on the modern Belarus–Polish border), but one must wonder if Balakhonov's words otherwise apply today. Conversely, challenging Russian imperial narratives was an essential catalyst in fostering a Ukrainian national identity. Ukrainian historian Mykhailo Hrushevsky's multi-volume *History of Ukraine-Rus'*, published between 1895 and 1936, was an important part of this process since it reclaimed Ukraine's national story, preventing it from being overshadowed by Russian narratives.[11] These contending Ukrainian and Russian historical narratives have clashed ever since.

The *proximity to imperial history* is also a live-wire issue for Russia and Ukraine because such little time has passed. Nevertheless, a distinction resides between directly held memories and memorialisation of much older events. David Rieff Sontag observes that 'once the transmission of collective memories continues for more than three or four generations, it can no longer be called memory other than metaphorically. To use a storied example, Irish men and women do not "remember" the Great Famine of 1845–9.'[12] As events pass from lived experiences to memorialisation of ancestral experiences, contemporary generations must be actively reminded of their ancestral suffering in order for it to retain the power of meaning. This is a common phenomenon that Sontag thinks can unwisely preserve a sense of collective trauma.

In Ukraine, the Holodomor remains in living memory and its remembrance has on occasion been sustained by politicians to foster national unity.*[13] The passage of time may take some of the bite out of memories of such traumatic events, even if forgiveness may never be automatic or expected between descendants of those involved in the traumatic event. Trans-generational healing requires dialogue between populations and responsible leaders. But truth and reconciliation is not a conversation that Russia has initiated with Ukraine; rather, the Russian government has been obsessed with continual commemorations of the Great Patriotic War, to restate its

---

*   Anne Applebaum describes Viktor Yushchenko, President from 2005 to 2010, as 'the first President of Ukraine without a Communist pedigree … He made references to the Holodomor in his inaugural speech and created a National Memory Institute with Holodomor research at its heart … Yushchenko understood the power of the famine as a unifying national memory for Ukrainians, especially because it had been so long denied.'

martial traditions, and to remind all and sundry of Russia's past and present power.

The unavoidable realities of *geography* are an exacerbating factor in the harmful preservation of imperial legacies, because Russia and Ukraine exist in adjacency. The realities of managing the legacies of a land empire like Russia's differ from maritime colonial empires. They too may have had bitter and blood-soaked colonial divorces, such as Britain in Kenya and India, or France in Algeria and Vietnam, or the USA in the Philippines – but there are seas and oceans to provide natural separation after imperial retreat and independence. Bitter feelings are likely to be present no matter the distance, but adjacency offers its own continuous reminder of past hierarchies, and it also explains why Russia itself remains huge.[14] 'Unlike other overseas empires,' writes the academic Domitilla Sagramoso, 'the Russian Empire and the Russian state had developed simultaneously, on the basis of the acquisition and colonisation of contiguous territory.'[15]

* * *

Taking all these factors together, it is clear why the Russia–Ukraine relationship was so danger-prone to the live wires of a difficult imperial past. Independent Ukraine inherited by necessity a number of tangible properties from the USSR; the Russian elites retained a wistful attitude to their former empire; the trauma of the USSR remains in living memory; and the two countries are geographically close to one another.

Having said this, history, like geography, never equates to destiny. There is no inevitability in how modern generations respond to and are shaped by imperial inheritances, whether leaving it to fester over time or using it as a basis for discussion and healing. Russia's nostalgia for empire and great-power status has instead been actively mobilised under Putin's presidency to justify policies at home and abroad. In his mind, Putin was living up to the legacies of the Soviet Union from thirty years ago and also of the Tsars of the Russian Empire that ended 100 years ago.

The immensity of Russia's imperial past must never be understated: for around 500 years, Russia's experience outside the confines of a formal imperial identity is limited to two relatively brief moments in history, one in the 1990s during Russia's flirtation with democracy under President Boris Yeltsin and the other in 1917, in the thin sliver of time between the fall of the Tsar's Romanov Dynasty and the rise of the Bolsheviks, which was filled by the Provisional Government led by Prime Minister Alexander Kerensky.

I still recall my astonishment when, as an undergraduate history student in a Russian Revolution class, Kerensky's grandson walked into our seminar. Kerensky Jr had settled in the UK and was a friend of my superb Russian history professor, who invited him in for a cameo talk with students.* Although not a historian by trade, Kerensky Jr set out to defend his grandfather's maligned legacy in failing to embed an openly elected Russian assembly, telling us that in war-torn lands of such vastness, his grandfather's Provisional Government was always likely to live up to its name.

Either side of the Kerensky interregnum are the two great empires of Russia's past, and Ukraine's prospects were not especially bright in either of these imperial incarnations. Before we resume the story of contemporary events, a short history class of our own is an essential precursor.

---

* With enduring thanks to Professor Christopher Reed for an outstanding primary source-led module on 1917.

EMPIRE OF THE TSARS

It was a request that should not have been beyond the pale: to translate the Bible into Ukrainian. But this was Kyiv in 1863 and the city's Russian Governor-General Nicholas Annenkov had other ideas. Born in the Russian oblast (region) of Nizhny Novgorod in 1799, and having fought Napoleon's army earlier in his career, the Kyiv governorship was Annenkov's final posting. As a typically conservative Russian official, Annenkov was determined to block the Bible translation, since it was part of a worrying trend of publications appearing in the Ukrainian language, including the poems of Taras Shevchenko, who was seen as a standard bearer for Ukrainian nationalism.

If the Bible now appeared in the Ukrainian language, Annenkov saw a slippery slope: it 'would achieve so to speak the recognition of the independence of the Little Russian language, and then of course they will make claims to autonomy for Little Russia...'[16] Annenkov's worries were read by the Russian Empire's Interior Minister of the day, Petr Valuev, who agreed that 'there has never been, is not, and cannot be any separate Little Russian language'.[17]

This condescending elite Russian attitude towards Ukrainian culture became typical in the Tsarist era, which spanned the sixteenth to the twentieth centuries. Rather importantly, this prejudice in turn had drawn its inspiration from an even earlier historical era.

Long before the advent of Tsarist Russia, the medieval kingdom of Kyvian Rus laid the foundations for the Slavic peoples in the mid-ninth century, when a mixture of Norse and Slavic tribes united around the Kyvian state. As American-Ukrainian historian Serhii Plokhii notes, 'ancestors of today's Ukrainians, Russians, and Belarusians adopted the name "Rus"...' and their ruler Prince Volodymyr the Great 'through his baptism would start the process of the Christianisation of Kyvian Rus'.[18] Ukraine commemorates this heritage, depicting Volodymyr and his son Yaroslav the Wise on the one- and two-hryvnia bank notes.

The kingdom of Kyvian Rus thrived until it was defeated by a Mongol invasion in 1240. Although Christianity continued to be practised by the Slavs during the era of Mongol dominion, they were very much the subjects. Centuries later, when the Slavic people gathered their strength and fought off Mongol rule, they did so not from Kyiv but from Moscow. Tsarist Russia began around this time, when Ivan IV ('the terrible') established the Russian Empire in the mid-sixteenth century by leading the city state of Muscovy to defeat the Mongol hordes who had swept over the Slavic lands. Ivan IV also promoted himself from 'Prince of Muscovy' to 'Tsar of all Russia', which is the origin of the title.

This basic chronology has given rise to a controversy in later interpretations: Russian rulers from the Tsars to Putin have tended to interpret this common lineage as a validation of Russia's hierarchy over Ukraine and Belarus. As the historian Dominic Lieven reminds us, this is a very old controversy that has lasted for centuries. He is concerned with the question of whether the Ukrainians and Belorussians were ever fully independent entities or simply extensions of the Russian whole, explaining that 'the official Tsarist claims that Ukraine and Belorussia were not imperial acquisitions but ancient Russian lands, however, did matter greatly as regards subsequent Tsarist policy in these regions'.*[19]

Putin gladly recycled this Tsarist-era interpretation in his history essay, writing that 'Russians, Ukrainians and Belarusians are all descendants of Ancient Rus' and 'the spiritual choice made by St Vladimir [Russian spelling] ... still largely determines our affinity

---

* After gaining independence in 1991, Belorussia began to refer to itself as Belarus.

today'.[20] Even if Russians, Ukrainians and Belarusians can trace their lineage, and their ancestral introduction to Christianity, to this moment in time, Kyvian Rus ended 782 years prior to 2022. Far from being a proximate historical influence, it is the sense of hierarchy inferred from this story by the later Russian Empire that is the decisive legacy.

*   *   *

The key event in imperial Russia's relationship with Ukraine took place a century after Ivan IV. As would happen so often in Ukrainian history, its lands were coveted by rival empires on all sides, which meant Ukrainians had to make tricky choices around who to side with.

This was the case in 1654, when the Cossack leader Bohdan Khmelnytsky led an uprising from Ukrainian lands against Polish rule and, fatefully for later generations, chose to side with the Russians. The Polish–Lithuanian Commonwealth (which formally confederated in 1569) was a formidable rival to the Russian Empire, and Ukraine was caught in the middle. Khmelnytsky (who is depicted on the five-hryvnia bank note) and his Hetmanate (kingdom) swore an oath of allegiance on 8 January 1654 to Russian Tsar Alexis Romanov in the town of Pereiaslav. This granted Russia control of central Ukraine and helped the Cossacks fight off the Polish. As Plokhii explains, 'The official Russian name of the Hetmanate, "little Russia", laid the basis for the tradition of treating Ukraine as "lesser Russia" and the Ukrainians as part of a larger Russian nation.'[21] Once again, the play of events allowed the Russian imperial elite to form a condescending view of their neighbours, and this has carried on through the ages.

For instance, in 1954, the Soviet Union celebrated the 300th anniversary of the oath at Pereiaslav, treating it as the 'reunification' of Ukraine and Russia. However, a careful look at this period reminds us that after the Polish–Russian war concluded in 1667, the Poles retained control of parts of western Ukraine while the Russians controlled territory east of the Dnipro River.

Another instance of picking sides arose in the eighteenth century, when Sweden went to war with Russia and fought its major battles on Ukrainian lands. The Ukrainian Cossack Hetman Ivan Mazepa (depicted on the ten-hryvnia bank note) saw an opportunity to side with the Swedes and their Polish allies and, in doing so, to unite Ukraine's divided lands. Sadly for Mazepa and his followers, he picked the losing side. The Swedish and Polish armies were beaten in a decisive battle fought in the Ukrainian town of Poltava in 1709 by the armies of Tsar Peter the Great. Mazepa's plan had failed: Sweden and Poland were banished from Ukraine and, in the ensuing partition, much of western Ukraine now also fell under Russian control. A notable exception was the far western city of Lviv, which would be absorbed into the Habsburg Empire and ruled from Vienna.

The Battle of Poltava's outcome has given rise to a joke that is told by Russians in the following way: *Have you ever noticed how similar the flags of Sweden and Ukraine are? It is because thrifty Khokhols* [slang for Ukrainians] *picked up Swedish flags after the battle of Poltava!* Incidentally, the term *Khokhol* referred to crop sheaves and was used by some Russians as a derogatory name for Ukrainians, but the Ukrainians later reclaimed the term for themselves and used it as a slur against Russified Ukrainians.

Russian imperial power was now in full ascent, as territories like the Baltic states also fell under Russian control. Peter the Great, who reigned 1682–1725, is a Tsar that Putin may well have liked to identify with. As Peter's biographer Vasily Klyuchevsky wrote, 'Peter had to solve inherited problems; since at least half of the Russian people lived outside the political boundaries of his state, he had to find a way of uniting them.' Moreover, 'War was the most important circumstance of his reign. Peter was rarely at peace ... with his principal enemies, Turkey and Sweden.'[22]

Russia's long imperial duel with the Turkish-centred Ottoman Empire unfolded around the Black Sea. The imperial Russian officer Field Marshal Count Alexander Suvorov (1730–1800) fought in the Russo-Ottoman War of 1787–92. His regent was Catherine the Great, who reigned 1762–96, and during this time, imperial conscription was extended from Russia's peasants to also cover Ukraine and the Baltic provinces. Crimea and the Black Sea coast was conquered by Russia in this era.*[23]

It turns out Marshal Suvorov was yet another of Putin's obsessions. 'In Ochakov [a city in south Ukraine] in the eighteenth century, soldiers of Alexander Suvorov fought for this city. Owing to their courage, it became part of Russia,' he said, while recounting how 'the lands of the Black Sea littoral, incorporated in Russia as a result of wars with the Ottoman Empire, were given the name of *Novorossiya* (New Russia)'.

Then came Putin's warning: 'Attempts are being made to condemn these landmarks of history to oblivion, along with the names of state and military figures of the Russian Empire without whose efforts modern Ukraine would not have many big cities or even access to the Black Sea.' Putin was annoyed that 'a monument to Alexander Suvorov was recently demolished in Poltava. What is there

---

* These Black Sea conquests brought into Russian control 'the mouths of the Dnieper and Dniester Rivers for the first time'.

to say? Are you renouncing your own past? The so-called colonial heritage of the Russian Empire?'[24]

Suvorov had been dead for 222 years before Putin cited him in his effective declaration of war on Ukraine. The real significance here, and the insight into Putin's motivations, circles around this term 'Novorossiya', used in imperial times to denote a new Russian province founded on lands north of the Black Sea. This land was annexed by Russia in 1764, its prize for victory against the Ottomans, and it was subsequently populated by Russians who were to serve as farmers and soldiers to bring these lands into the Russian Empire.[25] 'Novorossiya' would be resurrected by Putin's government to make its renewed claim in 2014 for the lands of Crimea, Donbas and southern Ukraine, an old colonial construct reused for modern purposes.

*   *   *

What of the fate of Ukrainian language and culture during the long centuries of Russian imperial rule? In the early nineteenth century, writing in Ukrainian was not especially frowned on, according to Paul Bushkovitch, who studied publications from the time that reflected the views of Russia's elites. However, 'The period of general Ukrainophilia in Russian culture came to an abrupt end after the Crimean War ... In contrast to the first half of the nineteenth century, the second half saw a public Russian culture much of which was hostile to Ukrainian aspirations.'[26]

Mention of the Crimean war of 1853–56 brings to mind the fact that Tsar Nicholas I is a much less auspicious reference point for Putin, given that he died of ill health after a failed war against a coalition of opponents, losing hold of Crimea in the process. Even then, Lieven writes that '90 per cent of the army's intake in 1870 were Russian, Belorussian and Ukrainian', and that for 'the Tsarist elite Belarus and Ukraine were beyond any question Russians, albeit Russians speaking a strange dialect and possessing some distinctive, though by no means objectionable or politically dangerous customs'.[27]

Whatever one may now think, empire meant a conjoined history for Russians and Ukrainians, who at times shared in the triumphs and the defeats of the Russian Empire, notably in Crimea. But the greatest defeat of all was to come in the Great War, which began in 1914 and proved to be a last throw of the blood-soaked dice of war by the Romanov Dynasty.

Russia hastily mobilised its army and joined the war on the Allies' side with the British and French Empires, lining up against the German, Austro-Hungarian and eventually the Ottoman Empires. The Russians fielded a parade ground-worthy army that met a bloody end after it invaded Germany. The Battle of Tannenberg, fought in east Prussia in August 1914, was a signature catastrophe for the Tsar's army. As the Russians retreated, their general, Alexander Samsonov, quietly snuck away from his fellow officers to commit suicide.[*][28] Three terrible years of battlefield defeats of this ilk followed, placing the Russian imperial state under the unbearable strain of shedding its blood, treasure and legitimacy. It was not only Nicholas II's army that was on the line but his entire regime. By 1917, revolution was in the air and the 500-year era of the Tsars ended.

---

[*] Adam Hochschild recounts, 'Unfortunately for the Allies, though Russia's army was the largest on earth, it was also the most inept ... Soon after this debacle [at Tannenberg], the Germans crushed a second invading Russian army ... The Russian commanding general fled home by car. All in all, during a month of fighting, the Russians suffered 310,000 men killed, wounded or taken prisoner, as well as the loss of 650 artillery pieces. Industrial war had taken an instant and devastating toll of their half-industrialised country.'

Sadly for the Ukrainians, what eventually followed the Romanov Dynasty was no better for their nation and was arguably far worse.

EMPIRE OF THE SOVIETS

Ukraine barely came up for air in the twentieth century, but it was briefly an independent republic between 1917 and 1920, in the sliver of time between the Tsarist and Soviet eras. The Great War of 1914–18 had collapsed the empires that ruled different parts of Ukraine – the Austro-Hungarian and the Russian. After the Bolshevik Revolution in October 1917, Russia's new leader Vladimir Lenin needed to swiftly end the war with Germany, and he did so through a capitulation, signing the Treaty of Brest-Litovsk, in which the new Bolshevik regime surrendered huge tracts of European Russia.[29]

This afforded Ukraine's nationalists a rare opportunity to make a break for freedom. In Kyiv, the 'Ukrainian People's Republic' formed and declared Ukrainian independence, electing the aforementioned Ukrainian historian Mykhailo Hrushevsky (depicted on the fifty-hryvnia note) as President of the Republic. A Unification Act was passed in 1919 uniting the cities of Lviv and Kyiv, which represented each side of divided Ukraine. National symbols like the trident, the hryvnia currency and the blue and yellow flag were adopted (and were later readopted after independence in 1991). But there was no time to consolidate this union, and independent Ukraine perished under the resumption of Russian empire in its Bolshevik guise.

In 1918, the German war effort fell apart and the Great War ended. The Bolsheviks' Brest-Litovsk capitulation was annulled, and Lenin rebuilt Russia's empire where it had been given up.[30] Independent Ukraine's republic could not survive in the wake of Germany's withdrawal. Lenin masterminded new 'organs of Soviet power' by establishing nominally independent Soviet republics in Estonia, Latvia, Lithuania, Belorussia and Ukraine – but with real power concentrated in Moscow.'[31]

As ever, westernmost Ukraine was at the edge of Moscow's grasp. In February 1919, the Red Army captured Kyiv, but in Lviv a 'West Ukrainian National Republic' was set up. This kicked off a seven-month war between Poland and Russia. The Polish commander in chief Jozef Pilsudski even had a plan to annex Ukrainian territory for Warsaw, and his army briefly captured Kyiv in May 1920, before the Red Army mounted a counteroffensive.[32] In the end, the March 1921 Treaty of Riga granted parts of western Ukraine to Poland and Romania, while Russia kept the rest. Ukraine was divided once more.

*   *   *

Lenin didn't have much time in power to bring suffering to Ukraine, since he died on 21 January 1924, barely a year after the official for-mation of the Union of Soviet Socialist Republics (the USSR for-mally amalgamated the Soviet republics, including Ukraine, under Moscow's rule). Nevertheless, toppling Lenin statues has in recent years become a national sport in Ukraine to protest these visible legacy symbols of Soviet rule. I saw one such Lenin statue felled in Kramatorsk, east Ukraine, in 2015, in response to a surge of anti-Russian sentiment to the war that had recently broken out. Those who toppled the statues tied a rope between Lenin's midriff and a truck, which they revved into life to pull the imposing statue to the

---

*   Robert Service: 'Withdrawal of the German forces gave Lenin his opportunity to invade these regions and set up organs of "Soviet power". The Red Army made rapid progress and at Lenin's insistence, it did not incorporate the region into the Russian Socialist Federal Soviet Republic but established independent Soviet republics in Estonia, Lithuania and Belorussia, Latvia and Ukraine ... His party were aghast at this; but he tried to explain that the communist parties in the republics would be treated as mere regional organisations of the Russian Communist Party. Real power would not be in the "independent" Soviet republics but in Moscow.'

ground. When it hit the concrete, a few dozen people ran over to kick the prostrate statue. Dozens more Lenin statues have met this fate across the country.

More so than Lenin, it was Joseph Stalin's long reign in power (1922–53) that heaped misery upon Ukraine. In the earliest days of the USSR, Ukrainian culture had been able to thrive, but 'the eruption of the Stalinist volcano reduced to ashes the high hope that Ukrainian nation builders had once had', in Plokhii's evocative words.[33] Stalin, a former Soviet Commissar for Nationalities from Georgia, meted out more suffering upon these nationality groups within the USSR soon after he had replaced Lenin. Ukraine's suffering was worse than in any other part of the Soviet Union and 4–5 million inhabitants of Soviet Ukraine died in the Holodomor (an eighth of the population).

Within a decade of the Holodomor, Ukraine became the site of Nazi Germany's *Lebensraum* ('living space') campaign of colonial destruction. Having decided that the Germans could not build an overseas empire, Hitler had fixated his imperial designs on eastern Europe. To this day, the Second World War is the signature event that shapes historical memories across eastern Europe. Memorialised in Russia as 'The Great Patriotic War, 1941–45', this omits the first twenty-two months of war during which time Stalin's USSR was in partnership with Hitler's Nazi Germany, as codified by the notorious Molotov-Ribbentrop Pact of 23 August 1939, named after the Foreign Ministers of these countries. The pact facilitated the carving up of Poland. Shortly after Hitler's army invaded from the west, Stalin ordered Russian troops into eastern Poland on 17 September 1939, citing the pretext of 'saving' Belorussians and Ukrainians in Poland. (A version of this pretext was used by Putin to invade Ukraine in both 2014 and 2022, this time to 'save' Russians.)

The rest of the story of the Second World War and its aftermath is fairly well known. Hitler turned on Stalin by launching Operation Barbarossa in June 1941 (the largest land invasion in military history), which was followed by four grim years of tank battles, city sieges, ethnic cleansing, aerial bombardment and all manner of other atrocities. Fully one-ninth of the Soviet population had perished by the time the Red Army had fought back the Germans and reached eastern Berlin. Contemporary accounts of the Second World War, including Western accounts since the 1990s, credit the Red Army for bearing an enormous brunt of the war effort against the Nazis.[*][34]

A Ukrainian colleague of mine has shared with me her personal view of the suffering borne by her family in the Donbas at this time:

> The Holodomor and later on World War Two killed over a half of the original population in Donbas. My grandma starved in 1933. My grandma starved again in 1943. When Stalin died my family closed all the windows and doors, covered them with thick blankets, made moonshine, killed a pig and celebrated for a week singing happy songs in whispers. If they were caught, they would have spent the rest of their lives in prisons.[35]

The darker side to Russia's victory in 1945 has been that successive Russian leaders (including Putin) have argued that the Soviet Union's sacrifice in the Second World War has given them a lasting justification for maintaining their influence in eastern Europe.

And why, they might argue, if the American military has remained in Japan as a legacy of its victory in the Pacific in 1945, should Russia

---

[*]   In Richard Overy's view, 'The Soviet Union bore the brunt of the German onslaught and broke the back of German power. For years the Western version of the war played down this uncomfortable fact, while exaggerating the success of democratic war-making.'

not take a similar prize? The big difference is the role of democratic permission in the stationing of foreign forces: such permission was granted by Japan to the USA but was absent as the USSR stayed in eastern Europe after 1945, later formalising Russia's command of the armed forces of occupied eastern Europe in the Warsaw Pact of 1955. Nevertheless, a persistent feature of Russia's latter-day disputes with the USA is the accusation of double standards, as in this instance.

*   *   *

During its existence as the Ukrainian Soviet Socialist Republic (1919–91), the Russian language became ever more dominant, especially in eastern Ukraine. As the Polish writer Ryszard Kapuściński sardonically observed, 'Ukrainian culture was better preserved in Toronto and Vancouver than in Donetsk or Kharkov,' referencing Ukraine's global émigrés.[36] Conversely, in western Ukraine, which was incorporated into the USSR only after 1945, Russians were still somewhat seen as outsiders.[37] The contrasting cultural and historical influences in these different regions in Ukraine, notably the contrasts between east and west, would be a defining theme for how Ukraine later evolved as a nation. During the repressive Stalinist era, however, there was little room for any kind of Ukrainian cultural self-expression, but this eased somewhat later on.

Nikita Khrushchev, a Ukrainian, led the USSR after Stalin's death in 1953 and until 1964. Under Khrushchev, Ukraine's status in the USSR was elevated to the most important of the Soviet republics behind Russia. In 1954, Khrushchev signed off on a symbolic

---

*   Anna Matveeva outlines how in western Ukraine 'attitudes towards the Soviet system, which was seen as "Russian", were negative and epitomised by discourse that presented Ukraine as a victim of Russian colonisation'.

handing over of Crimea to the Soviet authorities in Ukraine. Stalin had already deported most of the ethnically Turkic Tatar residents of Crimea to central Asia, and Khrushchev found it in Moscow's interests to leave Crimea in Kyiv's hands to further the job of 'Europeanising' the peninsula. This was 'the affirmative action empire' in practice, quipped Terry Martin, a scholar of the USSR, making reference to Russians always being at the top of the tree while various other nationalities were tolerated only to the extent that they didn't threaten this hierarchy.*[38]

Some of our most defining Cold War-era images of Soviet repression of national movements come from two episodes: in 1956, when Soviet troops brutally crushed the Hungarian uprising; and the 1968 Prague Spring, when a Czechoslovak attempt at local reform was met by an enduring Soviet occupation. It is important to recall that Hungary and Czechoslovakia had since 1955 been bound to Russia as members of the Warsaw Pact, and there was a big difference between this formula and the Soviet socialist republics (SSRs). Moscow saw in the SSRs an inner core to its sphere of influence, and assumed far more obedience from them as a result.

There were fifteen SSRs in the USSR's latter years: Armenia, Azerbaijan, Belorussia, Estonia, Georgia, Kazakhstan, Kirghizia, Latvia, Lithuania, Moldavia, Russia, Tajikistan, Turkmenia, Ukraine and Uzbekistan. Russia was the largest, followed by Kazakhstan and Ukraine. Of all the SSRs, Russia's cultural relationship and economic reliance on Ukraine was perhaps the strongest.

Russian empires had always benefited economically from possession of Ukraine. In the Tsarist era, Ukraine was initially a major agricultural region, and the Donbas was later built up as a centre

---

* Terry Martin called the USSR 'an extraordinarily invasive, centralised, and violent state formally structured as a federation of sovereign nations'.

for mining and metallurgical industries. In the Soviet era, Ukraine retained these functions and became the transit corridor through which the oil and gas industry in west Siberia could sell its commodities to Europe. The USSR invested in Ukraine's industrialisation, also building up its defence sector (Kharkiv housed a railway and tank factory, for instance, while warships were built alongside Ukraine's Black Sea coast). Under the USSR's command economy, the Russian and Ukrainian economies and defence sectors became increasingly fused together.[39]

Which is why, when the USSR fragmented, many people in Russia's economic and political elites felt a keen sense of loss as Ukraine split away, arguably more so than with the other SSRs. Conversely, Ukrainians who had longed for their nation's independence and had so far been denied any oxygen now came to the surface gasping for air.

THE LURE OF EMPIRE

In sum, Russia and Ukraine are the product of imperial legacies that come from different sides of the same coin: Russia on the 'head' side as the ex-imperial overlord; Ukraine on the 'tail' side of the ex-dominion. For Russia, the temptation for imperial revival in some form or another would always be present, and it would become especially acute under Putin's rule.[40]

An exemplar of the gravitational pull of empire is the contemporary Russian academic Alexander Dugin. Whether or not the Kremlin listens to Dugin, his views are of interest as a bellwether of intellectual opinion towards adapting Russia's imperial afterlife to the modern world. Born in 1962, Dugin has been banging this drum in his books since the 1990s, imploring Russia to avoid the temptation of globalism. He argued that 'adopting the

Western model [for Russia] would amount to geopolitical and cultural death', and that empire remained the only political system able to harness the national and religious diversity of the Eurasian space.[41]

Two weeks after Russia's invasion of Ukraine began in 2022, Dugin delivered a lecture: 'The language of the West does not want to hear anything of the language of Russia. And the language of the West is almost the language of the world, so we are isolated, and nobody is going to hear us … Now we are going to speak our own language.'[42]

Revelling in Russia's outsider status, Dugin referenced an old debate between two influential US political scientists from the early 1990s: '[Samuel] Huntington was absolutely right [with his *Clash of Civilizations* thesis] and [Francis] Fukuyama was absolutely wrong [with his *End of History* thesis on the final victory of liberal democracy].' Then came Dugin's chilling punchline: 'There are civilisations and one of them is Russia. And we had no other way of proving Huntington was right than attacking Ukraine. It's us who started this conflictual situation in order to be heard.'[43]

This astonishing diatribe conveys the Russian elite's sense of persecution, the only answer to which in Dugin's and Putin's minds was to come out fighting, if nothing else to prove to the USA and the Western world that Russia's imperial instincts could never be cowed. Whereas Fukuyama had posited the final victory of a US-led liberal democratic model at the end of the Cold War, Huntington argued against there being a universally applicable model for social and political affairs, pointing instead to the prevalence of many highly contrasting civilisational blocs.

The reference to Samuel Huntington also brings to mind the fact that Ukraine was always highly vulnerable to instability.

Huntington's passage on Ukraine from *The Clash of Civilizations*, written in 1993, became notorious for forecasting the coming problems. Calling Ukraine a 'cleft country with two distinct cultures', he says that

> at times in the past, western Ukraine was part of Poland, Lithuania, and the Austro-Hungarian empire … Historically, western Ukrainians have spoken Ukrainian and have been strongly nationalist in their outlook … practised Orthodox rites but acknowledged the authority of the Pope … The people of eastern Ukraine, on the other hand, have been overwhelmingly Orthodox and have in large part spoken Russian.

Most importantly, these are not ethnic but cultural differences, in which the inhabits of east and west Ukraine were the products of different historical and cultural influences, most obviously represented in the varying prevalence of the Ukrainian and Russian languages. Huntington quoted a Russian general speaking back in the 1990s, who said, 'Ukraine, or rather eastern Ukraine, can come back to us in five, ten or fifteen years. Western Ukraine can go to hell!'[44]

* * *

For its part, as this brief history lesson has demonstrated, Ukraine is itself a product of multiple imperial legacies, ranging from the Polish–Lithuanian Commonwealth to the Austro-Hungarian Empire in addition to its Russian influences.[45] Approximately a fifth of Ukrainians were ruled not by the Tsar but from Vienna, and in Austrian Galicia, Ukrainian high culture thrived. Indeed, Lviv was Galicia's chief city, and it was granted a degree of autonomy in

1871, four years after Austria and Hungary had amalgamated their kingdoms.[46]

The American academic Timothy Snyder has written of 'people today with great vested interests in showing, for example, that Ukraine was the "construction" of Austrian (German, Polish, whatever) agents', while 'others are committed to the view of an "essentially" continuous Ukrainian history'.[47] All nations come from somewhere, and all tend to have confusing and at times interrupted histories, and have origin stories that provoke the deepest emotions in those who endorse or condemn these narratives.

Two heads are good, but three teeth are better! So goes a Ukrainian witticism comparing Russia's two-headed imperial eagle and Ukraine's trident symbol. After 1991, keeping relations between these countries good humoured would be a challenge of the highest order.

CHAPTER 2

INDEPENDENCE AT LAST

A REFLECTION ON STATE-BUILDING

362 MONTHS BEFORE INVASION

On 25 December 1991 the Soviet Union ended. Mikhail Gorbachev resigned as its President and stepped down as the supreme commander of the Soviet Armed Forces, which was to be disbanded. The red and yellow hammer and sickle flag was lowered for the last time from above the Kremlin that evening, and the white, blue and red striped Russian Federation flag was hoisted in its place.

For Ukrainians who had aspired to independence, the long-awaited moment of freedom from the imperial yoke had come. Amidst the chaos and the euphoria of an imperial collapse, no one then could have predicted that 362 months later, Russia would invade Ukraine in a war of reconquest. This notion may have seemed absurd at the time, since Ukraine did not experience armed conflict during the breakup of the USSR, either between the constituent parts of its own populace or with its former imperial master, as happened with other former Soviet republics.

When we turn the clock back to the start of their post-Soviet journeys, it is clear that Ukraine and Russia may have been able to chart a different course in which some residual fraternity could have balanced out the enmity created by separation. Nothing is inevitable in the affairs of states, and it is worth remembering that the breakup of the USSR involved a relatively civilised divorce between Russia and Ukraine, and that the relationship featured no armed conflict for twenty-two years.[1]

That is not to avoid the difficult forces that had to be managed right from the start of the relationship. The breakup of the USSR deposited a sense of humiliation deep in the psyche of some of Russia's elite, while boosting nationalist pride in the other fourteen new states created from the SSRs. All of these states had to contend with the economic chaos of a single spluttering imperial economy being dismantled into its even weaker constituent parts. And, as with all imperial collapses, there were 'abandoned' decedents of settler communities now separated from the Russian metropole by new sovereign borders. Imperial collapses, especially if they are as sudden as that of the USSR, leave those who are affected no time to process what is happening, only a panoply of tricky transition issues to manage.

The USSR experienced its death throes between 1989 and 1991, and during this time Ukrainian independence was not always inevitable. With East and West Germany reunified on 3 October 1990, the Berlin Wall having been brought down the year before, the question of what to do with the USSR went through different phases. In the early stages of the USSR's demise, US President George H. W. Bush did not endorse Ukrainian independence since he was keen to preserve Gorbachev's authority and to avoid an uncontrolled disintegration of the USSR into outright war. Gorbachev had instigated negotiations to create a new and looser union of successor states to replace the USSR, and this idea was discussed in Kyiv on

18 April 1991 by representatives of the five biggest Soviet republics (Belorussia, Kazakhstan, Russia, Ukraine and Uzbekistan). The resulting treaty, signed after Gorbachev returned to Moscow from a summer holiday in Crimea, the Novo-Ogaryovo Accord (named after a retreat near Moscow), loosely reunited nine of the republics (Armenia, the Baltic states, Moldavia and Georgia all dissented).

This was Gorbachev's attempt to salvage a successor union to the USSR. He thought he had made sufficient concessions to the ambitions of these republics to preserve a modernised union where Moscow still called the shots on matters of core importance like defence and taxation.[2] Gorbachev wanted Russia to remain the 'big brother' and Ukraine's participation was crucial to the idea. His hopes would be dashed when, shortly after, Ukraine moved into the dissension camp by calling for full independence.

What changed for Ukraine? Moscow initially counted on the fraternal bonds between Russia and Ukraine, based on such factors as the considerable numbers of Ukrainians who served as bureaucrats and officers in the Soviet system, while also hoping that Ukraine's own dysfunctions, such as the divide between its eastern and western regions, would neuter some of the temptations of independence. But when Soviet authorities held a referendum on 17 March 1991 to suss out the demand for Ukrainian sovereignty, 84 per cent of Ukrainians turned out to vote, of whom 71 per cent voted for independence. Not for the last time, Moscow was a step behind popular sentiment in Ukraine.

On 19 August 1991 an attempted coup was mounted against Gorbachev by Communist Party hardliners who desperately wanted to forestall the liquidation of the USSR. The coup attempt was launched by the KGB chief and Interior and Defence Ministers while Gorbachev was away at his *dacha* in Crimea. After three tense days the coup failed, but when Gorbachev returned to Moscow he was effectively ousted by Boris Yeltsin, who took power on 10 July after being elected to lead the Russian Federation. Yeltsin stood atop a tank, in one of the abiding images from Russia's modern history, defying the hardliners and preserving the democratic systems that had brought him to power. And Yeltsin had told Bush that if over 70 per cent of Ukrainians voted for independence, he would grant it.[3]

Ukrainians saw the attempted coup and the power shift in Moscow and realised that time was up for the USSR. Ukraine's Parliament, the Verkhovna Rada ('Supreme Council'), voted for independence on 24 August by a majority of 346 to 1. The walrus-moustached veteran politician Levko Lukianenko (1928–2018), a long-time campaigner for Ukrainian independence, drafted a declaration: 'In view of the mortal danger hanging over Ukraine in connection with the coup d'état on 19 August 1991, and continuing the thousand-year tradition of state building in Ukraine, the Supreme Soviet of the Ukrainian Soviet Socialist Republic solemnly declares the independence of Ukraine.'[4] By deciding to take its own path, Ukraine delivered a final death knell to the USSR. Given its size and its criticality to past Russian empires, the USSR was truly finished once Ukraine decided to untether itself and attempt to forge its own future.*[5]

Events now moved quickly. Ukraine had previously voiced only cautious aspirations for independence, but now it announced some dramatic demands: total economic independence; an escape from a single monetary system; to print a specifically Ukrainian currency;

---

* Plokhii: 'Ukraine was the gravedigger of the last European empire.' See also Sarotte, *Not One Inch* (2021), pp. 130–31 on the Belavezha accords that ended the USSR signed by Russia, Belarus and Ukraine. Since these states 'had, on paper at least, founded the Soviet Union in 1922, they felt entitled to dissolve that union'.

to have a constitution; to refuse to contribute to a common army with Russia; and so on.[6] All these goals were later achieved.

The Rada now reaffirmed the popular mandate for its independence declaration in a referendum held on 1 December 1991. The turnout was 84 per cent and of those, 90.3 per cent voted for independence. Each region returned a majority for independence, with the lowest being 54 per cent in Crimea. Aside from the result in Crimea, there could be little ambiguity in these outcomes: Ukraine's Parliament and its people overwhelmingly wanted full independence. The vision of Ukrainian nationhood as articulated through the ages by Ukrainian nationalists during the long imperial epoch was finally a tangible reality.

*　　*　　*

Even if the collapse of the USSR was fairly sudden, the bonds of empire didn't vanish overnight. For instance, the old Soviet Olympic Committee was still in action and dispatched a 'unified team' of athletes from across the old SSRs to compete in the 1992 Olympic Games in Barcelona. The Ukrainian athletes acquitted themselves brilliantly. Of the 110 medals secured by the 'unified team', Ukrainian athletes were involved in securing ten gold, fourteen silver and ten bronze medals – a sizeable haul and a parting reminder of just how substantial a part of the USSR the Ukrainians had been.

So far so friendly, and it seemed as if fraternal relations could be maintained between people who for so long had lived under the Soviet banner but now forged ahead in separate successor states. Ukraine competed as an independent country for the very first time at the 1994 Winter Olympics held in Norway. And in these halcyon days of Russia–Ukraine relations, each country became accustomed to its new identity, learning to coexist alongside each other as separate sovereign states, even as the falling masonry of the USSR continued to crash down all around them.

KRAVCHUK, CREATING THE STATE

This is the tale of the 'Two Leonids', Kravchuk and Kuchma, who between them led Ukraine for the first thirteen years after independence. There were similarities between them, not least generationally since Kravchuk was born in 1934 and Kuchma in 1938. Their childhood experiences were of the Great Patriotic War against Nazi Germany, an event that claimed the lives of each of their fathers. As adults, the better parts of their lives and their careers were lived in the Soviet Union.

The big difference between them was that Kravchuk hailed from west Ukraine whereas Kuchma came from the Russian-speaking east. Both were committed to Ukraine's independence and tried to bring east and west Ukraine together in this endeavour, although each naturally had different instincts as to what this meant.

Kravchuk was Ukraine's first President; he was elected on 1 December 1991 and duly seen as the father of the nation, while Kuchma served as his Prime Minister for a year between 1992 and 1993.[7] On Ukraine's first independence day celebration, President Kravchuk addressed the nation by painting a picture of what Ukraine had sacrificed by being a Russian appendage: 'For us, as for other people, moreover, the time [of Ukraine's union with Russia] was not a time for developing our national culture, material and spiritual.'[8] Thus, Kravchuk, who had been a dedicated communist all his life, now adopted the language of proud Ukrainian nationalism. Straddling these worlds was the secret to his political success in navigating the choppy waters of independence.

Kravchuk had joined the Communist Party of Ukraine back in the 1950s, rising through the local party ranks until in July 1990 he had become the nominal head of state, also known as the 'Chairman of the Supreme Soviet of the Ukrainian SSR'. He used this communist pedigree to persuade his old local party comrades in Kyiv of the wisdom of backing Ukraine's independence from the USSR. But having originally hailed from west Ukraine, he now reached out to the Ukrainian nationalists based there to assemble a broad coalition to back independence. His nationalism was non-abrasive, and as well as adopting the yellow and blue flag, trident symbol and the national anthem, he made sure to emphasise that even if Ukrainian was the official language, Russian was also fully accepted.[9]

Keeping Ukraine together was not a foregone conclusion, since the country contained 11 million Russians at independence, many of whom would never become fully culturally Ukrainian. Crimea offered a very particular case: in the decades since 1954, when Moscow had transferred control of the peninsula to Kyiv, Ukraine had become convinced Crimea now belonged to them in perpetuity. A symbolic referendum was held for Crimea's independence on 20 January 1991, in which 93 per cent of the voters wanted to remain in the USSR. (This referendum had no legal power.) Passions ran high during demonstrations and there was even a hunger strike, coordinated by the newly formed Movement for the Republic of Crimea, all in the name of Russia taking Crimea back. Indeed, Crimea posed the only credible secessionist threat at the time of independence – offering fertile ground for Russia's later annexation in 2014.

The Crimean Peninsula had always mattered deeply to Russia because of its Black Sea Fleet naval base in Sevastopol, a site of strategic importance to the Kremlin. Ownership and access to the naval base was one of the biggest issues to negotiate between Kyiv and Moscow after Ukraine's independence. Kravchuk negotiated a deal with Yeltsin in 1992 to split the naval vessels of the old Soviet Black Sea Fleet 50/50 between the Ukrainian and Russian navies, although questions over costs associated with the facilities at the base itself remained trickier to resolve. In the end an agreement was reached whereby Ukraine owned the base but leased out the facilities to Russia.[10]

*   *   *

So far so amicable, and Ukrainians were no doubt counting their blessings as they gazed at other more bloodied territories of the former USSR, into which Russian soldiers poured ostensibly for 'stabilisation' missions, but gifting Moscow residual influence in the process. A quick tour of a handful of the former Soviet republics shows this in action.[11]

Russia intervened in Moldova in 1992, when Russian-backed separatists tried to build a breakaway republic in Transnistria. Russia's 14th Army was sent by Yeltsin to fight the Moldovan army in the early 1990s, and after securing victory, Russian soldiers have remained in Transnistria ever since. Today, the breakaway strip of land is not recognised by another state, and it remains almost stuck in time in the manner of a post-Soviet freeze frame. In Georgia, Russia supported the Abkhaz and South Ossetian separatists, and later brokered an end to the war between these breakaway states and Georgia. A Russian peacekeeping force entered and remained in both of the breakaway areas, along with relatively unobtrusive international ceasefire-monitoring missions. Yet another example of Russia's interventions was the Nagorno-Karabakh territorial dispute between Armenia and Azerbaijan, where Russia helped to broker a ceasefire in 1994. And to bring the Tajikistan civil war to an end in 1997, Russia intervened here as well. Whenever local unrest or an armed conflict in the former SSRs wasn't fully resolved, it left Russia with an excuse to move and keep its soldiers there.

These Russian interventions started a tradition that continued in Russia's wars in Georgia in 2008 and in Ukraine in 2014. More recently, in 2020, Russia (alongside Turkey) brokered an end to the latest round of fighting in the still-unresolved Nagorno-Karabakh war. As part of the deal, Russia inserted a 5,000-strong 'peace-keeping' force to provide security along the five-kilometre-wide Lachin Corridor, which connects Nagorno-Karabakh to Armenia. And in January 2022, just before it invaded Ukraine, Russia sent troops to Kazakhstan when unrest broke out in that country, help-ing President Kassym-Jomart Tokayev to remain in power despite popular unrest.

This was the Kremlin's post-imperial sweet spot: a privileged role as the stabiliser (and sometimes also the fomenter) of chaos in its old dominions. Russia wanted to retain this interventionist and policing role, with all the influence and great power pretension it afforded, seemingly in perpetuity following the end of its *formal empire* of direct occupation. Russia now shifted primarily into the realm of *informal empire*, which meant achieving and retaining a decisive influence over the security, economy and overall sover-eignty of a nominally independent state.

Enter NATO

The Kremlin, however, faced a growing problem: it was no longer the only big security presence in town. The NATO military alliance came swaggering into central and eastern Europe, flushed with its victory in the Cold War, and was now ready to field membership requests from the former Soviet satellite states who wanted a lasting guarantee of protection from Russia. The Kremlin watched aghast as NATO even courted some of the former Soviet socialist republics. It became clear that the Western powers had a compelling offer to bring to the table. NATO's growing role in Europe overlapped with the founding of the EU in 1993 (replacing the old EEC). Forming quite the power couple, NATO brought the protection and the EU brought the trading opportunities. Many of the former Soviet states were quite taken by the prospect of joining both organisations.

As the historian Mary Sarotte recounts, crucial decisions were taken by the USA as early as 1993, when President Bill Clinton made irreversible decisions around US support for NATO expansion. 'Thus began a slow train to dividing eastern Europe between countries that secured an Article 5 NATO defence guarantee and those that did not.' Article 5 was its mutual defence promise, of an attack on one NATO member being an attack on them all. The USA had abandoned any idea of creating with Russia a new security body that could include them both, or bolstering the existing options for doing so. Whereas 'the big play in Europe would have been to create a dynamic that established lasting cooperation, rather than confrontation, between Russia and the West', the USA opted to expand NATO.[12] If not betrayed outright, Gorbachev had certainly felt misled, and in his words, 'the decision for the US and its allies to expand NATO into the east was decisively made in 1993 ... It was definitely a violation of the spirit of the statements and assurances made to us in 1990.'[13] These statements, never recorded in a treaty, suggested that US officials had at the time of German reunification verbally assured Gorbachev that NATO would not expand further east.[14] Now that NATO was indeed expanding eastwards, a misunderstanding of epic proportions would develop between Russia and the USA.

Why did Russia's government despise NATO to such an extent? NATO was founded in 1949 explicitly to counter the USSR in Europe by tying the USA into Europe's defence. This was a different era: Europe was still reeling from the devastation of World War Two, and five of NATO's twelve founding members still ran colonial empires outside of Europe at its founding (Belgium, France, the Netherlands, Portugal and the UK). In Moscow, NATO was perceived as an anti-Russia vehicle for US neo-imperial aspirations in Europe. Whatever the veracity of this perception, that it has been held on to by Moscow since 1949 is significant. Jealousy also played a role in why Russian hardliners hated NATO, since their own security clubs could never compete. This was true of the Warsaw Pact (1955–91), which bound the Soviet satellite states into a creaky non-voluntary alliance. It has also been true of the Collective Security Treaty Organization (CSTO), founded by Russia in 1992, and which currently has just six members from amongst the former SSR states (Armenia, Belarus, Kazakhstan, Kyrgyzstan, Russia and Tajikistan). The CSTO cannot hold a candle to NATO in terms of military power and scope. Notably, Ukraine was not a member of the CSTO and did not aspire to be, much to Russia's disappointment.

Denuclearisation

At first, Ukraine was mercifully untroubled by these geopolitical developments since the Czech Republic, Hungary and Poland were first in the queue for NATO membership. These countries were deemed by NATO as being able to meet the alliance's criteria for membership, as relating to governance and military standards, while

Ukraine was considered to be near the back of the queue. The reasons for this will be explained in the chapters to come. Some credit must also go to Kravchuk, who skilfully managed Ukraine's foreign policy in the first years of independence. In January 1994, the joint US–Ukrainian–Russian Trilateral Statement agreed to the transfer of all nuclear weapons from Ukraine to Russia, an important step since the USSR had stationed a substantial nuclear weapons arsenal in Ukraine. In exchange, the USA, UK and Russia signed the Budapest Memorandum in December 1994, jointly agreeing to guarantee Ukraine's sovereignty. This was not a collective defence guarantee, only a diplomatic 'gentlemen's agreement' about the intentions of the signatories to respect the borders of Ukraine (which Russia renegaded on two decades later when it annexed Crimea).

Debate has emerged since then as to whether Kravchuk's decision to give up the nuclear weapons stationed in Ukraine left it defenceless, leading some to argue that had Ukraine kept them, it would never have been invaded. The Ukrainian government had weighed up the pros and cons of keeping the nuclear arsenal, but the Ukrainian Foreign Ministry had judged this to carry immense practical difficulties, not least since the command and control of these nuclear weapons had been in Moscow, and it would have been costly and complex to replicate these and other facilities necessary to operate an independent nuclear deterrent. The US government also offered Ukraine all kinds of incentives and help to denuclearise.[15] We will never know the counterfactual, but there is a more credible argument that had Ukraine retained nuclear weapons, Russia would likely have intervened much earlier.[*][16]

---

[*] Maria Rost Rublee: "'If only Ukraine had kept its nuclear weapons, this would never have happened." The counterfactual heard around the world after Russia annexed Crimea in March 2014 makes intuitive sense … I contend, if Ukraine had attempted to keep the Soviet nuclear arsenal for its own military purposes, Crimea most likely would have been annexed by Russia long before 2014.'

For Kravchuk, however, this was the end of the political road. Ukraine's denuclearisation, and all of the economic woes that came from the breakup of the USSR, had aggravated political divisions. Then Prime Minister Kuchma resigned in 1993 to challenge Kravchuk for the presidency, beating him in the 1994 presidential election. Kuchma campaigned on pursuing warmer relations with Russia, and he had mobilised Ukraine's Russian-speaking constituencies for support. In the run-off vote on 10 July, Kuchma won 52 per cent over Kravchuk's 45 per cent. Despite the country being mobilised into two rival linguistic camps during the campaign, Ukraine experienced a peaceful transition of power.

*   *   *

It is worth reflecting on the Kravchuk era and what it meant to create a Ukrainian state in the early 1990s. Some states are built rather more from scratch, perhaps born from a victorious secessionist war to be run by revolutionaries who have never before held power. Ukraine's experience was the opposite. At independence, Ukraine was painted onto a partially filled canvas; its borders were already drawn in as the old administrative borders of the Ukrainian Soviet Socialist Republic. Old sketches were given new life, with its first President being the former communist boss of this republic, now reinvented as a nationalist; and key assets like its fleet, army and metallurgical industry came from the breakup of old Soviet equivalents. But Ukraine was also fashioning something new out of these raw materials, using the cultural aspirations of the nationalist-minded western Ukrainians and the legacies of the short-lived Ukrainian Republic of 1917–20. The Ukrainian state that was created in the 1990s was undoubtedly on a pioneering journey.

KUCHMA'S EAST/WEST BALANCING ACT

It was a picture of post-imperial harmony, Putin and Kuchma walking side by side as they toured the Sevastopol naval base in April 2000. They stepped aboard the flagship of Russia's Black Sea Fleet, the guided missile cruiser *Moskva*, and were greeted by a ceremonial guard of sailors in dress uniform, standing erect with their bayonets pointing to the sky. Putin and Kuchma then stepped aboard the Ukrainian navy frigate *Hetman Sahaidachny*, named after a Zaporozhian Cossack leader from the seventh century. Earlier that day the Russian and Ukrainian national anthems were played, sailors from the Russian Black Sea Fleet and the Ukrainian navy marched by, and the dignitaries laid wreaths at a monument in Sevastopol's Nakhimov Square. In a joint press conference, Putin promised that the Russian Black Sea Fleet's debts to Sevastopol would be repaid. Acting President Putin, still a month shy of being officially sworn into the job, couldn't help but add that 'Russia [would] continue to defend its national interests and pay serious attention to NATO's possible expansion toward Russian borders'.[17]

Who could have imagined on the day of this visit that both of these ships would be sunk in a war between these two countries twenty-two years later?

The first to go was Ukraine's faithful frigate, *Hetman Sahaidachny*, in service for twenty years until it was scuttled in Mykolaiv to prevent it from falling into the hands of Russian forces as they advanced out of the Crimean Peninsula. The *Moskva*'s fate was even more dramatic, having approached Ukraine's Snake Island (also known as Zmiinyi Island) early in the war only to be greeted by the immortal line, 'Russian warship, go fuck yourself', the response of the island's small Ukrainian garrison in answer to a call to surrender. Later in the war, the *Moskva* was struck by Ukrainian Neptune anti-ship missiles, likely with remote US intelligence support to assist the targeting.[18] After the missiles struck, the *Moskva* was left listing helplessly, before it sank – a truly ignominious end to a warship that had served the Russian and previously the Soviet navy for four decades and had originally been built in Soviet Ukraine.

This was a history yet to be written when Kuchma met Putin aboard the *Moskva*. Kuchma accumulated immense experience helming Ukraine, having become Prime Minister in 1992 and then President in 1994, serving in the latter role for a decade.

During this time Kuchma managed a careful geopolitical balancing act between Russia and the US-led NATO alliance. In 1997, Kuchma and Yeltsin signed the 'Treaty on Friendship, Cooperation and Partnership', which agreed to leave the existing leasing arrangements for the Sevastopol naval base on Crimea intact for twenty years, and called for the 'strengthening of friendly relations, good-neighbourliness and mutually advantageous cooperation' between the countries.[19] This was a high point in Ukraine–Russia relations.

During his first term in office (1994–99) Kuchma also leaned tentatively towards the West. In 1995, Ukraine signed on to NATO's 'Partnership for Peace' (PfP) programme, a light-touch association agreement for non-members to access military training exercises and such like, with no commitment to future NATO membership (Russia also joined the PfP programme but didn't really participate in any exercises). A largely symbolic agreement between NATO and Ukraine was drafted in 1997. Called the 'Charter on a Distinctive Partnership between the North Atlantic Treaty Organization and Ukraine', it was a non-committal statement of intent, 'welcoming the progress achieved by Ukraine and looking forward to further steps to develop its democratic institutions, to implement radical economic reforms'.[20] The charter reads like a memorandum of understanding on general principles such as democracy and nuclear safety, and represented an early step in building a positive post-Cold War relationship between Ukraine and NATO.

Crucially, it did not prevent Kuchma from operating a 'multi-vector' foreign policy that also looked to Russia as a major trading partner for Ukraine.

Dealing pragmatically with the Russians came naturally to Kuchma, who, in his heart, was a Soviet-era factory boss. Early in his career, in his hometown of Dnipropetrovsk (latterly renamed to the less Russian-sounding 'Dnipro'), Kuchma was the director of the Yuzhmash missile and aerospace factory, which produced such advanced rocketry as inter-continental ballistic missiles.[21] In his second term (1999–2004), Kuchma began to lean more towards Moscow.

What happened to tip the balance? Foremost amongst the reasons was the dire state of Ukraine's economy: in 1994, for instance, the year-on-year decline in Ukraine's GDP was close to minus 25 per cent, and it was incredibly hard to reverse the trend lines.[22] Initially stuck in the rouble zone, Ukraine also suffered immense hyper-inflation, reaching 10,000 per cent, which contributed to a growing black-market economy, and a growing culture of oligarchic politics amidst the privatisation of industries. Ukraine could not turn to the EU or the USA for massive economic help at this time, and so it turned to Russia for the most favourable terms of trade, for access to the Russian market, and to purchase Russian energy.

There were also political reasons for Kuchma's tilt towards greater Russian patronage. In October 1999, Kuchma was re-elected to the presidency in a vote that was marred by irregularities, leaving him open to Western criticism. Kuchma's style of rule also took an authoritarian turn. In 2000, Kuchma was loosely implicated in the kidnapping and killing of investigative journalist Georgiy Gongadze, who had started to dig into the business dealings of oligarchs in Ukraine. Kuchma denied involvement and was never prosecuted, but accusations tainted his rule.[23] Separately, in June 2002, Kuchma appointed Viktor Medvedchuk his chief of staff, who helped to enact strict controls on the political opposition.[24] (As a contemporary footnote, Medvedchuk was chosen by Russian intelligence officers two decades later in their failed bid to topple Zelensky's government in favour of a puppet regime. Medvedchuk was arrested by Ukrainian security forces and, at one point in the war, the Russians tried to get Medvedchuk back in a prisoner exchange for two British volunteer soldiers captured while fighting for Ukraine.)

In the early 2000s, Kuchma's second term coincided with the start of Putin's first presidency. The pair met repeatedly. Kuchma must surely have been keen, anxious even, to see what Putin would bring to the Russian presidency and would have had few illusions about how the skills and proclivities of a former KGB intelligence officer might influence the Kremlin's stance towards Ukraine. Kuchma, a relatively diminutive man, stood only a little taller than Putin, but the latter had already carved out in blood a fearsome reputation for himself by presiding over Russia's second war in the breakaway republic of Chechnya. Putin wielded all the power in the relationship with Kuchma.

Ukraine gained from its warming economic ties with Russia. In his hometown of Dnipropetrovsk, Kuchma hosted Putin in February 2001 and signed agreements that brought Russian investment into Ukraine's energy infrastructure. Kuchma agreed to connect the power grids of both countries and to cooperate further in the production of military equipment. In October 2002, Russia and

Ukraine agreed to a deal that created a consortium for the transport of gas.[25] In the early 2000s, therefore, Putin's first few years in the Russian presidency involved a pliant and cooperative Ukraine.

At this time, the gulf between the West and Ukraine seemed vast, and Ukraine was an unlikely candidate to receive the full benefits of association with either the EU or NATO. On 1 May 2004, the EU inducted ten countries as new members (Cyprus, Czech Republic, Estonia, Hungary, Latvia, Lithuania, Malta, Poland, Slovakia and Slovenia). As for NATO, the military alliance had admitted the Czech Republic, Hungary and Poland in 1999, and on 29 March 2004 admitted another seven counties (Bulgaria, Estonia, Latvia, Lithuania, Romania, Slovakia and Slovenia). Ukraine was nowhere near either membership list since it was still perceived as lacking the requisite domestic reforms, and was also considered far closer to Russia in distance and in spirit than the others.

Having left office, Kuchma published a book called *Ukraine Is Not Russia*, a title certainly intended to defend his legacy and to convey his dedication to Ukraine's independence. Given how precipitous the plummet latterly became, it seems almost quaint that Kuchma had proudly walked a high-wire balancing act between Russia and the West.

* * *

On 9 October 1999, an international football fixture took place in Moscow's Luzhniki Stadium that has never since been repeated. The Ukrainian team took the field against Russia, and the match ended in a 1–1 draw. The first goal was scored by Valeri Karpin, born in Soviet Estonia and who went on to manage Russia's national team. The equaliser was scored just three minutes from full time by Andriy Shevchenko, a Ukrainian who later played for Chelsea under the ownership of Russian oligarch Roman Abramovich. This dramatic end to the match meant Ukraine progressed to the Euro 2000 finals whereas Russia did not. How humiliating it must have felt for Russia, bested by Ukraine.

To date there has been no rematch. Indeed, since 2014 Russian and Ukrainian footballers have been banned outright by the football authorities from playing competitively against each other. If sport can be a healer, it would not be employed in this instance.

INDEPENDENCE SQUARED

The Maidan Nezalezhnosti, translated as Independence Square, sits at the heart of Kyiv. It has a storied history that mirrors the vicissitudes of the city. Pyotr Stolypin, the Prime Minister of the Russian Empire under the last Tsar, Nicholas II, was assassinated in Kyiv Opera House in 1911. The Maidan later hosted a statue of Stolypin, who was associated with brutal repression; in his day the hangman's noose was nicknamed 'Stolypin's necktie'. In Soviet times, the Maidan was used to celebrate the Bolshevik Revolution, and hosted an imposing October Revolution monument that depicted a huge Lenin, standing imperiously over smaller figures of revolutionary workers and soldiers. This is the exact spot where, in October 1990, protesters announced a hunger strike and began to demand political reforms.[26] If the square could talk, it would tell its own story of the divergent paths of Ukraine and Russia.

By the early 2000s, it was abundantly clear that Ukraine and Russia were pulling in very different directions domestically. Putin was centralising political power in Moscow and creating a near-feudal, patronage-based economy, key parts of which were operated by his former KGB colleagues. Whereas Russia was reconciling the loss of empire, Ukraine was building a nation, and its democracy was starting to show signs of flourishing.

Key to this was the generational change now under way, from Kravchuk and Kuchma to aspiring leaders who were born two or three decades after them. For instance, Kuchma's Prime Minister, Viktor Yushchenko, was dismissed in April 2001 after pursuing what were seen as policies that were too Western-leaning. Yushchenko (born in 1954) formed his own political party. Alongside his sometimes-ally Yulia Tymoshenko (born in 1960), he looked away from Russia and towards the West for inspiration and allyship.[27] As the story of Maidan Square demonstrated, times change even though the surroundings remain the same. Ukrainians born in the early days of the USSR, whom Russia knew how to deal with, were now retiring.

Aside from the generational changes threatening to drive a wedge between Russia and Ukraine, the geopolitical tides were choppy. The post-Cold War world was maturing around Ukraine, and the 'multi-vector' foreign policy practised at the start of Kuchma's tenure in 1994 would become less feasible at the end of his time in office a decade later.

*   *   *

During the 1990s, US ambitions had grown regarding what could be achieved by continually expanding NATO. In 1997, Secretary of State Madeleine Albright explained that 'the prospect of [NATO] enlargement has given central and eastern Europe greater stability than it has seen in this century' and, in the process, 'we have made a particular effort to reach out to Ukraine'. The prospect of friction between Russia and Ukraine was never seriously mentioned, and

Russia was dismissed as an irrelevance with no say in the process, aside from in the relatively toothless 'Russia–NATO Council', which was created in later years to at least provide a forum for discussion, between two sides who openly distrusted each other.

'I do not believe that the debate about NATO should be reduced to a debate about Russia,' Albright explained, because 'we do not *need* Russia to agree to enlargement. The point is to advance a goal that is worthwhile in its own right.' She was bullish:

I do not expect the Russian government to change its mind about NATO's plans to take in new members. We must face this fact squarely, but we should also recognise it for what it is: an issue of perception, not of military reality ... We do no favour to Russia's democrats to suggest otherwise.[28]

For Albright's deputy, Strobe Talbott, NATO expansion was all about maximising the upsides and minimising the downsides. Optimistically, 'the very prospect of NATO membership has already begun to encourage positive, peaceful trends in central Europe' as it became a vehicle for democratisation. Luckily, thought Talbott in 1997, the downsides were negligible:

As everyone knows, the issue of NATO enlargement is acutely neuralgic in Russia, especially for the political elite there ... There are Russian hard-liners who long for what they remember as the glory days of the USSR and who exploit what they depict as the spectre of NATO to whip up nationalistic passions. There are also plenty of Russian reformers and democrats who worry – and warn – that NATO enlargement threatens to strengthen those reactionary forces. We believe that that risk is both exaggerated and manageable.[29]

As it transpired, the passage of time proved Talbott's and Albright's assumptions about Russia to be incorrect. NATO expansion delivered a gift to Russia's hardliners, because the perception of Western threat was enough to allow Putin to justify tough policies at home and abroad. Putin would repeatedly complain that by expanding NATO, the West threatened Russia's security, and was moving into its old sphere of cultural influence. It was a powerful argument despite being only partially true. Even if NATO expansion posed no actual security threat, Russia was still left smouldering with rage over losing influence in its immediate neighbourhood. In short, NATO's eastward expansion would over time have a big impact in shaping Russia itself.

It is an easy thing to argue with moral clarity that Russia has had no right to contest the expansion of NATO and, given its imperial past, that Russia did not deserve any say in the affairs of its old spheres of influence. But it is harder to argue this in practice, since power and size tell their own story. At the time, Talbott admitted that 'unlike Germany in 1918 or again in 1945, Russia in 1997 is not a defeated power'. NATO expansion played an important, albeit indirect and inadvertent, role in sowing the seeds of the virulent Russian imperial-revivalist traditions of statecraft, which germinated during the next two decades under Putin's rule.

Was the USA unwise to expand NATO? In the historian Mary Sarotte's estimation, based on her study of US diplomacy at the time, the US got carried away with itself as the winds of change swept across Europe: 'The US realised it could not only win big, but bigger' by continually adding new NATO members. This was a delicate matter, says Sarotte. 'The expansion of NATO was a justifiable response to the challenges of the 1990s and to the entreaties of new central and eastern European democracies. The problem was *how* it happened.' The advent of democratisation in eastern Europe needed a response, and Washington threw caution to the wind by dealing with the people once ruled by Moscow, while essentially ignoring Moscow itself. Moreover, the USA did not take incremental steps towards the accession of new NATO members; it extended full NATO Article 5 defence guarantees to them right away, effectively dumping the use of the NATO PfP mechanism as a precursor step to slow the passage to full membership. The outcome was that 'Washington and Moscow snatched stalemate from the jaws of victory', since both sides contributed to driving a permanent wedge between them over NATO's expansion.[30]

In 1995's Operation Deliberate Force, and in 1999's Operation Allied Force, NATO was used to launch air strikes across the former Yugoslavia. Russian anger towards NATO grew, notably when Serbia, a state it was historically sympathetic to, was targeted by NATO air strikes. 'It should astonish no one', judged Samuel Charap and Timothy J. Colton, 'that a country of Russia's capabilities and ambitions will seek influence over its periphery; the US or China are no different in that respect', even if their methods of influence vary. Moreover, 'the psychological fallout from the heir to a superpower being denied an authentic voice in shaping the regional order and being told to wait its turn to get in' was a deeply impactful factor.[31]

In its waning years, the Clinton administration sensed how tricky further NATO expansion may be in the wake of the Kosovo war, so they slowed the process of admission and kicked the can down the road for their successors in the White House's next administration to deal with. At NATO's fiftieth anniversary summit in April 1999, held a month after the Czech Republic, Hungary and Poland joined the alliance, Clinton and the other NATO leaders decided to push the question of further expansion to no later than 2002, and thus to the administration of George W. Bush.

There was simply no way to reconcile the triplicate forces of the democratisation wave taking hold in Europe, the expansion of NATO, and Russia's desire to remain a great power with a direct stake in the region. 'Ukraine was the place where democracy and independence most challenged Russia's conception of its national interest,' judged the academic Paul D'Anieri. 'It was not inevitable that this conflict would lead to violence, but neither was it likely to resolve itself.'[32]

Such is the fate of countries like Ukraine, large in their own right but minnows in a world of mammoths like the USA, Russia and NATO. For the first era of independence, Ukraine was out of the crosshairs, as international attention focused on the Balkans, then on the countries of the old Warsaw Pact now joining NATO, and eventually on the Middle East and Afghanistan after the 9/11 terrorist attacks. The question was this: for how long could Ukraine duck out of the crosshairs and pursue a path that was independent of Russia? Perhaps Kuchma's balancing act could never have been sustained indefinitely, but the USA, NATO and Russia each played their own role in ensuring that such a balancing act would never again be possible for a future Ukrainian President. For a country that measures nearly 1,300 kilometres east to west and is populated by a huge mixture of people, having to swing fully into either the Western or the Russian camp untroubled was simply never going to be possible.

CHAPTER 3

PUTIN SEES ORANGE

A REFLECTION ON REVOLUTION

THE PENDULUM

The roar of the audience cut through the snowfall in Dynamo Kyiv's football stadium, and now they cheered every time the ball was struck, including by the visiting Italian team. The football had itself become a symbol of pure joy to the home crowd due to a trick of fate: the November snowfall had rendered the normal white ball invisible to the players, so the referee replaced it midway in the match for the bright orange all-weather ball. This was standard practice for a professional football match, but it happened to coincide with the Orange Revolution, named by Yushchenko's supporters after he adopted orange as the colour of his election campaign. Revolution was in the air in Kyiv, but here it felt more like a party, and I noticed the hundreds of young police officers keeping security at the game took their seats in the stadium to watch their team beat the Italians.*

---

* The match finished Dynamo Kyiv 2–0 AS Roma and was part of the 2003–04 UEFA Champions League. It was played at Valeriy Lobanovskyi Stadium in the heart of Kyiv, close to the Dnieper River.

The stadium was freezing, and I was encouraged to stay warm by downing shots of vodka handed to me by friendly Dynamo supporters. This was my first taste not only of Ukrainian vodka in the snowfall but of Ukrainian political tumult. Like many of the best adventures, I was there by happenstance. Having graduated from university that year and as yet without a job, I bumped into a fellow graduate from my university who recruited Brits for election monitoring missions around the word run by the UN, the EU and, in the post-Soviet space, by the Organization for Security and Co-operation (OSCE), a club of fifty-seven states that is headquartered in Vienna.*

This election was expected to be an obscure event, which is why a rookie such as myself was encouraged to apply, so they could boost numbers. Indeed, hundreds of election monitors were needed in total to cover Ukraine's expanse. I ended up observing all three rounds of the 2004 presidential election and coming back in later years to observe two subsequent parliamentary elections.

Thanks to these experiences, I ventured far out of Kyiv, to the east and the west, noticing how it still exuded a very dense Soviet feel in some of its cities, shops, railways and other environments. Ukraine was a beguiling country to visit, clearly on the move but as yet unsure where it was headed.

The 2004 presidential election ended up being anything other than an obscure event – far from it, since it snowballed into, at the time, independent Ukraine's most seismic moment to date. The

---

* The OSCE originated from the detente that helped to thaw out the Cold War. It convened in 1973 as the Conference for Security and Co-operation in Europe (CSCE) and was renamed the OSCE in 1995. It has fifty-seven member states including the Russian Federation, other Soviet successor states, western European counties, Canada and the USA. The standing of the OSCE as a multilateral club capable of playing a lead role in regulating European security affairs has been eclipsed by the expansion eastwards of NATO and the EU. The OSCE's own need for consensus decision-making between its member states has been another limitation.

election result was bitterly disputed, leading to a popular revolution and exposing deep regional divisions as the country momentarily threatened to pull itself apart over who should be the next President. A geopolitical tug of war was precipitated over Ukraine's fate, which turned into the first key event in Russia's falling out with Ukraine. The Orange Revolution was the moment Russia's elite first seriously feared they were losing influence over Ukraine. The genesis of the crisis was, however, internal to Ukraine, an outcome of domestic machinations accompanying the maturation of a sovereign country that, with each passing year, moved further from its Soviet backstory.

*   *   *

The path to the Orange Revolution began at the tail end of the Kuchma presidency. After nearly a decade in power, domestic opposition forces were mobilising against him, staging a 'Ukraine without Kuchma' publicity campaign that came after the Gongadze scandal in 2000. The political opposition did well in parliamentary elections held on 31 March 2002. In this vote, seen as a preview of the forthcoming presidential election, Viktor Yushchenko's 'Our Ukraine' bloc won 23.57 per cent; the Communist Party won 19.98 per cent; the pro-administration 'For A United Ukraine' bloc received 11.77 per cent; and Yulia Tymoshenko (whom Kuchma's government had once tried to arrest due to a scandal around an energy deal) fronted a party that won 7.26 per cent. In other words, the field was wide open. Kuchma must have feared history would repeat itself: just as he, a former Prime Minister, had replaced his old boss Kravchuk in 1994, now Kuchma's own ex-Prime Minister Yushchenko was poised for power.

Following the 2002 parliamentary election, the pro-Kuchma bloc assembled a slim majority in the Verkhovna Rada of just 226 seats and were forced to rely heavily on unaffiliated parliamentarians to prop up the majority. Opposition figures complained about the manner of forming the majority and accused the government of using blackmail and bribery to secure the support of the independent Members of Parliament. Eventually, Our Ukraine, the communists, the Tymoshenko bloc and others began to call for an early election and issue joint statements questioning Kuchma's legitimacy to rule.*

It is important to note that the loose coalition of opposition parties to Kuchma at this time could hardly be called 'pro-Western'. For instance, the leader of the Communist Party, Petro Symonenko, pursued a traditional Marxist line, wanted stronger links with Russia and had once questioned if the Holodomor was a man-made famine. Rather, this was Ukrainian democracy in all its rawness of the time, with a rich diversity of views that reflected the different heritages and complexions of Ukraine's populace.

Despite having secured for himself the right to contest a third presidential election, somewhere along the line, Kuchma decided not to run again for President. Instead, the government's old guard, including Kuchma's chief of staff Medvedchuk and the Rada Speaker Volodymyr Lytvyn, backed a candidate who could defend their vision of Ukraine. Kuchma endorsed the candidacy of his current Prime Minister, Viktor Yanukovych. The stage was now set for a duel between 'the two Viktors'.

Unbeknownst to me at the time as I tucked into my first servings of *vareniki* (dumplings) and buckwheat, while also taking in

---

* This analysis draws on the OSCE's pre-election analysis for its observer mission. Documents in possession of author.

the vicissitudes of Ukrainian politics, the geopolitical 'great powers' were now lining up their own goals for Ukraine. Within the corridors of Washington and Brussels great hope was being placed on the outcome of Ukraine's 2004 election. The US State Department, in conversations with EU officials, thought that 'the October presidential election would be a watershed for Ukraine – a free and fair election would be a huge step toward the consolidation of democracy, and the opposite would be a huge setback', and they discussed 'the multiplier effect of strong, coordinated US and EU messages on democracy'.[1]

Ukraine was becoming ever more interesting to Brussels and Washington, and ever more anxiety-inducing for Moscow.

For the Russian government there was scant interest in the electoral process itself, only on its preferred outcome: a Yanukovych victory preserving the interests and pro-Russian sympathies of Ukraine's 'old guard'. Yanukovych hailed from east Ukraine and if he won power, he was likely to strengthen the status of the Russian language amongst the Ukrainian populace, while reorienting Ukraine's foreign and economic policies further towards Russia. 'Of all the former Soviet republics,' wrote the former *Financial Times* Moscow correspondent Catherine Belton, 'Moscow had always felt the loss of Ukraine following the Soviet collapse most keenly, as if it were a phantom limb of empire that Russia believed was still attached.'[2] For pro-Russian minds, that missing limb was about to start twingeing uncontrollably as the election played out.

Compared to the increasingly open field of Ukrainian politics, Russia's domestic politics was moving in precisely the opposite direction. Putin's political vehicle, 'United Russia', began to base its own nationalist rhetoric on uniting the country against all manner of external and internal enemies, from Islamist terrorists in the restive Russian north Caucasus region to the supporters of so-called 'coloured revolutions'. Putin's United Russia wanted to offer a vision of renewal in the aftermath of an imperial collapse, and was busy restoring the Soviet national anthem with new words along-side various Tsarist symbols because, according to political scientist Marlene Laruelle, who wrote a book on this phenomenon, 'they are part of the common cultural background and seen as an indication of normalcy' by Putin.[3]

In stark contrast, 2004 was the year that Ukraine truly began its journey of forging a different path to Russia by breaking away from its Soviet past. Or at least, a certain part of the country did, since Ukraine was at this time a deeply divided country in which far from all of its inhabitants felt that way about Russia, the West, and wher-ever else in the world to look when locating bastions of support for one's own identity.

ROUND ONE, 31 OCTOBER 2004

Only by traversing the length and breadth of Ukraine does the size of the country dawn on you. Sure, it cannot compare to the vast-ness of the Russian Federation, which can require weeks aboard the Trans-Siberian Railway to cross even a subset of the country's eleven time zones, but Ukraine's 600,000-odd square kilometres make it the largest country wholly in Europe. To travel between the city of Lviv in the west to Kyiv in the centre to the Donbas region in the east, one can hop on board an overnight train, set out for a long drive or take a domestic flight. Ukraine seemed huge to me when I first arrived, from the cavernous National Aviation University au-ditorium in Kyiv, used to brief the hundreds of election monitors assembled by the OSCE, to the deep descents into Kyiv's artful sub-terranean metro, to the considerable local distances we would drive to reach remote polling stations – once we were assigned an area of responsibility to cover.

My first destination was Lviv, having been assigned to monitor the first round of voting there, and my first taste of the city was being greeted by a TV news channel film crew awaiting our arrival on the tarmac of the airport. Lviv seemed to be a world unto itself and far away, geographically and spiritually, from what I later experienced in east Ukraine. Lviv, after all, was the former Austro-Hungarian city of Lemberg, as was pointed out to me by my German colleague, but I also heard Polish colleagues wisecracking that the city 'really still should belong to us and be named Lwów', referring to the various stages of the life of the city. This was a stark reminder of how much Lviv in particular and Ukraine in general had been subjected to contention over their borders and sovereignty, contention that led eventually to the 2014 and 2022 invasions. Back in 2004, however, the issues that mattered to Ukrainians were of a different nature. The clamour of the news team to record our arrival, and indeed the enthusiasm of the locals more generally for the presence of monitors from EU states and from North America, suggested a genuine hunger for international engagement – and a genuine fear that forces in the east were about to steal the election by rigging it.

Lviv is the unofficial capital of pro-Western Ukrainian sentiment and, unsurprisingly, Yushchenko's forward-looking, pro-Western message was popular in Lviv and its surrounding environs. *Tak* – 'yes' in Ukrainian – was the simple one-word slogan of Yushchenko's campaign along with the orange ribbons and scarves worn by his supporters (it was simply a striking colour that had no particular link to Ukrainian history). *Pora* – meaning that it was calling 'time' on defunct regimes – was the name of the student groups that campaigned for Yushchenko's candidacy. Yushchenko and Tymoshenko had also united their campaigns to create a wider movement they dubbed 'Power of the People'. It was a well-organised opposition campaign and its supporters in western Ukraine were vocal and abundant.

The same could not be said nationwide, and favourable coverage of Yushchenko's campaigns was conspicuously absent in parts of the broadcast and print media – social media still being in its infancy, of course. Most major Ukrainian TV channels failed to offer Yushchenko wide-ranging and favourable coverage, with the exception of Channel 5, which was owned by the businessman and future Ukrainian President Petro Poroshenko, and even this channel could transmit to only one-third of the country, and at one point it was simply taken off the air. Some opposition-leaning media outlets even received anonymous death threats by telephone. The opposition voice could be heard in some places, but the state was attempting to crowd it out.

When this didn't work, the forces conspiring to stop Yushchenko resorted to more brazen means: poisoning. In the evening of 5 September 2004, Yushchenko attended a dinner with his advisor David Zhvania and two other men, the chairman and deputy chairman of the SBU (the Ukrainian domestic intelligence service), Ihor Smeshko and Volodymyr Statsyuk. Yushchenko fell violently ill after the dinner. He was flown to a specialist clinic in Vienna soon after, where it was determined that he had been poisoned by the chemical dioxin, and although Yushchenko's life was saved he emerged from his ordeal with a badly disfigured face. Culpability for the poisoning has never been fully established, but there were certainly enough people in Ukraine and in Russia who did not want to see a pro-Western President of Ukraine. Needless to say, for the Russians, Yushchenko was anathema.[4]

The braided visage of Yulia Tymoshenko had become the face of the opposition in Yushchenko's absence, and he delivered his first speech after the poisoning on 18 September. Yushchenko delivered his speech while wiping sweat from his brow and still visibly ill. His words now carried their own venom, and Tymoshenko was herself a firebrand speaker. This suitably riled up the opposition movement, and on 23 October they staged a final pre-election rally in Kyiv with the message of stopping election fraud, delivered when some of the protesters marched on to Ukraine's Central Election Commission building.[5]

In the first round of voting, the electorate were selecting from twenty-six candidates for the subsequent run-off between the top two. On the day, Yushchenko won 39.9 per cent of the vote and only narrowly beat Yanukovych's 39.3 per cent. Yanukovych had campaigned on a platform that was sympathetic to Russia bolstering the official status of the Russian language in Ukraine and against closer cooperation with NATO, as two key positions. Ukraine was divided regionally and quite neatly, as Yushchenko won with a tally of 78 per cent of the votes in seventeen western and central regions, whereas Yanukovych won an average of 71 per cent in ten eastern and southern regions. The communist vote fell to just 5 per cent and never recovered again, as Yanukovych stole the pro-Russian vote in Ukraine with a brand of populism that appealed to the proletariat and pensioners particularly in the east.[6]

What flummoxed Russia's government was its sense that the West was stealing the election: that Yushchenko's popularity was mainly the result of Western meddling, and that Ukraine truly belonged at Russia's side. Before examining the evidence behind these allegations, it is worth stepping back to the world of 2004 to understand why this explanation seemed compelling to Putin.

Foreign intervention

In the early 2000s, the notion of democracy promotion was buoyant in US government circles. These were the heady days of US unipolarity and Fukuyama-infused confidence in the emerging spread of Western-style liberal capitalist democracies the world over. In a striking artefact from that era, former Reagan-era US ambassador to Hungary Mark Palmer authored a book in 2003 entitled *Breaking the Real Axis of Evil: How to Oust the World's Last Dictators by 2025*. Palmer, as a former diplomat, wrote with authority about transforming US embassies around the world into bastions of democracy promotion that could unleash local pro-democracy forces. Books like this gained attention for having arrived at the time of the neo-conservative Bush administration's invasion of Iraq, which intended to topple Saddam Hussein and to instil democracy by force. It followed the campaign to weaken and topple Slobodan Milošević, who lost power in a popular uprising in 2000 and ended up on trial in the Hague for crimes against humanity conducted by the Serbian forces he led during the Yugoslav wars.

Even if there was no war being waged by US forces in east Europe to instil democracy, the language of 'free and fair elections', and the accompanying certification by authorised international monitoring missions (like the one I was part of), was very much part of the toolkit of Western foreign policy. Jean-Jacques Rousseau's famous line that 'man is born free but is everywhere in chains' had seemingly been adopted by the USA as its foreign policy credo under the neo-cons who governed in Washington DC during the Bush administration (2001–09).

Was Yushchenko's popularity Western-backed? The answer is less than clear, and it depends on what is inferred by external support. The student activist group *Pora* was built with Western technical help but little financial assistance, and this seems to be all that the USA has admitted to in terms of leveraging its influence in Ukraine at this time.[7] For instance, the future US ambassador to Russia Michael McFaul, then an academic, wrote an article in the *International Security* journal where he gathered evidence of external support to the Orange Revolution. He wrote, 'Although the US government never targeted its financial resources at fomenting revolution, it spent more than $18 million in election-related assistance efforts in Ukraine in the two years leading up to the 2004 presidential vote,' adding that 'these were official figures produced to the author by staff in the Office of the Coordinator for US Assistance to Europe and Eurasia, US Department of State.'[8]

American groups like the International Republican Institute (IRI) and the National Democratic Institute (NDI) gave 'ideas and know-how' to Yushchenko's party Our Ukraine, but 'there is no evidence that the US or any European government contributed financial resources directly to the campaign of Viktor Yushchenko and Our Ukraine'. Groups like the IRI, the NDI, International Renaissance Foundation (the local Ukrainian affiliate of the Soros Foundation), Freedom House, Internews-Ukraine and the Eurasia Foundation 'contributed direct financial assistance to the get-out-the-vote projects organised by their Ukrainian partners' to encourage the high turnout in Yushchenko's core areas that boosted his vote tally.[9] In short, foreign NGOs helped Yushchenko, and the work in the US embassy almost certainly added focus to these efforts, making it look like 'the will of the people' but at the same time helping to boost the campaigning techniques of Western-leaning candidates.[10]

By comparison, the tricks employed by Russians who backed Yanukovych's campaign were blunt, menacing and out of date. The brazen act of poisoning a rival was in a league of its own insidiousness. Other tactics involved Putin publicly endorsing Yanukovych, and Yanukovych's supporters smearing Yushchenko as being an anti-Russian Western puppet.

Just days before the first round, Putin travelled to Kyiv to appear alongside Kuchma, Yanukovych, the Belarusian President Alexander Lukashenko and Azerbaijan's President Ilham Aliyev. Incidentally, Putin, Lukashenko and Aliyev all remain in power in their respective countries at the time of writing, eighteen years after this vignette. On 28 October, they all attended a military parade that was staged on the central Khreshchatyk boulevard to celebrate the sixtieth anniversary of the liberation of Ukraine by the Red Army in World War Two – the first time this commemoration had ever taken place. Its messaging was clear: Ukraine remained in a post-Soviet cultural and historical space and Russia would always be the big brother. The parade was one of Putin's multiple visits to Ukraine in 2004, another of which took place in July when Putin met Yanukovych in Yalta, Crimea – a location rife with World War Two symbolism after Stalin had attended the famous Yalta Conference in 1945 with Roosevelt and Churchill.

The Kremlin's tactics for backing Yanukovych belonged – almost literally in the case of the World War Two parade – in a museum. By comparison, the Western approach was to arm the Ukrainian candidates it favoured with the techniques to compete convincingly in the election. Whether outside powers had any right at all to influence Ukraine's political destiny is another matter entirely. We may consider some interventionist tactics as being more morally virtuous than others, or we may deem all foreign intervention as being beyond the pale. Regardless of which stance we take on the matter of principle, there was a competitive game at play between Western countries and Russia to increase the chances of their favoured Viktor. At the time, Yanukovych had genuine grass-roots support in east and south Ukraine, but his backers in the Kremlin were starting to fear that this would not be enough, thus more dirty tricks would be needed to sway the vote.

ROUND TWO, 21 NOVEMBER 2004

In the next round, as the tug of war over Ukraine's fate intensified, the rope itself began to fray and threatened to be torn apart. This time, my area of monitoring responsibility was Kuchma's home-town, the eastern city of Dnipropetrovsk, to be renamed Dnipro in 2016. As previously mentioned, this name was considered more 'Ukrainian-sounding', despite the majority of residents in this in-dustrial metropolis traditionally being Russian speakers. Here, in eastern Ukraine in 2004, we encountered grim-faced apparatchiks manning local electoral offices and polling stations, with some less than welcoming to Western outsiders.

One abiding memory is of pulling up at a polling station in our white OSCE-emblazoned vehicle, only for a young chap seeing us approach run into the station, shouting at the top of his voice in Rus-sian, *'The Americans are here!'* This was an amusing blanket char-acterisation of the international community since the two OSCE observers in the car comprised myself, of British-Indian origin, and my Hungarian colleague, who happened to be called Attila.

This latter fact amused everyone present and helped to break the ice when we introduced ourselves in some of the polling stations we visited. But no amount of levity could hide the fact that election monitoring in the east was uncovering serious ballot fraud. Attila and I heard stories, which we later verified, of people being bussed between polling stations to vote multiple times. We saw irregulari-ties in the voting lists that were later found to involve names of dead voters being inserted into the lists to justify carrying extra ballot papers, inevitably marked for Yanukovych.

If you can't win fair, win dirty was the mantra for those backing Yanukovych. It worked, with another extremely tight race that was won by Yanukovych, who secured 49.5 per cent of the vote over Yushchenko's 46.6 per cent. Immediately after the results were announced, Putin congratulated Yanukovych on his victory and followed this up on 25 November with a congratulatory official letter. This time Putin had spoken too soon. The run-off was so marred by allegations of electoral fraud that the Supreme Court declared Yanukovych's apparent victory void. Manipulating the voter lists was one tactic used to steal the election; others involved pressuring state employees to vote a certain way, with police and military personnel having their votes 'approved' by their officers. Reports even surfaced of some hospital staff pressing patients on how they should vote. There were suspicious turnouts of almost 100 per cent in some eastern regions. Back in Kyiv, the focus of attention now became the Central Election Commission (CEC), which had initially declared Yanukovych's victory. The CEC was now effectively placed on trial by the Supreme Court, as witness testimonies and evidence of electoral fraud began to spread.

Yushchenko's orange-clad supporters now took to Kyiv's streets in their thousands. In response to the political and legal stalemate, Kyiv was brought to a virtual standstill by massive street demonstrations by opposition supporters. The Orange Revolution was in full flight, and the US Secretary of State Colin Powell made a statement of support for the protesters on 24 November that further buoyed the pro-Yushchenko protesters: 'Today the United States stand with the people of Ukraine and their effort to ensure their democratic choice … It is time for Ukrainian leaders to decide whether they are on the side of democracy or not.' The USA rejected the vote due to reports of fraud and abuse, and as Powell demanded, 'We call for a full review of the conduct of the election and the tallying of election results.'

To Western governments and publics this was developing into the perfect story: it was a continuation of the post-Cold War liberation of eastern Europe, and it involved striking a blow through people power against Russia's freedom-hating ambitions. It was the ultimate validation of the key assumptions underpinning US foreign policy at this time: of the superiority, perhaps even the ultimate inevitability, of the spread of liberal democracies all over the globe.

Riding the overnight train back from Dnipropetrovsk to Kyiv, a more seasoned American colleague speculated that 'the Russians won't let this happen. I've heard rumours they are sending snipers up to the roofs in Kyiv to target the protesters.' This American colleague had been around the block, observing elections all over Europe and Africa, and had seen his fair share of post-election violence. As it turns out, his prediction was a decade too early as a version of this was Russia's response to the 2013–14 Maidan protests (documented in Chapter 5). There was indeed some anecdotal evidence and warnings by the Orange leaders to suggest that Yanukovych wanted to use force to disperse the protests, and that the Kremlin would have backed him, but there was no definitive evidence of any tangible Russian military involvement in November and December 2004.[11] As our train arrived in Kyiv, the scene was tense, but it was not violent.

Walking through the Maidan, the scene that greeted me looked like a snow-draped Woodstock Festival. Lots of young Ukrainians, huddling in tents to keep warm, with supplies at hand, were enjoying the vibe of political activism plus the acts taking to the huge and modern-looking stage that had been erected to host speeches and musical performances. In some respects, it was no different from the music festivals young people attended, the big change being the weather. I recall purchasing a hotdog from a well-provisioned food stall in a bid to warm myself up, only to see the end of it begin to freeze as I hurriedly tried to eat the rest. Clearly, as Michael McFaul later wrote,

> the protest was not spontaneous. Months in advance of the presidential election, Our Ukraine campaign leaders made plans to organize street demonstrations in what they believed was the likely event that the election results would be falsified. At the last minute, the location of their protest changed, and some tactics of mobilisation misfired, such as a planned parallel vote count to be conducted in the tents in Maidan Square … The quick appearance of truck-loads of tents, mats, and food supplies, which had been secured weeks before, demonstrated the opposition's preplanning.[12]

I wove a path through the encamped protesters and through the crowd that stood in front of the stage on Maidan Square, taking in the atmosphere. Revolution was in the air but felt good-natured and non-confrontational. Riot police surrounded the nearby Parliament building, and despite the clatter of their shields making the protesters there jump, it remained only a stand-off. Yanukovych's supporters organised a big rally to back his claim in the Donbas mining town of Severodonetsk on 28 November, in which noises were made about holding a possible referendum on the federalisation of

Ukraine, which was, according to the economist Anders Åslund, 'an old eastern demand, which aroused new worries about the breakup of Ukraine, but it led nowhere'.[13]

During the seventeen-day crisis, the fracturing of Ukraine between eastern regions that mainly voted for Yanukovych and western regions that mainly voted for Yushchenko was a real possibility. Kuchma had appealed to all sides to avoid such an eventuality, and foreign leaders began to fly in for talks. These included Lech Wałęsa, former Polish President and leader of the Solidarity movement that managed Poland's transition to democracy, the serving Polish President Aleksander Kwaśniewski, the Lithuanian President Valdas Adamkus, and Javier Solana, a senior EU official and ex-NATO Secretary General. These talks helped to break the logjam, as Yushchenko, Kuchma and Yanukovych thrashed out an arrangement with enough concessions for each side to agree to a rerun of the elections.[14]

Yushchenko told the protesters to remain *in situ* until the election results were reversed or annulled. Only through a complete rerun of the run-off vote was this most bitterly disputed of polls resolved; the cost of doing so was to arm Putin for ever with the argument that the USA and the EU were hypocrites who respected democracy only to the extent that it delivered their preferred result. In Putin's Russia, 'managed' democracy and rigged election campaigns became the norm, since the purpose of politics was to ensure continuity of governance for a ruling elite that channelled a non-negotiable version of national destiny. There was little compatibility with Western notions of electoral politics. Aside from the exercise of dropping ballot papers into a ballot box, much else varied, and in Putin's eyes the net result of Western influence in Ukrainian politics was simply a different version of stealing an election. Make of this Russian grievance what you will, but it was genuinely felt in Moscow.

ROUND THREE, 26 DECEMBER 2004

Rural Ukraine, like so many rural places in other countries, can appear like a land that time forgot. This time I was sent to an obscure and remote area in the Khmelnytskyi Oblast, which is roughly midway between Kyiv and Lviv. Walking across sodden tractor trails pressed deep into the mud to reach one particular polling station, aside from the vehicles, the scene before me could have been dated from any time in the past hundred years.

Inside the polling station, which was little more than a shack with no heating, I was astonished to see several pensioners enter, one after the other, each donning a communal pair of spectacles that was being offered to older voters who did not bring their own so they could decipher the words on the ballot paper. Surely they had different optical prescriptions? The next day, when I came to settle my hotel bill the day after the election, I could not fathom why the receptionist seemingly ignored me and instead began to fiddle with a bunch of coloured beads on a risen wooden rack. Then it hit me: this was an abacus, and the receptionist was calculating my hotel bill! In 2004, every day brought instances like these highlighting the extent of Ukraine's underdevelopment.

At the time of the rerun, as I navigated the ploughs and tractors, I could not shake the feeling that I was missing out since I was far away from the Orange Revolution's tent city in Kyiv, which had by now became a fixture in the international news.

Ukraine's Supreme Court had concluded its rumination in early December, dismissing several members and scheduling the rerun for 26 December. To avert another fraudulent election fiasco, electoral law amendments were made to address some areas of concern highlighted by international observers. In particular, the supply of absentee ballots was capped, and the procedure tightened so that just one specially designated polling station per constituency could accept them. This virtually eradicated absentee ballot fraud. In addition, the rerun was praised for reduced reports of coercion by state employees, and for a greater plurality of views being presented by the media.[15]

As we patrolled the area, we noticed that the Russian-run Commonwealth of Independent States (CIS) had deployed its own observation mission. The CIS was another 'USSR-lite' voluntary club of states. Both the initial rounds were declared perfectly democratic by the CIS executive secretary Vladimir Rushailo (a former Russian Interior Minister) while the rerun incurred criticisms of fraud. This sequence was so perfectly in tune with Moscow's unequivocal backing of Yanukovych that the mission's independence was questionable. One must be sceptical of election observers from countries that are themselves in varying stages of democratic transition, I was reminded by my senior OSCE colleagues.

The result this time was unequivocal, with Yanukovych gaining 44.2 per cent of the vote and Yushchenko securing 52 per cent. At one point, as McFaul recounts,

the Yanukovych campaign called his opponent 'Bushenko' and circulated posters and leaflets warning of a US-orchestrated civil war in Ukraine similar to those in Bosnia, Serbia and Iraq, should Yushchenko come to power. The campaign strategy worked. Yanukovych won smashing victories in the December round of voting in the eastern regions of Donetsk [93 per cent], Luhansk [91 per cent], and

Crimea [81 per cent], but he failed to break double digits in the western regions of Ternopil, Ivano-Frankivsk, Lviv, and Volyn Oblast.[16]

The Orange Revolution was the top news story for nearly a month. As the tents were taken down, the outcome was an important victory for the Westernising forces in Ukraine, but the election had shown that Ukraine was a country of many parts, and some of these parts had little interest in a Westernising agenda.

UKRAINE'S GOVERNMENT TRIES TO LEAVE RUSSIA BEHIND

The Orange Revolution changed everything for Ukraine, and moreover Russia's perception of its supposed little brother. In early 2005, Yushchenko took power with a desire to lead Ukraine out of the Kremlin's orbit, and to renew Ukraine's efforts to join NATO and the EU. These institutions did not play a particularly big role in the 2004 election, but they would thereafter. This was the moment that Ukraine became a competitive battleground for rival geopolitical ambitions in a way that it never had before, when at least some goodwill allowed for misunderstandings between the major players circling around Ukraine to be resolved constructively. Now, the ties were loosened and the competition between the West and Russia to be able to determine Ukraine's future became much more intense.[17]

From Putin's perspective, an array of colourful tides were turning against Russia across the region. In the space of barely eighteen months, Georgia experienced the Rose Revolution in November 2003 that saw old Soviet Foreign Minister Eduard Shevardnadze replaced by Mikheil Saakashvili; Ukraine's Orange Revolution ended in December 2004 with Kuchma out and Yushchenko in power; and over in former Soviet central Asia, the Tulip Revolution in Kyrgyzstan took place in April 2005 whereby Askar Akayev's fifteen-year hold on power ended, removing yet another Soviet-era political whom the Kremlin had trusted to run a now-independent former Soviet republic. This trend worried Moscow as it would mean losing its cultural and coercive influence on these capitals. But what was truly alarming was that the Colour Revolutions in Georgia and Ukraine in particular were happening at the time of Western club expansion. As ever, some may find these Russian worries 'manufactured', 'absurd' and any other sentiment when it comes to what Moscow should be 'allowed' to do. Yet as we know, international affairs don't work like this: we cannot mirror-image or foist our set of priorities and per- spectives onto other countries, especially those run by regimes that are convinced by their own interpretations of history.

Russia also took particular umbrage at the phenomenon that these Colour Revolutions followed remarkably similar patterns. The academics Donnacha Ó Beacháin and Abel Polese looked into this matter and found the repeated use in different countries of local activist NGOs that received training from international bodies in order to work with the political opposition against a decrepit in- cumbent regime. This fusion of NGOs and opposition politicians then worked hard to maximise the voter turnout to win the election, and if this failed to force the incumbent out of power, to mount street protests until it did so.[18] The authors surveyed the process of 'trying to go post-Soviet' in Slovakia (1998), Serbia (2000), Georgia (2003) and 'perfecting the post-Soviet' in Ukraine (2004), judging it to be a formulaic set of tactics being used to reshape the politics of the region.[19]

Russia was not going to take this passively: it tried and succeeded in slicing the Orange coalition from afar by using Ukraine's con- sumption of Russian energy as a weapon of coercion. The Ukrainian state oil and gas company Naftogaz proposed a price change in July 2005, and in subsequent negotiations with the supplier, Russian gas giant Gazprom, a dispute spiralled out of control and Russia briefly cut off all gas supplies to Ukraine. 'It is no secret that Russia uses its energy resources for ensuring the political loyalty of some countries,' reported the Ukrainian media at the time.[20]

Russia intended to hike up Ukraine's gas prices in a politically motivated move. In November 2005, Oleh Rybachuk, President Yushchenko's chief of staff, tried to broker a new agreement on buying Russian gas. Dmitry Medvedev, the Russian chief of staff, offered Ukraine a dodgy deal in which gas would be sold via an intermediary company, RosUkrEnergo. The Kremlin wanted to punish Ukraine for its westward drift, so it hiked up the prices, believing that Ukraine was now receiving copious amounts of Western money and did not deserve Russian concessions any more. Gazprom was being used as the perfect coercive tool by Russia, given that it operated much of the gas trade across the former USSR. Ukraine was an especially important transit location for Gazprom's energy exports, particularly for selling Russian gas to other parts of Europe.

As the Ukrainian government prevaricated over the deal, Russia took drastic measures and on New Year's Day it turned off gas supplies to Ukraine. As Belton reminds us, though, 'Russia could not leave the gas turned off for longer than three days, otherwise it would damage its own pipeline network. At 3 p.m. the following day the gas supply was suddenly turned back on.'[21]

The pressure tactics forced Yushchenko's hand, and he took up the deal proposed by Medvedev, in which the middle company RosUkrEnergo gained a monopoly on Russian gas supplies to Ukraine plus a chunk of the domestic distribution market. It also had the effect of sowing division in Ukraine's government, as

Yushchenko came under intense criticism from his Orange Revolution Prime Minister Yulia Tymoshenko for accepting the Kremlin's RosUkrEnergo gas deal. The falling out between Yushchenko and Tymoshenko on this and other matters became so toxic that the latter was dismissed as Prime Minister in late 2005. Eventually, Yushchenko was forced to accept the old adage 'better the devil you know', working more closely with Yanukovych, who began to stage a political comeback almost immediately. Yanukovych had taken advantage of the infighting taking place under the collapsing Orange Revolution tent to rebuild his own political and parliamentary base. Although Yushchenko remained the President, he installed Yanukovych as his Prime Minister in August 2006, simply to ensure the government could function with enough support in the Rada.

* * *

After the Orange Revolution, the gulf between certain regions in Ukraine widened further. I had already experienced the innocent differences between certain parts of west and east Ukraine, but I had not yet visited the Donbas, where the contrasts were immense. According to a resident from the Donetsk Oblast that I spoke to about this era, 2004 was the point at which petty prejudices between some people in different parts of Ukraine worsened:

> Regarding prejudices towards the residents of the Donbas, I have to mention the idiotic politicians and other public people who occasionally uttered unpardonable, emotional things that were completely detached from reality. It started with the Orange Revolution of 2004 and peaked by the end of 2013, when Maidan started. Those were statements directed against people in the south and east of

Ukraine who did not display the fervent patriotism people from the west did, or who voted for those that they felt understood the needs and specifics of industrial areas like the Donbas [there is a detailed discussion both of the Maidan and of the Donbas's industrial history and the influence it has had on regional identity, national unity and geopolitics in Chapter 5].[22]

The prejudices could travel in both directions. Some western Ukrainians thought the easterners to be backward in their cultural predilections, voting habits and such like. Conversely, some easterners thought their western compatriots presented themselves as superior by propagating notions of Ukrainian patriotism that worked well in Lviv but did not necessarily resonate everywhere in Ukraine. Care must be taken with such generalisations, since many people were more than capable of forming more nuanced opinions than these, but there was indeed something nasty in the air after 2004.

The regional divisions exposed by the Orange Revolution ended the national togetherness fostered by politicians like Kravchuk in the early days of independence. Hereafter, managing Ukraine's regional contrasts became an ever more important factor in ensuring the stability of the country. Intra-Ukrainian regional stereotyping also increased Ukraine's vulnerability to Russian predation. Indeed, Russian propagandists were already having a field day during the Orange Revolution, quoting for instance Tymoshenko in December 2004 as saying the 'Donetsk, Luhansk and Dnepropetrovsk regions should be isolated from the rest by putting barbed wire around them'.[23] The veracity of the original quote as attributed to Tymoshenko may be questionable, but this is a secondary matter to the widespread coverage it received in Russian media, and the ill-feeling this stoked between Ukrainians.

* * *

At the geopolitical level, seeing how badly Ukraine was exposed to Russian pressure on the energy question, President Yushchenko's government began to prioritise its bid for NATO membership. Ukraine was far from a model candidate for NATO, given the domestic reforms it still needed to achieve to meet NATO's admission standards. Moreover, there were several international organisations still on Ukraine's list to join, not only NATO and the EU, but also the World Trade Organization (WTO), which Kuchma's government had seemingly never gotten round to completing.

Despite his dreams of Ukraine joining NATO, Yushchenko knew his neighbourhood, and his first official foreign visit was to Russia. 'I think Ukraine has gone through a very difficult time, especially over the last six months. We have just witnessed the most complicated elections in our history,' he told Putin, stating the obvious. Putin responded that he was 'very happy about your decision to make your first foreign visit to Russia. We see in this a sign, a very good sign.'

Along the way Putin brazenly lied by claiming that 'as you know, Russia never works behind the scenes in the post-Soviet area', before saying that he hoped to 'build new relations in the post-Soviet area in the area of integration, above all in the economic sphere', confident that in his accounting of the situation, Russia was responsible for 60 per cent of Ukraine's foreign trade at this time. Putin told Yushchenko that 'our position is that Russia is a permanent strategic partner for Ukraine'.[24]

No one mentioned Ukraine's approach to NATO in the press conference, since to do so would now derail any Russian–Ukrainian meeting like this. Elsewhere, in an interview on French television in 2005, when asked about NATO expansion, Putin singled out Ukraine for comment: 'Certain problems could arise in the context of our military cooperation with Ukraine' if Kyiv ever joined NATO, especially 'if there was to be a [NATO] military presence in Ukraine.'[25] In 2005, Ukraine's bid to join NATO was only just revving up, but the prospect alone riled up Putin. The matter would only become more controversial during the coming five years of Yushchenko's presidency.

CHAPTER 4

NATO'S FATEFUL OFFER

A REFLECTION ON HARSH GEOPOLITICAL TRUTHS

QUEST FOR THE MAP

Dinner was laid on by the US ambassador, but there was one thing above all else that his Ukrainian guests had an appetite for: a NATO Membership Action Plan, or MAP, which specifies the political, economic, defence and legal reforms a prospective member state needs to achieve to be allowed into the military alliance. The date of the dinner was 19 April 2006, and the high-powered Ukrainians present (Defence Minister Anatoliy Hrytsenko, Foreign Minister Borys Tarasyuk and the point person on NATO matters, Anton Buteyko) were keen to impress Ukraine's enthusiasm to join NATO on the American officials around the table. An American official told the Ukrainians that while the USA backed its NATO bid, other members did not, and that America had also noted the deep split within the Ukrainian public between those who did or did not want their country to join NATO.

Defence Minister Hrytsenko implored the Americans not to use these reasons as an excuse to block Ukraine's path into NATO, and he began to list the things Ukraine's armed forces had busied themselves with to prepare for a MAP. For instance, remodelling its command and logistics management along NATO rather than Soviet lines, actively helping to support the Americans in the Iraq war, providing airlift capabilities to the international community in Sudan, and so on.[1]

Based on a US State Department write-up of the meeting, at times it sounded like the Ukrainians were pleading. The Americans listened carefully and offered their support, but the fact of the matter was this: Ukraine's post-Orange Revolution government thought that it was gearing up for a sprint to secure entry to NATO; in fact, they ended up on a wild goose chase.

Did the Americans unrealistically raise Ukrainian expectations of NATO membership at the time? The record of private conversations between 2006 and 2008 (from which the account of the meeting above is taken) supports this view, that the US officials of the day at times preferred to speak in aspirational terms rather than address the harder issues, such as: what Russia's likely response might be to the Ukraine–NATO courtship; whether US assumptions from a decade ago as articulated by Albright and Talbott, of simply ignoring Russia, still held; and if there were any serious defensive alternatives for Ukraine to consider rather than joining NATO.

Because it had already extended the full Article 5 guarantee to new NATO members in the 1990s, rather than offering a more gradual accession process, the USA – unquestionably the leading NATO member – had boxed itself in when it came to the options for bringing in more members. This became especially telling as the issue of prospective Ukrainian and Georgian bids to join NATO came into view. It was a path to full NATO membership and the Article 5 guarantee or nothing, it seemed. Options for a richer variety of defensive relationships with Ukraine and Georgia did not exist or were not explored.[2]

There was no option being pushed other than to offer a complete NATO security guarantee further down the line, and for Washington it was easier and more gratifying simply to expand the existing NATO alliance than to create something new that was specifically designed to safeguard European security.

This is the story of how the Yushchenko government tried and failed to get to the starting line of NATO accession, a story that is now more instructive than ever in light of the 2022 war.

Public support for NATO membership

On 24 January 2006, Ukrainian official Volodymyr Khandohiy told a pair of his US counterparts (Peter Flory and Daniel Fried) that Ukraine wanted the MAP that very year, so Ukraine could enact the requisite reforms and join NATO by 2008. Flory and Fried said Ukraine still needed to demonstrate the 'political, economic, and social values required to meet the performance-based requirements for NATO membership'. Fried added that 'membership in NATO hinged not so much on NATO's views but on the determination of the candidate country to join', before citing Poland's and Romania's successful membership bids. He added, 'Public attitudes in NATO candidate countries were more important than many people realised.'[3] This was the part that was not looking too good for Ukraine in 2006.

At this time, the US State Department assessment was striking: 'The low level of public support for NATO membership may well prove to be the Achilles' heel of Ukraine's ambitions to be invited sooner (in 2008) rather than later to join NATO.' According to this assessment, 'There is an unusual chasm between the views of

Ukraine's policy and opinion-making elite, which overwhelmingly supports NATO membership, and the general population, which currently does not.' Joining NATO was at this stage an elite project, and opinion polls estimated that just '25–30 per cent of Ukrainians are in favour of NATO membership', with '30–35 per cent strongly opposed' to it and the remainder uncertain. Apparently, media coverage of NATO's role in the Balkans had harmed NATO's reputation in the country, especially from Russian news channels that were popular in some parts of Ukraine.[4]

When Yushchenko met Flory, he went into sales mode to convey the extent of Ukraine's military reforms to emulate NATO standards, recounting an anecdote from his own service as a conscript soldier in the USSR when 150 soldiers crammed into a single overcrowded barracks. Now, Ukraine was experimenting with brigades of contract soldiers (professionals, in other words, not conscripts), and it anticipated fielding a fully professional military by 2010.[5] It would not be possible to achieve this goal by 2010, given the deep Soviet legacies in materiel, mindsets and manpower that had to be unlearned (these in fact would only truly be shed under the pain of war when the fighting started in 2014). For now, the old USSR conscript system of two years' mandatory service, which had been halved by the independent Ukrainian army after independence, remained the backbone of the force, and it hampered Ukraine's NATO prospects.

The quest to secure a MAP was not achieved in 2006, and by January 2007, Ukraine had not advanced much further. Although nobody at the time could have known it, January 2007 was the equidistant moment in time between Ukraine's full independence in 1991 and Russia's all-out invasion of Ukraine in 2022; it was fifteen years either side of each event, and serves as a symbolic moment in the story.

At the start of 2007, Yushchenko's government considered staging a referendum on whether Ukraine should join NATO while, for the sake of balance, asking the electorate at the same time if they wanted to join Russia's new economic club, the Single Economic Space (SES). Ukraine's Central Election Commission had received over 4 million signatures asking for such a referendum, but it was not simple to find a legally permissible way to pose the question to voters. *'Do you agree that Ukraine should become a member of NATO?'* could not be used, since as per Ukrainian regulations, the question had to relate to a specific legal act. A bigger concern was that Yushchenko's government did not think they would even score a positive referendum result on joining NATO, and Yushchenko feared that the very act of staging the referendum could aggravate the social cleavages that opened in the 2004 election.[6]

Ukrainian officials were scrabbling for ideas. Presidential advisor Oleh Rybachuk suggested pop-culture tactics for making a public case for NATO: he wanted to enlist celebrities like Ukraine's 2004 Eurovision song contest winner Ruslana Lyzhychko and Ukrainian boxing brothers Vitali and Wladimir Klitschko to advertise the appeal of Western values.[7] But Yushchenko's government was way ahead of the majority of Ukrainians on the NATO issue: most did not consider it urgent, or thought it to be unnecessarily divisive, inimical to some people's Russian-leaning sympathies. Despite US encouragement Ukraine's quest for a MAP was faltering – but the fact it was under way had been noticed elsewhere.

*   *   *

In an attempt to pour cold water over the idea of further NATO expansion, Putin travelled to Munich and delivered a strident address on 10 February 2007. Even if one considers him a man in league with the devil, he cannot be accused of inconsistency on the issue of NATO expansion. He began with a general complaint: 'One state and, of course, first and foremost the US, has overstepped its national borders in every way. This is visible in the economic, political, cultural and educational policies it imposes on other nations. Well, who likes this? Who is happy about this?' asked Putin rhetorically. His specific complaint followed:

> I think it obvious that NATO expansion does not have any relation with the modernisation of the alliance itself or with ensuring security in Europe. On the contrary, it represents a serious provocation that reduces the level of mutual trust. And we have the right to ask: against whom is this expansion intended? And what happened to the assurances our Western partners made after the dissolution of the Warsaw Pact? Where are those declarations today? ... NATO is not a universal organisation, as opposed to the UN. It is first and foremost a military and political alliance, military and political![8]

After his speech, he delivered a parting shot in the Q&A session, pointing out that the deployment of military infrastructure should be related only to dominant security threats of the day, which he surmised to be the war against terrorist armed groups. The audience of Western officials was utterly unmoved by Putin's words, seeing them as self-serving, which they surely were, but also irrelevant because Russia was still the defeated power from the Cold War and could be ignored. As before, no heed was paid to Russia's disquiet, not even treating it as part of the puzzle that needed to be solved to engender lasting European security. Perhaps the puzzle could never have been solved, but as we know, this dismissive approach in fact contributed to the deterioration of Russia–NATO relations and later provided Putin with a core part of his public justification for the invasion of Ukraine.

For NATO, it was business as usual with Ukraine, encouraging the furtherance of their mutual ties. NATO's Secretary General Jaap de Hoop Scheffer flattered Ukrainian officials by telling them that theirs was the only partner nation to contribute to every one of the alliance's ongoing operations. He reaffirmed NATO's open-door policy, telling them that the future of NATO–Ukraine relations is 'in the hands of Ukraine's people and their elected leaders'. US ambassador Victoria Nuland agreed wholeheartedly that NATO was getting a good deal from its cooperation with Ukraine, adding for good measure, 'Only you can decide Ukraine's future with NATO; our door is open.'[9]

No serious effort, including by Yushchenko, was made to manage the impact of Kyiv's desire to join NATO on Ukraine–Russia relations. As before, Russia had to accept the self-evident truth that it was on the losing side of history. Operation Ignore Russia remained in full swing, empowered by a moral certitude underpinned by the USA that this was the right thing to do, given Russia's past crimes of totalitarian aggression in east and central Europe.

In Moscow, the political classes were increasingly irate at the NATO–Ukraine courtship. A Russian politician, Vladimir Ryzhkov, warned that unless a moratorium was placed on further NATO expansion, Putin, 'who has a long memory' and may remain at the top of government for some time, would not forget this.[10] Foreign Minister Sergey Lavrov called NATO enlargement 'artificial and unnecessary' in an address to the Russian Parliament, the Duma.[11]

And then, in an unnecessarily inflammatory move to rub salt in ancestral wounds, on 2 April 2007, the Duma passed a resolution on the seventy-fifth anniversary of the Holodomor to honour the victims of the 1930s famine but to reject the Ukrainian government's claim that the famine was targeted against the Ukrainians on the basis that Stalin targeted many nationalities, including Russians. The motion passed 370 to fifty-six votes by Russian MPs, some of whom lumped together the Ukrainian government's desire to join NATO and its attempts to reclassify the Holodomor as different versions of Russophobic tactics.[12] The gradual impact of NATO's dismissal of Russian opinion on its eastward expansion was clear to be seen in the bitterness of this domestic political debate in Moscow.

* * *

NATO is a defensive alliance in which countries join of their own volition – at least, this is the bumper sticker explanation propagated by the USA and its allies, and on one level it is true. Its mutual defence clause, Article 5, is indeed defensive, and its prospective members do ask to join. At the same time, NATO has been used to launch sustained military operations in the Balkans in the 1990s, in Libya in 2011 and for a military occupation in Afghanistan between 2001 and 2014. Only the latter instance has its roots in collective defence, due to the 9/11 attacks on the USA and the role of al-Qaeda, which was partly based in Afghanistan at the time. To see matters from different perspectives is a prized ability, and when it comes to NATO, the perspective that it is not wholly defensive but also an enabling body for US-led military actions in a variety of different circumstances must be taken on board. No matter how often NATO and its supporters say that it is purely a defensive alliance, its immense offensive military power projection capabilities that have been used in past wars say otherwise.

Regarding NATO accession, the notion of voluntary requests to join happily juxtaposes with the obvious fact that the USA and NATO cannot be rendered mere passive players in the accession process. Just because prospective members request to join, the shepherding and admission process itself places the USA in an incredibly powerful position in European security affairs. Put simply, NATO could not expand in any direction if it wasn't in US interests at the time.

This is not to give credence to Putin's well-documented lines, for instance in his later interviews with the US filmmaker Oliver Stone, in which he complained that:

> nowadays NATO is a mere instrument of the foreign policy of the US. It has no allies, it has only vassals. Once a country becomes a NATO member, it is hard to resist the pressures of the US. All of a sudden, any weapon system can be placed in this country. An anti-ballistic missile system, new military bases and if need be, new offensive systems. And what are we supposed to do?[13]

These lines from Putin are rather overblown and not terribly convincing, but the sentiment is worth paying attention to, especially in relation to future events in Ukraine. In Putin's mind, if a territorially intact Ukraine had ever joined NATO, then by definition, NATO's soldiers (Ukrainian or otherwise) would be stationed in Kharkiv, in Luhansk, in Donetsk, in Mariupol. Forcing Russia to subscribe to the most benign view of NATO remained the basis of a foreign policy of continual NATO expansion. When it involved countries like Ukraine and Georgia, in particular, it was heading to disaster.

NATO'S FATEFUL OFFER IN BUCHAREST

By coincidence, the Romanian capital city of Bucharest had been the location of the signing of the 1994 deal whereby, after Ukraine had given up its old Soviet nuclear weapons arsenal, the defence of its sovereign security was guaranteed by a tripartite pact between the US, the UK and Russia. Bucharest also happened to be the location of the NATO summit in April 2008 where Ukraine's efforts to secure a path to NATO membership came to an abrupt standstill. Despite backing for their candidacy by the USA, and by NATO's east European members, other European states blocked it. Without unanimity, Ukraine's application could go no further for now.

The summit was held in Bucharest's gigantic Palace of the Parliament, a vanity project and quite possibly the world's largest building, the construction of which was commissioned by the Cold War-era Romanian dictator Nicolae Ceauşescu, in power from 1965–89. The repressive rule of the Ceauşescu era had scarred Romania and afforded its post-communist leaders a deep yearning for integration into structures like the EU and NATO.[14] Now, Romania was a poster child for the expansion of Western clubs into the former Warsaw Pact countries, having been admitted to NATO in 2004 and to the EU in 2007.

These days, three flags can be seen flying outside some of Bucharest's government buildings: Romania's blue, yellow and red tricolour, the EU's circle of stars and NATO's compass emblem. NATO membership had long been sought by Romania in the 1990s. During their accession process, former Romanian Chief of the General Staff Constantin Degeratu noted, 'It is fair to say that no state has conducted a more vehement campaign for NATO membership than Romania. Because Bucharest could not portray itself as a leader in democratisation or economic reforms, it has put the emphasis on

Romania's strategic location.' For Romania, it was therefore a matter of great pride and importance to host a NATO summit just four years after joining, and the agenda was broadly divided between NATO's war in Afghanistan, the active operational matter of the day, and NATO's presence in eastern Europe.[15]

In the symbolic surroundings of Bucharest's Parliament Palace, Ukraine wanted to emulate what Romania had achieved, jumping through the hoops that NATO places in front of prospective members. Instead, while Albania and Croatia were officially invited to join, Georgia and Ukraine were placed on the waiting list with no firm promise of future admittance. Instead of a MAP, both Tbilisi and Kyiv were placed in a half-way house, as the Bucharest summit declaration of 3 April 2008 conveys:

> NATO welcomes Ukraine's and Georgia's Euro-Atlantic aspirations for membership in NATO. Both nations have made valuable contributions to alliance operations. We welcome the democratic reforms in Ukraine and Georgia and look forward to free and fair parliamentary elections in Georgia in May. MAP is the next step for Ukraine and Georgia on their direct way to membership. Today we make clear that we support these countries' applications for MAP. Therefore, we will now begin a period of intensive engagement with both at a high political level to address the questions still outstanding pertaining to their MAP applications.[16]

With these fateful words, Ukraine and Georgia entered a kind of NATO purgatory, a perpetual waiting room in which these countries attempted purification with no guarantee of ascension. Worse still, Russia was angered by the language of inevitability surrounding their eventual membership prospects. What had happened at the summit to result in such an unsatisfying outcome?

President Bush was in attendance and the USA pushed for a MAP for Ukraine, as did Poland and other eastern European NATO members, no doubt keen to insert another alliance member between them and Russia; but France under Nicolas Sarkozy and Germany under Angela Merkel staunchly refused. The transatlantic rift between these NATO allies over the divisive US invasion of Iraq was yet to heal sufficiently, adding to their mistrust. Indeed, other members of 'old Europe' resisted too, such as Italy. The Italian Ministry of Foreign Affairs had warned that Ukraine and Georgia were in 'a different basket' when it comes to NATO, that these countries were insufficiently prepared for a MAP, that the idea of Ukraine joining was only a recent one, and that the political situation in Ukraine was 'very shaky'.[17] The Netherlands, often a country willing to back US leadership on security matters, decided that it had 'no objection in principle' to Ukraine's membership in the alliance but that the time was not ripe.[18]

For France and Germany, the important blocking countries, their intention was to slow down to a virtual halt the process of admitting new members. In Merkel's words about Ukraine and Georgia, 'it is their destiny and vocation to be partners in NATO', warning that 'criteria need to be met and we need another phase of intense commitment'. To this, a Polish delegate to the summit accused Germany of being 'more worried for Moscow than for your allies'.[19] Passions ran high and those NATO members that were fence-sitters ended up placing their weight against the MAP for Ukraine and Georgia when they realised it was not going to be granted.[20] Long to-do lists emerged from the summit for Ukraine to take home, for instance with Germany, Greece and the Netherlands asking Kyiv to reform its security services and judiciary, to renew its fight against corruption, and to secure more domestic support for joining NATO.[21]

In a subsequent post-mortem of the summit, the *New York Times* journalist Steven Erlanger spoke to some of those people present, who were keen to wash their hands of the unsatisfying outcome. Fiona Hill, who attended the summit as a US intelligence officer, recounted how Bush had been advised by the US intelligence community not to offer membership to Georgia and Ukraine because of a lack of support by other NATO members, but Bush didn't listen. The final statement 'was the worst of all possible outcomes', said Hill. Ivo Daalder, a later US ambassador to NATO, recounted how a late-night compromise reached by Bush had tried to bridge the gap created by the German and French veto. Carl Bildt, a former Swedish Prime Minister and Foreign Minister and long-time proponent of NATO expansion, thought 'the Bucharest compromise was the worst of both worlds' because 'it created expectations that were not fulfilled and fears that are grossly exaggerated'.[22]

Sadly, the Bucharest summit declaration convinced Moscow that NATO – and the USA in particular – was determined to ultimately admit Georgia and Ukraine. The fact that so many other NATO members had opposed it, and that the statement had still asserted the inevitability of the outcome, was interpreted at face value by the Russians. One would have thought that Russia would have been pleased that Ukraine and Georgia were not offered a MAP – but the opposite was true. Russia was now more alarmed and angered than before.[23]

*   *   *

Beaming photos can be found online of Putin and Bush dining together at the closing dinner of the summit in Bucharest.[24] Putin was invited to the conference, participating in the NATO–Russia Council on 4 April 2008, and also dining with Romanian President Traian Băsescu. Putin revisited all of his bugbears, vehemently denouncing US plans for east European countries to host ballistic missile defence bases, for instance. But he added something far more sinister at the conference. As recounted by the US official Kurt Volker, Putin 'implicitly challenged the territorial integrity of Ukraine, suggesting that Ukraine was an artificial creation sewn together from territory of Poland, the Czech Republic, Romania, and especially Russia in the aftermath of the Second World War'. Moreover, Putin stated that 'Crimea was simply given to Ukraine by a decision of the Politburo of the Soviet Communist Party Central Committee', which mattered because Russians made up '90 per cent' of people in Crimea, while '17 out of 45 million Ukrainian citizens are Russian', and that 'Ukraine gained enormous amounts of its territory from the east and south at the expense of Russia'. And, most ominously of all, 'If we add in the NATO question and other problems, the very existence of the [Ukrainian] State could find itself under threat…'[25]

As a threat and as a statement of intent, it was all there, back in 2007 after a calamitous NATO summit, many years before Putin decided to match these words with his military deeds.

*   *   *

When Russia's 2022 invasion of Ukraine was in full swing, Merkel delivered her first public comments on the 2008 Bucharest summit since leaving office. After expressing sorrow at the war, she stood by her decision for Germany to block Ukraine's path to a NATO

MAP. 'Ukraine was not the country that we know now. It was a Ukraine that was very split ... even the reformist forces Tymoshenko and Yushchenko were at odds. That means it was not a country whose democracy was inwardly strengthened,' said Merkel, looking back after fourteen years. She reasoned that 'you cannot become a member of NATO from one day to the next ... It's a process, and during this process I knew Putin would have done something to Ukraine that would not have been good for it.'[26] Merkel praised Zelensky for his wartime leadership, but her comments attracted his outrage. 'I invite Ms Merkel and Mr Sarkozy to visit Bucha and see what the policy of concessions to Russia has led to in fourteen years,' said Zelensky, referencing the location of Russian killings of Ukrainian civilians in 2022.[27]

These conflicting perspectives remind us that while the failure to begin Ukraine's admittance into NATO in 2008 was consequential, Merkel's suggestion that Putin may have intervened in Ukraine even earlier to stymie Ukraine's NATO journey cannot be dismissed. We are in the realm of counterfactual history and can never know if NATO's offer of a MAP in 2008 would have been a panacea or would have inadvertently invited a quicker Russian invasion. Events in Georgia after the 2008 Bucharest summit give credence to the latter possibility.

WAGERING ON THE WEST

As a child of the 1960s, Mikheil Saakashvili was born in the Georgian Soviet Socialist Republic but lived most of his young adulthood in a world filled with the American dreams that drifted across the rubble of the Berlin Wall, settling into the minds of the youth of Tbilisi and Kyiv. The Soviets were the past and the West was the future for Saakashvili, who began his university education in

Ukraine and completed it in the US in the 1990s, before entering Georgian politics. Saakashvili was swept into presidential power in 2003's Rose Revolution at the age of just thirty-six, an improbably youthful challenger to the Soviet-era statesman Eduard Shevard-nadze, who previously ran the Georgian SSR and was the Soviet Union's final Foreign Minister.

At first, Saakashvili wagered his country's future on NATO mem-bership, a talisman that his government pursued at the same time as Yushchenko's government in Kyiv. Of these two countries, Georgia was in the greatest hurry because, unlike Ukraine, independence from the USSR had involved armed conflict and lingering, violent border disputes. When this wager backfired at Bucharest, he still bet on the West coming to his aid if he challenged Russia – a bet that failed spectacularly.

Georgia contained a pair of recalcitrant provinces, South Osse-tia and Abkhazia, which border Russia. Russia's neo-imperialism was in full swing when Moscow had brokered an end to the wars between the Georgians and South Ossetians in 1991–92, and be-tween the Georgians and the Abkhaz in 1992–94. These provinces, semi-autonomous in the Georgian SSR, had now resisted full con-trol by Tbilisi. This afforded Russia a reason to station its troops there, and gave Putin an obvious lever to antagonise Georgia by supporting the Ossetian and Abkhaz separatists.

Saakashvili was not a man lacking in confidence and, having won a second term as President in January 2008, decided to do some-thing about the situation: he thawed these frozen conflicts to launch a military offensive against the separatists with the aim of restor-ing Georgian control over Abkhazia and South Ossetia. Over the summer, skirmishes intensified between Georgian forces and the South Ossetian separatists. Russia, watchful of the situation at its border, maintained its contact with the separatists and kept peace-keeping troops in both provinces. On 7 August, Saakashvili ordered a Georgian military assault on South Ossetia, which also targeted the Russian troops based there.

Armed with the perfect pretext, Russia unleashed its own snarl-ing dogs of war: a massive Russian counteroffensive drove the Georgians out of South Ossetia and then pushed deep into the rest of Georgia. It was a short war, with Russia's offensive taking place across a few very violent days before a ceasefire was brokered by French President Sarkozy, which came into effect on 13 August. By that time, the Russian armed forces had smashed the Georgian armed forces, wrecking their ground forces and sinking their naval vessels in the Black Sea. All wars are unique outcomes of their own peculiar circumstances, and the circumstances in Georgia in 2008 favoured by far the Russian military.

What is all the more astonishing is that Saakashvili initiated the war mere months after Georgia was placed in the slow lane of NATO membership at Bucharest. Why had Saakashvili escalated the war regardless? As the authors Samuel Charap and Timothy Colton sum up, 'Either Saakashvili fell into an elaborate Russian trap or he launched a murderous *Reconquista* war with a tacit green light from Washington.'[28] Both explanations are too extreme, as the authors conclude, but the American factor was a critical part of Saakashvili's calculation.

Between 2002 and 2004, US soldiers ran a 'Georgia Train and Equip Programme' that involved several hundred US troops train-ing and modernising Georgia's armed forces. Washington was after allies in its global war on terror, and some of these US-trained Georgian troops went on operations in the Pankisi Gorge, next to Chechnya. This may have accustomed Saakashvili to American help, but if he thought the Americans could stick around to fight the Russians, he would be sorely disappointed.

The outcome of the 2008 Russia–Georgia war was a success for Moscow. Russian authority was forcefully reasserted, and Georgia was 'disciplined' for its westward drift. In later years, Russia continued to 'passportise' Abkhazia and South Ossetia, meaning it managed the widespread issuance of Russian passports to inhabitants in these areas. And, as of 2020, 'the de facto governments' relations with Russia are so close that both Abkhazia and South Ossetia have former Russian officials serving in senior roles', according to analysis from International Crisis Group.[29] This was the kind of war, waged decisively to punish disobedience and censure westward drift by a former SSR, that the Kremlin almost certainly wanted to emulate in its recent invasion of Ukraine.

A war foreshadowed

Geopolitics involves cruel games, the rules of which are frequently defined by the most powerful states dishing out harsh lessons. For the weaker, smaller and more disunited states, their fates can depend on how skilfully they play a game that is weighted against them, and whether they can attract powerful friends in binding alliances. It is not a game for the faint-hearted, and Ukrainians were learning quickly, through Georgia's example, of what may one day be in store for them.

On 26 August 2008, Ukraine's Ministry of Foreign Affairs strongly condemned Russia, describing its actions in Georgia as a 'gross violation of the norms and principles of international law and bilateral and multinational treaties', before stating that 'actual annexation of part of Georgia's territory through the creation of puppet regimes and support for them is evidence that the doctrine of the "law of force" in resolving international problems is being reinvigorated in the Russian Federation". Reactions in Ukraine predictably enough broke down along party lines, and alongside the condemnation of Russian actions from Yushchenko, there were curious comments from Yanukovych, who spoke out in favour of the independence of Abkhazia and South Ossetia, alongside comments that Russia's actions were a consequence of recent decisions by some countries to officially recognise Kosovo as a sovereign state. A decade after NATO's aerial bombing campaign against Serbia had allowed Kosovo to retain its de facto independence, the full diplomatic recognition of Kosovo by a selection of other countries began in 2008, which Yanukovych seems to have interpreted as being an insult to Russia, which had supported Serbia and not Kosovo.[30]

A dispute then broke out between the Russian and Ukrainian governments over the Georgia situation. Dmitry Medvedev, serving since May 2008 as Putin's stand-in in the Russian presidency, was indignant. Medvedev wrote a letter to Yushchenko that expressed a hardline view:

I must frankly say that the position of the Ukrainian authorities regarding Georgia's aggression arouses deep resentment in Russia. Officially, Kyiv has in fact taken the side of Saakashvili's criminal regime, which it actively armed during recent years, including supplies of heavy weaponry. One still has to look into the role of Ukrainian military experts in training the Georgian army, and their actions during military operations against South Ossetia. Attempts to hush that up will fail. Unqualified interference in these matters may have a negative impact on the range of Russian–Ukrainian relations.[31]

Was there anything to Medvedev's allegations? What truth to the allegation of Ukrainian arms sales to Georgia? The sale of arms to Georgia is a window into the often under-appreciated extent of Ukrainian defence industry exports, rooted in its past as a centre of Soviet arms manufacturing. Data gathered by the UN Register of Conventional Arms Sales found that 'Ukraine was the main supplier of weapons to Georgia in 2007', with exports significantly higher than in 2006. The weapons systems sold by Ukraine included 'seventy-four tanks, six armoured vehicles, nine large-calibre artillery systems, 10,800 rocket systems, and 28,800 small arms'.[32]

This was enough to leave the Russian armed forces deputy Anatoliy Nogovitsyn livid, accusing Georgia of using air defence systems that it had procured from Ukraine and which had proven effective against Russian aircraft. Colonel-General Nogovitsyn further complained that if the Ukrainians hadn't 'armed Saakashvili to the teeth', and if US advisors had also not helped to train the Georgian military, then the Georgian army would not have mounted its offensive in South Ossetia. For Nogovitsyn, 'the death of our boys is on the conscience of these two countries', meaning Ukraine and the USA.[33] Russia's Deputy Foreign Minister Grigory Karasin went even further, implying that all of these countries were operating in what he called an 'anti-Russian "International"'.[34]

The Russian Black Sea Fleet in Crimea was now a source of disagreement between Russian officials and Ukraine. At one point during the war in Georgia, Ukraine threatened to close Sevastopol port to Russian warships involved in the war. Russia's government referred back to their countries' 1997 Treaty of Friendship, Cooperation and Partnership, which indeed had only obligated Russia's Black Sea Fleet ships to offer a notification of departure and did not constrain how they could be used operationally once they were at sea.[35] Nevertheless, Kyiv's threats over port access in Crimea must have scared Moscow's military officials enough to make them consider the importance of taking direct control of the port in the future.

Indeed, many of the ingredients of future Russian interventions in Ukraine were on display in 2008 in the Georgian context: false pretexts, narratives of 'helping' separatist republics, issuing Russian passports in breakaway republics, stoking tensions around post-imperial borders and, ultimately, using the fire and steel of war to ram Moscow's points home. It was a clear preview of how Russia later sank its sharp teeth into the Donetsk and Luhansk regions in east Ukraine. In the Rada, Ukrainian MPs debated Ukraine's vulnerabilities in this light, and whether Crimea in particular was open to the same Russian pretext of issuing passports, springing to the defence of local residents and so on. One MP claimed Russia was already issuing passports in Crimea and wanted to find out which Crimean people already had dual citizenship.[36] War, however, was not imminent in Ukraine, and it was certainly not inevitable at this stage, despite the barbs being traded between leaders in Kyiv and Moscow.

* * *

In the fallout after the Russia–Georgia War, Saakashvili clung on to his job as President until 2013 before leaving Georgian politics. He the resurfaced in Ukraine in 2015, giving up his Georgian citizenship to become Ukrainian, and serving in a controversy-ridden term as the Governor of Odessa. He had become a living artefact connecting the stories of these two former SSRs, an embodiment of the portent offered by the Russia–Georgia War as to what may one day come to Ukraine.

OPEN DOORS IN BAD NEIGHBOURHOODS

Fateful or fatal, when NATO made its offer of eventual membership in 2008 to Ukraine and Georgia, it doesn't seem to have seriously contemplated the fact that Russia could wage war to preclude it. In Georgia, Russia had done precisely this within months. NATO carried on regardless in its attempts to prepare Ukraine for one day joining the alliance, but in the fourteen years that elapsed between the Bucharest summit declaration and the war in Georgia in 2008 and Russia's full-scale invasion of Ukraine in 2022, readers can come to their own conclusions on whether NATO handled its offer of eventual membership to Ukraine well or not.

For Ukraine, NATO membership became the proverbial pot of gold at the end of the rainbow. It is questionable, with the benefit of hindsight, whether NATO was the best option for providing security to Ukraine at this time, and whether US enthusiasm for Ukraine's NATO candidacy, and lack of thinking around other options for Europe's security, did more harm than good. George W. Bush's *Bonhomme* approach to the issues seemed to take at face value the appeals by Yushchenko and Saakashvili. And even after the summit and the Georgia War, US Vice-President Dick Cheney persisted with articulating a heavily ideological view of Ukraine's and Georgia's NATO membership prospects. During a visit to Italy in September 2008, Cheney seemed to act as if the past few months had not even happened:

> I have come here from the East, by way of Azerbaijan, Georgia, and Ukraine. These lands, once held in the grip of a totalitarian empire, now stand proudly as independent nations – setting their own course and engaging the world with confidence. That is as it should

be. Since 1989, the lamps of liberty have been coming out again, and millions have walked in that light toward a future of prosperity, security and peace.

Regardless of what one now thinks of Cheney, his views offered US policymakers an ideological inheritance: to keep expanding NATO for the good of all mankind, it would seem. Cheney appeared to believe in the rhetoric of historical inevitability to an extent that would make even a Marxist blush:

> NATO's alignment is with the forces of freedom; it exists to preserve liberty, not to oppose any country. It is a growing community of values – a voluntary, defensive alliance that is devoted to freedom, and is a threat to no one. Russia now enjoys the most benign western border ever in its history – from its very edge, all the way to the cliffs of the Atlantic.

Getting into specifics, Cheney reached this crescendo:

> The world must also pay attention to Ukraine, which Russia has attempted to intimidate by threats and severe economic pressure, and the Baltic states, which have also been subjected to Russian pressure. Let us make clear that the enlargement of NATO will continue as and where the allies decide. We have long held those meeting the standards for membership and having the desire to join have every right to do so. At Bucharest only five months ago, we considered extending a Membership Action Plan to Georgia and Ukraine but did not do so. But allies agreed that those nations will be NATO members, and the time to begin their Membership Action Plans, I believe, has come.[37]

At the time of writing in 2022, this moment had still not come, and tens of thousands of people have perished along the way of proving the point that NATO's open door should always remain open, no matter the neighbourhood. NATO has, of course, no blood on its hands here, but as an exercise in effective statecraft, NATO's past record of handling Ukraine's and Georgia's membership aspirations is a shoddy one.

*   *   *

Hardline opinion in Russia was becoming harder, as the hawks considered how to hold the line against further NATO expansion into the former SSRs. Already in 2008, in the assessment of the US State Department, the Russian government would have ideally liked to secure from Ukraine a written neutrality pledge that would preclude future NATO membership. Lavrov told his Ukrainian opposite number that Russia would always resist a MAP for Ukraine, and its advent would invite 'disastrous consequences for Europe, Russian–Ukrainian relations and NATO–Russia relations'. Although Russian officials like Lavrov spoke at the time of Georgia and Ukraine in the same breath, it was the thought of Ukraine's possible accession to NATO that hit them in the guts the hardest. The Russians still believed that the Ukrainian public did not really want to join NATO at the time, and that it was just the whipping up of anti-Russian sentiment by Yushchenko driving the whole thing. Given the polling of Ukrainian opinion at the time, cited earlier in this chapter, one must add that this was not a totally inaccurate view to hold. But there was still hope in Russian elite circles that their version of imperially tinged 'common sense' would prevail, and that the deep economic ties between Russia and Ukraine might dampen down Ukraine's westward drift.[38]

Of the things Russia feared about Ukraine's destiny, its democratisation was not the big problem – it was the overlap between democratisation and NATO membership (as per the terms of the MAP). Russian officials would cite Article 6 of the 1997 Russia–Ukraine Friendship Treaty – 'Neither party shall allow its territory to be used to the detriment of the security of the other party' – which is why NATO always asserted that it was a 'defensive alliance', and why Russia pointed to NATO's record otherwise, arguing that Ukraine joining NATO was a detriment to Russian security.[39]

Conspicuously absent in Russia's approach to Ukraine, however, was any real offer of positive incentives, of reassurances in exchange for Ukraine's neutrality, or an even-handed attempt to manage the various emotive post-imperial issues lingering between the countries, such as the Holodomor. The coercive instincts of the Russian state left its officials only ever talking the language of power and obedience, and the unattractiveness of such sentiments to many in Ukraine was clear.

*　*　*

There is a chicken-and-egg argument to all of this: had NATO enlargement motivated Russian coercion and aggression? Wasn't NATO membership the ultimate guarantee against this very aggression? Which one came first? After all, Russia attacked Georgia in 2008, and Ukraine in 2014 and 2022, whereas the tiny Baltic states have not been attacked by Russia despite also being ex-SSRs with Russian minorities, but their safety has been guaranteed precisely because they are in NATO. The argument thus seems simple: Ukraine and Georgia should have been awarded a NATO MAP much earlier to protect them from Russian aggression.

As this chapter has shown, this is not so simple. It wishes away the finicky realities of NATO accession, dependent on the individual politics of many member states, made so much harder in the wake of the transatlantic Iraq war rift. It downplays the reality of the 2000s, that the USA's major priorities were elsewhere: in Iraq, Afghanistan and the war on terror, not in eastern Europe. And it takes at face value the idealism of Bush, Cheney and others who thought it a cost-free exercise to admit to NATO the one Soviet republic that Russia cared about more than the others: Ukraine.

The USA did not display a nuanced understanding of the conduct of its superpower statecraft amidst an imperial collapse in a historically volatile region, and with a still-powerful rival former superpower waiting in the wings. US officials just kept trying to spread NATO further, believing this to be unquestionably the correct thing to do. No other ideas for European security were seriously mooted.*[40]

The US knew which side of the debate it was on, as the US official Kurt Volker explained in temperate language:

[NATO] allies are divided on their perception of how the Bucharest Summit pledge of future membership to Georgia and Ukraine affected the current crisis [of the Russo-Georgia war]. The German-led allies argue that the Bucharest decision on eventual membership

---

* Michael O'Hanlon wrote in 2017 that 'whether most Russians truly see NATO as a physical threat is a question, but many do see it as an insult – a psychologically and politically imposing former enemy that has approached right up to their border', which is why he advocated a different approach, in which the 'core concept would be one of permanent neutrality' for states like Ukraine and Georgia. The ship has now sailed on this idea, but it is important to recall past discussions on options for the region short of further NATO expansion.

provoked the Russian aggression, while most others (new members and Canada) see it as we do: that Russia interpreted the denial of MAP as a green light for action against Georgia.[41]

To 'see it as we do' is, by definition, to see only one side of a complex matter. And this in turn was the essence of the tussle over Ukraine's fate.

Back in Kyiv, in the wake of the dramatic events of 2008, Yush-chenko had found his political lustre increasingly tarnished. Even his core supporters could not ignore Ukraine's failure to make meaningful headway with its entry into either NATO or the EU; in fact, Ukraine was still only at the start of an arduous journey towards both of these bodies. And Yushchenko did not have all the time in the world for this journey, since Russia was gathering its own political forces to wrest back its influence in Ukraine.

CHAPTER 5

YANUKOVYCH, VIKTOR AND LOSER

A REFLECTION ON CORRUPTION

TRUMP AND YANUKOVYCH, THE MISSING LINK

Washington DC is a world away from Kyiv, which is why it is was surprising to see Ukraine feature so prominently in Special Counsel Robert Mueller's investigation into Donald Trump's victory in the 2016 US presidential election. The missing link to Ukraine was Paul Manafort, the veteran Republican political strategist who ran Trump's presidential campaign. Previously, Manafort had earned vast sums of money, at least $60 million and likely much more, from helping Viktor Yanukovych, the loser in the Orange Revolution, in seeking re-election. As Mueller reported:

Manafort was introduced to Rinat Akhmetov, the Ukrainian oligarch who hired Manafort as political consultant. In 2005, Akhmetov hired Manafort to engage in political work supporting the Party of Regions, a political party in Ukraine that was generally understood to align with Russia. Manafort assisted the Party of Regions in regaining power, and its candidate, Yanukovych, won the presidency in 2010. Manafort became a close and trusted political advisor to Yanukovych during his time as President of Ukraine. Yanukovych served in that role until 2014, when he fled to Russia amidst popular protests.[*][1]

In one way the story made complete sense: Yanukovych needed expert help to repair his image as an election loser. The help he received from Russia in 2004 had not worked: the Kremlin had dispatched two advisors, Gleb Pavlovsky to Kyiv, and Vyacheslav Nikonov to work in Yanukovych's campaign office in Donetsk. Both Kremlin insiders at the time, Pavlovsky was a behind-the-scenes political operator and Nikonov a political scientist who happened to be a grandson of legendary Soviet Foreign Minister Vyacheslav Molotov (the namesake of the Molotov cocktail). In 2004, Yanukovych's campaign had tried to frame the choice facing voters as being between Russia and the West, tarring Yushchenko with the name 'Bushenko' and other such messages, but the campaign obviously failed.[2]

What did Manafort advise Yanukovych to do this time round? Some of it was rudimentary, oft-practised in Western elections, like giving the campaign a weekly focus on a message of importance to the targeted constituencies and increasing his hold over his base in east Ukraine. This helped Yanukovych's political fortunes, as I saw for myself on repeat visits to observe Ukraine's parliamentary elections in March 2006 and in September 2007. As you can deduce from this, Ukraine holds a lot of elections, to which the OSCE always

---

[*]   The report explains that 'Manafort's Russian contacts during the campaign and transition periods stem from his consulting work for [the Russian-born Ukrainian billionaire Oleg] Deripaska from approximately 2005 to 2009 and his separate political consulting work in Ukraine 2005 to 2015'.

sends a monitoring mission. Ukraine's presidential-parliamentary system of government has both a directly elected President plus elections for the Rada, to which each electoral district returns a Member of Parliament. Power ultimately sits with the President, who appoints the Prime Minister, but this appointment must reflect the balance of power in the Rada. Majorities in the Rada therefore count for a lot.

Western narratives painted the Orange Revolution as a decisive defeat of Yanukovych's Party of Regions, but these later parliamentary elections said otherwise. In March 2006, I was deployed to south-west Ukraine near the Carpathian Mountains, to the city of Uzhhorod and its surrounding region, which borders Poland, Slovakia and Romania. In the election, of 450 seats in the Rada, Party of Regions won 32.1 per cent of the vote (which amounted to 186 seats); Yulia Tymoshenko's Fatherland party won 22.3 per cent (129 seats); and Yushchenko's Our Ukraine just 14 per cent (eighty-one seats). The rest of the votes were distributed amongst other parties, including the Socialists at 5.7 per cent (thirty-three seats), who also belonged to the Orange coalition. With the largest single party in the Rada, Yanukovych now became Prime Minister under Yushchenko's presidency, already an astonishing turnaround to the Orange Revolution.

This was a fragile governing arrangement and tensions between the President and the parliamentary majority led to its collapse in 2007. To resolve the ensuing political crisis, the two Viktors agreed to hold an early parliamentary election in September 2007, and this time I was deployed closer to Kyiv. Proving that its previous showing was no fluke, this time the Party of Regions secured an even better result of 34.4 per cent (175 seats); Fatherland won 30.7 per cent (156 seats); and Our Ukraine won 14.2 per cent (seventy-two seats).

With Yanukovych's Party of Regions doing so well, Manafort's reputation grew with the oligarchs who funded his advisory work, so much so that he started spending more time in Ukraine and billing ever greater amounts for his work. 'Having spent so much time in the company of oligarchs,' opined *The Atlantic* magazine, 'Manafort decided to become one himself.'[3] Eventually, his business dealings in Ukraine landed him in jail back home in the USA.

Yanukovych was still riding high on his parliamentary success and as he approached the 2010 presidential elections, he knew that he had another shot at the highest office in the land. Yanukovych's campaign capitalised on Yushchenko's failures to bring Ukraine meaningfully closer to either EU or NATO membership. Indeed, the 2010 election campaign featured muted messaging from all of the major candidates on the theme of European integration, aside from Yushchenko, called by some as a pause in Ukraine's 'Euro-romanticism'.[4]

Conversely, the Party of Regions 'was not "pro-Russian" in the sense of being a puppet, but it was Russia-leaning', the US State Department assessed, meaning the Kremlin would need to curry favour and devise ways of influencing Yanukovych, rather than controlling him outright. Russia itself and the Russian language were undeniable parts of Ukraine's history, said Borys Kolesnikov (who later served as Deputy Prime Minister under Yanukovych), and according to him, the Party of Regions had polling data showing 66 per cent of people supported Ukraine's neutrality (in other words, no to NATO membership).[5]

These Russian-leaning messages did not hinder – and in some regions helped – Yanukovych to win the presidential election in 2010. According to the OSCE's monitors, Yanukovych had defeated his chief rival Tymoshenko fair and square, exploiting her own uneven personal popularity due to a string of controversies that had damaged her image. The result was clear cut. In the first round on 17 January, Yanukovych received 35.32 per cent of the vote and Tymoshenko 25.05 per cent (others included Tihipko with 13.05 per cent, Yatsenyuk with 6.96 per cent and Yushchenko with a paltry 5.45 per cent). With no candidate receiving more than 50 per cent of the vote, a second round was held.

This time, Yanukovych was the winner with 48.95 per cent against Tymoshenko's 45.47 per cent, and the Central Election Commission announced the results on 14 February. After another narrow margin victory, Ukraine was still very much a divided country. The regional spread of votes showed that in the east and the south, Yanukovych tallied well in the round two run-off: 90.44 in Donetsk, 88.96 in Luhansk, 84.35 in Sevastopol City, 78.24 in Crimea, 74.14 in Odessa, 71.53 in Mykolaiv, 71.50 in Zaporizhzhia, and 71.35 in Kharkiv. Cheating and fraud were not prominent features of the campaign, and despite the defeated Tymoshenko's claims of irregularities, the OSCE had judged that 'the [2010] presidential election met most OSCE commitments and other international standards for demo-cratic elections and consolidated progress achieved since 2004'.[6]

THE DONBAS REGION

The Donbas was key to Yanukovych's victory, but where did this region fit in the wider Ukrainian body politic? At a glance on the map, the Donbas looked partially encased by Russia's borders, with key Donbas cities like Donetsk, Luhansk and Mariupol geograph-ically close to the big Russian city of Rostov-on-Don. The Donbas was truly a world away from Lviv and also quite a distance from

Kyiv, until a relatively quick Intercity express train service began to connect the capital to the Donbas town of Kramatorsk in seven hours (although the cheaper tickets still left you on a longer overnight Kyiv to Donbas train).

Although a touchy subject, and one that should be conveyed while avoiding gross generalisations, I encountered some Kyivites and western Ukrainians who held ill-conceived and occasionally prejudicial opinions of Donbas residents, which were sadly in line with those identified by the Donbas resident interviewed in Chapter 3. One story that occasionally surfaced was 'they are all descendants of prisoners over in the east', which was largely baseless.[7] Plenty of Ukrainians from elsewhere in the country had never visited Donbas, although this is a perfectly innocent phenomenon and hardly the makings of a civil war.

There are versions of this all over the world. For instance, in my home country of the UK, there are plenty of Londoners like myself who have not spent much time in north England, or in Wales or Scotland, let alone in Northern Ireland (I never visited any of these places until my twenties). Unlike the example of the United Kingdom's four nations, however, where the three smaller nations were granted their own regional assemblies in the 1998 devolution reforms, no devolution has occurred in Ukraine. When it gained independence Ukraine was a centralised state, exacerbating the tendencies of some Donbas residents to hold sceptical views of

---

* The notion of Donbas residents as the descendants of criminals has origins in the USSR. Some people displeased with the USSR and its methods of rule moved to the Donbas in the hope they would be left alone by the authorities. Fervent Bolsheviks and Lenin-Stalin supporters called them 'criminal elements' who were inclined to betray their motherland. In addition, when the USSR forcefully deported Polish and Hungarian people from their lands in the west of Ukraine, these 'unreliable and potentially criminal elements' were first brought to Donbas, which was used as a transition camp before they were moved elsewhere. This is where the term 'criminal' comes from. The theory of prisoners being brought to the Donbas from all over the USSR to work in coal mines is not confirmed by historical research. Quite the opposite, in fact: Donbas 'mines were a refuge for those who aspired to freedom. People from all over the country and from beyond settled here,' according to historical research quoted in BBC News Ukrainian.

Ukraine's other regions and of central rule in Kyiv, which can seem far away in distance as well as in spirit, unlike Russia, which is immediately next door.

In the Donbas, Yanukovych was one of their own. Having been born in the village of Zhukovka in the Donetsk Oblast, and later studying at the Donetsk Polytechnic, his regional identity was more important to the locals than his pro-Russian sympathies. The Donbas residents themselves have an interesting lineage that is very much tied to the colonisation of the region by the later Tsars of the Russian Empire. Until about the 1750s, the Donbas had actually been rather empty of people (the name 'Donbas' refers to the basin of the River Donets, which is the largest tributary of the River Don in Russia).

As the writer Anna Reid points out, 'Ukraine's Russians are fairly recent arrivals. They came in waves that mirrored the empire's belated industrial revolution: at the end of the nineteenth century, with the first industrial boom.' Thanks to their arrival, 'in the Donbas coal basin, equidistant from Kyiv and Moscow, Russians form a majority'. Donetsk City was founded in 1869 to house the workers at the metallurgical factory, which was owned by a Welshman named John Hughes. The Imperial Russian Government had commissioned the Millwall Iron Works Company to develop the metallurgical industry. Luhansk City's history was not dissimilar, and involved an English industrialist named Charles Gascoigne who in 1795 founded a metal factory near a Zaporozhian Cossack settlement which, in 1882, was expanded and merged with another settlement to found Luhansk City. Further industrial development of the Donbas took place in the Soviet era, and more Russians moved there in the pre- and post–1945 eras. As my former locally hired OSCE colleague, who was a Donbas resident, explained to me, a unique regional pride developed in the Donbas around its industrial identity:

> Donbas for over a century now was always giving people a real chance to lay bread on their tables, even when villages around starved to death from Holodomor. But it has always been and still remains bloody bread – coal mining (always) and metallurgical production (quite often) are very dangerous professions. Donbas coal and metal is paid for in human lives and injuries. In Soviet time there was a scary statistic about how many hundreds of tons of produced coal/metal goods/steel per one death of a coal miner/metallurgist is considered normal. I know what I am talking about. Both my grandfathers were coal miners. My father was a metallurgist engineer. People in Donbas for several generations lived with the understanding that their father/husband going underground now might never return alive. Our perception of death is a bit distorted because of that.[8]

For Ukraine, the Donbas's heritage has hindered the Westernising visions of other Ukrainians. As Anna Reid observes, 'Lviv may be unmistakably Ukrainian and Donetsk unmistakably Russian, but the vast swathe of country in between is neither quite one nor the other. The population is thoroughly mixed.'[9] Hence, if one imagines Ukraine as a seesaw, the USA and the EU wanted to tip the country on the basis of the dominant sympathies in its western regions, whereas Russia wanted to tip the country towards the dominant sympathies in its eastern regions.

In 2010, the Ukrainian seesaw had tipped decisively towards Russia. But the trick to tipping the seesaw also involved manipulating the one thing that really made Ukraine tick: the extreme wealth of a very small number of individuals, and the corruption that bedevilled the rest of them.

UKRAINE'S OLIGARCHIC POLITICS

'All animals are equal but some animals are more equal than others.' So ran the immortal line in George Orwell's satire on the hypocrisy inherent in the Soviet Union's purported socialist republics. Despite its avowedly egalitarian ideology, there was little distinction between power and wealth, and as the USSR collapsed, this legacy was passed to the Russian Federation, where its developing market economy was captured by a relatively small number of oligarchs who built their unfathomable wealth by taking over businesses amidst the chaos of privatisation. This phenomenon occurred across the former Soviet republics, and Ukraine was no exception. The Ukrainian version of oligarchic politics developed differently from the Russian Federation, where Putin ensured after he came to power in 1999 that the security state would tame Russia's oligarchs, ensuring that the state through its cronies and ex-spies retained its hold over critical industries like energy production and the media.*

In Ukraine, where there was no equivalent security state with unrequited imperial ambitions, this left the Ukrainian oligarchs relatively free to roam for many years, building not only financial but also political power. During the 1990s, Ukraine's richest businesspeople tended to build their wealth through the gas trade, by importing Russia's natural gas at a subsidised exchange rate only to resell it at a higher domestic price. In the early 2000s, the metalworks owners had the most lucrative businesses, especially as the requisite materials were sourced locally for regulated low prices and

---

* This is one of the main themes in Belton, *Putin's People* (2020).

sold abroad for higher sums. This had been enabled by the way in which privatisation had been handled, notably during the Kuchma years, since he had encouraged the growth of the oligarch class not only to provide himself with some very rich friends but also to reform Ukraine's Soviet-era command economy. Compared to the last year of the USSR, when the share of its GDP from private enterprise was just 10 per cent in 1991, by 2001 privately owned businesses accounted for 60 per cent in 2001.

According to the economist Anders Åslund, the patterns of ownership in the energy and the metal trade, as well as industries like agriculture, banking and property, meant that 'Ukraine remained an oligarchic state, where a club of big businessmen dominated the government, parliament, and media'. Importantly, that 'power was not consolidated but divided' between different oligarchs.[10]

Yanukovych's billionaire supporters included fellow Donetsk native Rinat Akhmetov, who had originally introduced Yanukovych and Manafort, and whose businesses interests spanned the metallurgical industry and ownership of Shakhtar Donetsk football club. In 2021, Akhmetov was ranked Ukraine's richest person in a tally published in the *Kyiv Post*, followed in the number two spot by Victor Pinchuk, whose main business involved churning out steel pipes and railway wheels but had also made sure to sponsor Kyiv's modern art gallery, the Pinchuk Art Centre. The third was Vadym Novynskyi, who was born in Russia but had been awarded Ukrainian citizenship in 2012 by Yanukovych and had also acquired vast wealth in the metallurgical industry.

Extreme wealth was not only limited to Russian-leaning circles, and fourth on the list was future President Petro Poroshenko, who owned the Roshen confectionary company as well as a TV channel.[11] Indeed, when the Pandora Papers scandal broke and disclosed the tax haven holdings of wealthy individuals from around the world, thirty-eight Ukrainian politicians were implicated – included the latter-day favoured son of Ukrainian politics, Volodymyr Zelensky, who had parked much of his wealth in offshore accounts. There is no getting away from it: politics in Ukraine is a sport open only to the wealthy, and regardless of whether we call these honestly earned or ill-gotten gains, the old Soviet tradition of a mix between wealth and political power has persisted in a modern form.

*   *   *

The moment the depth of Ukraine's corruption really struck me was in a conversation with my regular taxi driver in Kyiv. He always looked somewhat stressed and one day, after we had known each other for some time, he told me his story. His postgraduate university degree at a leading Kyiv university had become hostage to a bribe still due to be paid to someone in the university. He remarked wistfully to me that in Britain a student could earn a degree through merit and by paying the publicised fees, before rueing the fact he had to continue driving his taxi to feed his family and save up to pay the bribe.

Stories like this were all too common; whether it related to trying to get treatment in a hospital, or clearing up a bureaucratic logjam, bribes often changed hands.

If the oligarchic basis of Ukraine's economic and political systems appeared one side of the gilded coin, then on the other side was the everyday corruption that bedevilled ordinary citizens. Transparency International, an NGO that describes itself as 'the global coalition against corruption', produces an annual 'corruption perceptions index' in which Ukraine is ranked the 122nd most corrupt in the world. Russia is not far behind, ranked at 136th place, placing both countries very much in the bottom half of the overall list of 180 countries.[12]

According to an authoritative study of Ukraine's crony capitalism, versions of this appeared at the national and the local levels, where elites 'and their accomplices in regional governments and councils' subverted established systems and siphoned off money for personal gain. Four factors have kept Ukraine deeply corrupt:

1. 'Deep penetration of government decision-making processes via senior officials who favour the interests of big business and benefit from these connections';
2. 'Influence over the legislative process including through paid-for support of MPs who either have direct business interests or stand to benefit indirectly from their support of the business interests of others';
3. 'Influence over the judiciary and law enforcement agencies through the appointment of loyal individuals, as well as the use of bribery';
4. 'Control of the media through ownership of the main outlets that provide a platform for selected politicians to develop their careers and for big business to shape public opinion'.

This resulted in 'rigged public procurement tenders and privileged access to state aid, tax benefits, soft loans and debt guarantees from state banks', and all manner of other schemes.[13]

The system of corruption survived the Orange Revolution and worsened under Yanukovych's presidency, when 'mafia structures in Donbas colluded with government agencies, including the Security Service'.[14] Luckily, I never had any run-ins with Ukrainian organised criminal gangs, but I did note the reference to them in the naming of a popular restaurant chain I ended up visiting in Kyiv and Dnipro called Mafia. Ostensibly a nod to the Italian part of its menu, I'm sure the locals chuckled at the name.

According to the Global Organised Crime Index, which ranks Ukraine third in its 'criminality score' on a list of forty-four countries in Europe, Ukraine was a hub for human trafficking, arms trafficking, drugs trafficking and wildlife trafficking.[15] Ukraine is a point of origin for human trafficking (as 'one of the largest countries of origin for people subject to forced labour in Europe') and arms trafficking (thanks to the abundance of small arms littering Ukraine, from when the Red Army downed tools and disbanded in 1991). The drugs and wildlife, conversely, don't originate in Ukraine, but it is used as a transit route thanks to its coastal access. Perhaps some of this is par for the course in a relatively poor country with a big black market, but it brings home how endemic the challenges of criminality in Ukraine have been.

*　*　*

In years gone by it was perfectly normal for someone to personally profit if they held public office or a position of administrative authority. Indeed, British parliamentarians used to purchase their seats in past centuries, using their newfound power to pay back their creditors. As Francis Fukuyama reminds us in his study of decaying political systems, the 'distinction between the public and private sphere' has only developed in recent centuries, and prior government 'was patrimonial', especially since monarchs owned the territories they governed. Corruption tends to be based on one of two basic practices: either 'the creation and extraction of rents' that are 'created by natural scarcities but can also be artificially created by governments' or 'patronage or clientelism' involving 'a reciprocal exchange of favours between two individuals of different status'. While patronage is 'sometimes treated as highly deviant forms of political behaviour', in fact, the 'political patronage relationship is one of the most basic forms of human social organisation. It is universal because it is natural to human beings.'[16]

In Ukraine, patrimony involved people who wanted influence bandwagoning around whomever was in power. Although fighting corruption became a massive undertaking in recent years, it took the massive corruption of the Yanukovych era to enlighten many more Ukrainians as to just how much of their country's wealth was being siphoned off for personal gain by those in power. Confronting corruption has often been an uphill struggle, but it has also been an essential part of Ukraine's modernisation.

YANUKOVYCH REBUKES THE EU

Dmitry Medvedev never transcended the image of a stand-in, having first been cultivated by Putin as a 25-year-old lawyer in St Petersburg before keeping Putin's seat warm in the Russian presidency between 2008 and 2012.[17] In August 2009, after a year in the driving seat of the presidency, Medvedev wrote a letter to Ukraine's government, bitterly criticising Yushchenko as an 'anti-Russian', and hoping for 'new political leadership of Ukraine' in 2010.[18] Russia got its wish with Yanukovych's election victory. The problem for Moscow was that, rather that Yanukovych simply being their vassal, he wanted Ukraine to have its cake and eat it by seeing what he could get from both Russia and the West. Yanukovych was going to try to play all sides for as long as he could, seeing how much he could get from all of them.

He explained his philosophy shortly after coming to power: 'Ukraine will embark on a foreign policy that will allow our country to fully benefit from equal and mutually beneficial relations with Russia, the EU and the US.' This meant that seeking 'cooperation between the Ukraine and Russia was in everyone's interest' and that 'a stable and solid partnership with the European Union, Russia and the United States would be provided to broaden democracy in Ukraine in every area.'[19] Whereas Kuchma did something similar in 1994–2004, now it was harder to play all sides.

Yanukovych gave Russia an early windfall on 21 April 2010, when he met Medvedev in Kharkiv to sign a deal between their countries extending Russia's lease on the Black Sea Fleet for twenty-five years. In return, Ukraine could buy Russian gas at a discounted price. But Yanukovych ran into problems with the EU, who looked dimly upon his authoritarian tendencies when he jailed his electoral rival Tymoshenko and barred the boxer Vitaly Klitschko from running for President on the basis that he paid taxes abroad.

Even if Yanukovych wanted to play all sides, his sympathies and tendencies leaned more naturally towards Russia. Nevertheless, if you didn't look hard enough, it seemed around this time that Ukraine was also becoming a part of mainstream Europe.

Ukraine co-hosted the Euro 2012 football tournament with Poland. The opening ceremony was held in Poland and featured bunting dropped from the stadium roof in the red and white of Poland plus the yellow and blue of Ukraine, a nice moment after the historical wars between these nations. The choice of the countries was part of the 'sport as a healer' philosophy.[*][20] Ahead of this

---

* Peter Kennedy and Christos Kassimeris assert that 'from UEFA's perspective, the choice served as a reminder of the wider European project to which it aspires ... The Euros and UEFA itself have come full circle from the post-'45 Cold War climate of East vs West.'

tournament, a revamped stadium was built in Donetsk, to be used by the Shakhtar Donetsk club once the tournament was over. In the end, both Ukraine and Russia were knocked out of their separate groups early on in the tournament, and western European teams dominated the semi-finals played in Donetsk and Warsaw and the final in Kyiv. As a reminder of how far Ukraine still had to go to find its home in Europe, EU officials boycotted this because Yanukovych had jailed Tymoshenko.

* * *

At first, Yanukovych benefited from a less pernicious international environment. With Medvedev in the Kremlin and Obama in the White House, the ideological edge to the preceding Putin/Bush years softened. In 2012, Putin returned to the presidency for a third time, causing the first big protests against his personal rule in Russia. Putin brushed these off with the expected repression he meted out to Russia's dissidents. With Yanukovych in Kyiv, it seemed to Putin that Moscow's influence in Ukraine was on the up.

Moreover, when Ukraine's prospects for NATO membership faded after 2008, joining the EU resurfaced as Ukraine's main hope of entry to Western structures. For the oligarchs, the EU promised better access to Western markets, but there was a problem.

> While some oligarchs [...] had much to gain from access to the European market, they also had much to lose from laws that undermined their control of the Ukrainian economy. Yanukovych was more interested in the symbolism of integration than the substance, and when it clashed with his interest or those of the powerful oligarchs, it lost out ... Ukraine said it could not generate the sacrifices

for far-reaching reform if membership was not promised in return, and the EU could not make a membership commitment to a country that needed so much reform.[21]

Nevertheless, Yanukovych was out to get what he could from the EU, even if it was only the flattery of their attention. The Brussels–Kyiv courtship began to take centre stage, until the stage itself collapsed under contradictory impulses arising from Yanukovych's parallel courtship with Moscow.

In Brussels, the EU Enlargement Commissioner Štefan Füle, who served in this post from 2010 to 2014, wanted to ensure the EU's courtship of Ukraine would not fail in the same way as NATO had in 2008. 'I participated in the Bucharest NATO summit,' said Füle in a conversation at a US think tank. 'NATO promised membership to Ukraine and Georgia, which was quite a political achievement [but] in a quite surprising move, it has not acted in a MAP.' Füle wanted the EU to do better: 'This time the approach is a clear message to these countries: you help to build more of the EU in your countries, with our assistance – indeed using instruments and lessons learned from enlargement – and it will be you, quite logically, who will put this issue on the table.'[22]

Someone in the audience quipped, 'NATO gives Ukraine and Georgia a destination but won't give them the instruments; you turn around, give them the instruments but won't give them the destination.'

The EU was a process-obsessed entity. After the Orange Revolution, the European Parliament voted for Ukraine to be offered 'a clear European perspective, possibly leading to EU membership'. Brussels duly reached out to Kyiv (as it did to the EU's neighbours) via the European Neighbourhood Policy. Then, in 2009, it set up a specific vehicle to cultivate relations with the former Soviet socialist republics, called the Eastern Partnership (Ukraine plus five other former SSRs: Armenia, Azerbaijan, Belarus, Georgia, Moldova). Finally, the courtship with Ukraine culminated with Brussels offering a draft association agreement in 2012, which kicked off a major crisis.

These were the EU equivalents of the NATO MAP, but progress was difficult, as the reforms needed to meet EU criteria clashed with the interests of the oligarchs.

*   *   *

Meanwhile, in the Kremlin, Putin decided that Russia needed to make a rival offer to Kyiv. To Russia, EU expansion was not quite as offensive as NATO expansion, but only just. Lavrov once told a Brussels audience, 'We are accused of having spheres of influence. But what is the Eastern Partnership, if not an attempt to extend the EU's sphere of influence, including to Belarus?'[23] After the Eastern Partnership was launched, Russia announced its own customs unions (also called the Eurasian Union). Belarus and Kazakhstan joined right away, and Russia's intention was to lure Ukraine into it, too.

Playing along, Yanukovych, on 31 May 2013, sent Ukrainian Prime Minister Mykola Azarov to sign an agreement with Russia to become an 'observer' of the customs unions. Russia assumed this meant a path to full membership, but Yanukovych did not necessarily want to join Russia's customs union if it meant ending his EU talks.[24] In July 2013, on a charm offensive rooted in historical ties, Putin visited Kyiv for the 1,025th anniversary of the adoption of

Christianity by Kyivan Rus to again reflect on his vision of a shared civilisation space between Ukraine and Russia.

This is when things got tricky. To use a crass analogy, Yanukovych was encouraging Ukraine to be courted by two suitors, in Brussels and Moscow, but they wanted Ukraine to choose one or the other. Yanukovych kept refusing to choose until the whole situation ended in a catastrophe.

The EU, through its Eastern Partnership, offered Ukraine an association agreement (AA) in 2013. This was a significant technical offer, with a Deep and Comprehensive Free Trading Agreement (DCTFA) through which the EU offers benefits like visa-free travel and smoother trade to countries that aspire to full membership, providing they follow the three Copenhagen criteria: consolidation of democratic institutions and protection of human rights, a market economy, and adoption of the full body of EU laws and regulations.[25]

Fatefully, the EU attached an unofficial deadline to its offer, telling Ukraine that the AA should be signed at the EU's Vilnius summit in November 2013. 'The effect was to light the fuse on a slow developing crisis by appearing to set a deadline for Ukraine to make a choice between Russia and the EU.'[26]

Ukraine couldn't join both clubs – the terms of their respective memberships wouldn't allow for it. Russia now piled on both the pressure and the charm, at first offering more gas price discounts and favourable tariff terms on key goods, but Yanukovych rejected Moscow's offer. So, Russia shifted to bullying.

Beginning in July 2013, Russia imposed trade sanctions on Ukraine, first by cutting off imports of certain food products. It then hit steel manufacturing and other exporters with cumbersome new customs procedures. Although trade resumed in less than a week, the message was clear: if Kyiv were to proceed with the EU offer, expect a disruption in bilateral trade … A few weeks after Vilnius, Putin received Yanukovych in Moscow. Russia promised to purchase US$15 billion in Ukrainian Eurobonds and to cut the gas price for Ukraine by more than US$130 per thousand cubic meters.[27]

It was a serious offer, and the EU wasn't going to offer as much money simply for signing its agreement.

So, Yanukovych finally made a choice, right at the last minute. He left the EU jilted at the altar in Vilnius, abandoning the EU deal.

At the summit itself, with the cameras rolling, EU officials like José Manuel Barroso and Herman Van Rompuy were livid at Yanukovych, who still showed up at the summit. 'I regret this decision,' Füle said in Vilnius. 'Many of the new opportunities for modernisation and investment that the association agreement would have brought for Ukraine and its citizens will now be delayed.'[28] But it was never that simple: EU membership was not simply about modernising Ukraine; it was about doing so on Western terms. Moscow and Brussels had tried to play each other off, and Moscow had won, albeit temporarily.

*   *   *

A rather vulgar Russian joke did the rounds at the time, making light of Ukraine and the EU:

Imagine if Ukraine entered the EU. Two Khokhols sit and drink. One asks how things are.

'EU is shit. I am without a job. My wife washes floors in Italy. My son married a German man. My daughter is a hooker in France. All because of damned Moskals!'

'Moskals knew everything when they told us repeatedly, "Do not join EU!" They knew we would join it out of sheer spite!'

The *Khokhols* and *Moskals* were slang for Ukrainians and Russians respectively, and the point about clashing world views was clear.

Ukraine should have been developing as a place where a plurality of cultural influences and international connections mingled and merged, but this is far too idealistic a notion for the competitive world of geopolitics. Ukraine's reality was instead defined by the vanity of statesmen and their notions of zero-sum gains and losses based on different conceptions of civilisation.

Almost as egregiously as NATO, albeit in a very different way, during its courtship with Kyiv, Brussels acted as if Moscow did not matter. Operating with the absolute conviction of the righteousness of its enlargement agenda, convinced it was on a civilising mission and that the reforms that it fostered were a good in their own right, the hard power of Russia's objection was ignored. Füle referenced Carl Bildt, the Swedish Foreign Minister and former Prime Minister, who once said that Russia was never likely to join an 'Eastern Partnership' with the EU because 'I don't think they want to be included'.[29] For Bildt and other European officials pushing Brussels's relationship to deepen with the former Soviet republics while leaving Russia out, the logic was simple: Russia was on the wrong side of history and had squandered its stake in Europe's future until it modernised itself.

In a later speech, Bildt explained that 'our expectation [of Russia's development] was that there would be the emergence of a middle class; that there would be an opening up of society; and that there would be a gradual Europeanisation of Russian society'.[30] The fact that Russia was primarily located in Asia, and was the product of very different cultural, geographical and historical influences, was not of interest to Bildt in this speech, since he preferred to convey 'our way or the highway' as a mantra for the future of Europe, given how far behind in the modernity stakes Russia was compared to the EU. Whether one believes EU standards to be generally morally superior, more humane and modern compared to what Russia has offered (which I happened to agree with) is hardly the point. The point is that Russia retained the power to forcefully disagree that it should be shut out of Europe's evolution.

Putin used to hold forth about Ukrainian history back then, too, but he sounded less deranged. In 2013, speaking to the Valdai Discussion Club think tank, Putin's take was moderated: 'Ukraine, without a doubt, is an independent state. That is how history has unfolded,' balancing the fact that 'we have common traditions, a common mentality, a common history and a common culture. We have very similar languages,' before fawning over the fact that

> the Ukrainian people, the Ukrainian culture and the Ukrainian language have wonderful features that make up the identity of the Ukrainian nation. And we not only respect it, but moreover, I, for one, really love it, I like all of it. It is part of our greater Russian, or Russian–Ukrainian, world.[31]

This is perhaps because back then, Putin still smelled victory in Ukraine: getting their man in power in Kyiv and his decision not to join hands with Brussels. But it was a fleeting victory that would fall foul of people power, resulting in a toppled government and something Ukraine had avoided for twenty-two years – massive violence via domestic repressions and, eventually, armed conflict. This was the moment the intensifying geopolitical contest over Ukraine began to involve the shedding of Ukrainian blood.

DIGNITY AMIDST THE BLOODSHED OF 'EUROMAIDAN'
The ethnic diversity of the populace is not the first thing one thinks of when in Ukraine, aside from the visiting communities of students from South Asian and African countries and a few other relatively small communities. The last Ukrainian census is rather out of date, having been conducted in 2001; the two largest groups are those who identify as Ukrainians (77.8 per cent) and as Russians (17.3 per cent), while a multitude of other identities and nationalities comprise the remaining 4.9 per cent.[32] Which means someone like me stands out a mile away in Ukraine, aside from city centres in big pre-war student towns (although I barely experienced any hostility, only the occasional surprising question, such as from an old taxi driver who had been raised on regular broadcasts of Bollywood films on Soviet-era TV and wanted to talk about India).

All of which made the career ascent of Mustafa Nayyem truly impressive, having been born in Kabul to an Afghan father and a Ukrainian mother, and later moving to Ukraine to avoid the Soviet war in Afghanistan in the 1980s. The millennial Nayyem was amongst the first journalists with social media reach to call on Ukrainians to head to the Maidan in the wake of the EU's Vilnius summit in late November 2013.

One day out government said 'stop, don't dream about it.' And it was a very sad day for me. I saw there were a lot of [online] posts on this issue [of the signing of the EU agreement], and I was wondering if it was only likes or if people were ready to go offline. And it was a very symbolic day because nine years ago on that day the Orange Revolution started.

Nayyem played a role in kicking off the 'Euromaidan', as it became known, and he would later become a Ukrainian Member of Parliament.

The protests that Nayyem's Facebook post galvanised had two motivations: the 'Euromaidan' one being a demand by the protesters for Yanukovych to reverse his decision and to sign the EU's association agreement; later, as the protest gathered momentum and numbers, it also became known as the 'Revolution of Dignity', with a more general call to clear up the graft in Ukraine's politics and to realise the unfulfilled potential of the Orange Revolution from nearly a decade ago.

Had Yanukovych allowed the initial protesters to vent at his decision not to sign the technocratic EU association agreement, then the stand-off at the Maidan may have fizzled out. But there was tension and violence almost immediately, as the Interior Ministry's Berkut security forces brawled with the protesters, who later moved to St Michael's Square, just up Mykhailivska Street from the Maidan. 'You know, the government of Yanukovych, they did something that never happens in Ukraine; they used brutal force against a peaceful demonstration,' Nayyem told the US broadcaster CNN.[33] He was right to single out this fact: as we have seen, until then, state violence had not blighted Ukraine, quite unlike so many countries around the world born from an imperial collapse.

Thousands of people now came to the Maidan, outraged at the heavy-handed security response, and determined to vent their outrage at a regime they wanted to stand down in shame over its sanctioning of violence. The protesters stayed out over the winter.

Yanukovych realised that he needed to start speaking to opposition politicians and offering concessions, for instance firing his Prime Minister, the Russian-born and later Donetsk-based Mykola Azarov, on 28 January, for an opposition replacement.

The softly spoken Arseniy Yatsenyuk would be his replacement after he was selected from amongst the three leading opposition politicians (the others being the hulking ex-boxer Klitschko and the far-right leader of the Svoboda party Oleh Tyahnybok). Just how Yatsenyuk made the cut became mired in its own controversy, after the USA was portrayed as being puppet master and kingmaker following a bugged telephone call between Assistant Secretary of State Victoria Nuland and US ambassador to Ukraine Geoffrey Pyatt was uploaded on YouTube for all the world to hear on 6 February.[34]

In the call, Pyatt says to Nuland, 'I think Yats is the guy who's got the economic experience, the governing experience ... What he needs is Klitsch and Tyahnybok on the outside.'

Nuland responds:

OK ... one more wrinkle for you Geoff ... When I talked to Jeff Feltman [UN official] this morning, he had a new name for the UN guy, Robert Serry. Did I write you that this morning? ... Serry could come in Monday or Tuesday. So that would be great, I think, to help glue this thing and to have the UN help glue it and, you know, fuck the EU.

Pyatt references the Russian response:

No, exactly. And I think we've got to do something to make it stick together because you can be pretty sure that if it does start to gain altitude, that the Russians will be working behind the scenes to try to torpedo it ... So let me work on Klitschko ... We want to try to get somebody with an international personality to come out here and help to midwife this thing. The other issue is some kind of outreach to Yanukovych, but we probably regroup on that tomorrow as we see how things start to fall into place.

Nuland responds:

So on that piece Geoff, when I wrote the note [National Security Advisor to the US Vice-President Jake] Sullivan's come back to me VFR [direct to me], saying you need [US Vice-President Joe] Biden and I said probably tomorrow for an atta-boy and to get the deets [details] to stick. So, Biden's willing.[35]

The headlines focused on the invective directed at the EU, but beyond this the whole thrust of the leaked call was a fascinating moment of diplomatic indiscretion. It left little to the imagination about how these US officials viewed the situation in Kyiv, in competitive terms with the Party of Regions and Russia and even the EU. The US ambassador wanted to 'midwife' the transition to a more Western-leaning leadership. Biden when President would have many more chances to 'atta-boy' future leaders in Kyiv, but for now, around the time of the leaked call, the situation on the Maidan was tense and about to break.

Yanukovych was about to lose all control of the situation and lose his own job in the process. The day of reckoning on the Maidan came on 18 February 2014, when thousands of protesters marched toward the Rada building to demand the reinstatement of the 2004 constitution, which had weakened the range of presidential powers. (Yanukovych reversed these changes when he came to power years later, in effect undoing one of the gains of the Orange Revolution.) These protesters were fired on by the security forces with a mixture of rubber bullets, tear gas and live ammunition and they retreated to the Maidan. The site already resembled a medieval battlefield with makeshift barriers built by the protesters, but it could not last for ever. Everyone present, protesters and security forces, were getting jumpier and more agitated, and the situation descended into outright tragedy two days later.

On 20 February, the protesters breached a wall of barriers manned by police at one end of the Maidan and were met by deadly force. Sniper fire from the Berkut security forces was directed into the unarmed protesters, killing forty-six within two hours and bringing the number killed in the protests to seventy by the end of that day, with hundreds more injured. Places where protesters had been slaughtered would afterwards be marked by murals of the faces of the dead and a 'museum to the heavenly hundred' was also opened in Kyiv.*[36]

After the massacre, Yanukovych was on borrowed political time as his regime had the blood of so many people on its hands, regardless of who it was that ordered the shootings on 20 February. Various officials who had formerly worked with Yanukovych, including the mayor of Kyiv, resigned in light of the horrendous violence, and some members of the police and security forces simply gave up their posts. On 22 February, Yanukovych fled the country in the dead of night to Russia, thinking his life was now in danger if he remained in Kyiv.

The Revolution of Dignity had succeeded.

---

* As the Maidan Museum recounts, 'The participants of the Revolution of Dignity, who were killed by the security officers and their mercenaries, received a name of the Heavenly Hundred. The official count of them is one hundred and seven … The youngest one, Nazarii Voitovych, was sixteen. The oldest one, Ivan Nakonechnyi, was eighty-three.'

* * *

Jean-Jacques Rousseau's seminal work *The Social Contract* explains that 'despotism, instead of governing the subjects in order to make them happy, makes them miserable in order to govern them'.[37] The Ukrainians who gathered at the Maidan wanted to oust their own despot and to have a chance at rewriting their social contract. Putin would rather subscribe to the views of a very different eighteenth-century thinker, the famous counter-revolutionary writer Edmund Burke, who wrote *The Evils of Revolution*. Of the French revolutionaries in 1789: 'This sort of people are so taken by their theories about rights of man, that they have forgotten his nature.' Putin was about to remind Ukraine about the nature of man.

Just five days after Yanukovych fled, early on 27 February, armed men with no military insignia took over the Crimean Parliament building and raised the Russian flag – Russia's first 'special military operation' in independent Ukraine began, although it naturally wasn't called that, or indeed called anything at all by Putin, who had moved swiftly after, in his eyes at least, a Western-manipulated mob had effectively staged a coup against Yanukovych, Ukraine's elected leader.

War, something Ukraine had avoided during the breakup of the Soviet Union and had never experienced for twenty-two years afterwards, would now become Ukraine's reality.

CHAPTER 6

THE INTELLIGENCE OFFICER'S WAR

A REFLECTION ON DECEPTION

A BARELY DENIABLE INVASION

'Welcome to Ukraine. You will all be heading east – to our patrol hubs in Donetsk and Luhansk.'

This was the greeting from the head of operations, a silver-haired retired British army officer who now worked for the OSCE 'Special Monitoring Mission Ukraine' in its headquarters in Kyiv. Bang went my chance of sipping coffees and admiring the architecture in Lviv or Ivano Frankivsk, where we also inexplicably had patrol hubs, since these towns were as far from the war as you could get. So, towards the trenches it was. After all, this was what I wanted and why I signed up, but as the reality of it dawned and I was handed my regulation body armour and helmet, all of a sudden, it didn't seem quite as appealing.

I looked around the briefing room, at the mixed bag of former soldiers, policeman, diplomats and aid workers from different countries. They didn't seem to flinch, or at least, they didn't show it, most of them being far closer to the ends of their careers than I was as well as being seasoned veterans of other wars.

At the same time as the annexation of Crimea, a series of uprisings and armed conflicts was taking place in the Donbas region of eastern Ukraine. Beginning as local protests against Yanukovych's ousting, Russian-backed separatist fighters had quickly joined the conflict to take it to the next level. This was where I had been deployed as part of the monitoring mission, and we were there to try to prevent the conflict from escalating further.

We had just completed our war zone hostile environment training, with a particular emphasis on 'coping with capture', in light of the two patrols of OSCE monitors who had recently been kidnapped by the Russian-backed separatists. They were mercifully released without harm, after their kidnappers were satisfied that their point over who controlled the easternmost parts of the Donbas was proven.

The OSCE had the virtue of including the Western countries and Russia in its member states, which is why it was used in Ukraine. All fifty-seven OSCE member states signed off on the mission on 21 March 2014, soon after the fighting began. It was to be a non-coercive civilian mission, aimed at 'reducing tensions and fostering peace', and supporting future ceasefires, but with no ability to enforce the peace or to prise apart the warring sides.[1] Naturally, Russia would not have endorsed an international mission that could have stopped the war in its tracks, as I was about to find out.

For the next year, across 2014 and 2015, I shuttled between ceasefire monitoring work, which often involved heading out on patrols to obscure parts of the Donbas, and spending time in Kyiv on rotations at headquarters, where the OSCE briefed diplomats from around the world about what was really going on in Ukraine's war-torn east, and on the talks it was mediating between the warring sides.

At other times, I would head back to Kyiv or elsewhere on man-dated rest and recuperation trips. As we all found, the Donbas war zone could be stultifying and it forced you to come up for air once in a while. It was remarkable to me that the rest of Ukraine was entirely peaceful and, frankly, safer than my hometown of London. Cities like Lviv or Ivano Frankivsk continued to gleam. For this was a localised war, ringfenced in the Donbas, lethal to those caught in the crossfire but far away from much of the rest of the country.

The overnight train between Kyiv and the Donetsk region became the main artery to get in and out of the Donbas. One night, heading out on my mandatory R&R trip, I boarded a regular train that con-tained what seemed like an entire battalion of Ukrainian soldiers; to reach my cabin I walked past carriages full of them, weaving past camouflaged figures sprawled over the seats and in the aisles, with their unslung rifles and tired eyes.

The following morning, as the train rolled into Kyiv, their wives, children, girlfriends, parents lined the station platform and greeted them with embraces and tears of relief. The intimacy of their re-unions made me feel like an interloper, but it highlighted to me an important fact. In the coming eight years of what military analysts call 'low-intensity war', thousands upon thousands of Ukrainian soldiers made similar rotations. The impact on Ukrainian society was considerable. After picking itself up from the shock of finding itself at war for the first time in its independent history, Ukraine's army had to mobilise some personnel with no prior military service, reinstating conscription to create a mixed army of professionals and conscripted personnel.[2] Many families felt the impact of war all over Ukraine.

February and March 2014 marked the start of the Russo-Ukrainian war, and the fighting claimed an estimated 14,200 lives from then until January 2022. If the first incarnation of the war paled in comparison to the invasion unleashed by Russia in 2022, it was still no mere dress rehearsal: it was a real war, and the people of east Ukraine were suffering, dying and fleeing.

Putin's smoke and mirrors

Unlike his invasion in 2022 when he played at being 'general', back in 2014, Putin stuck closer to his real professional identity as an intelligence officer. He may have held the colonel rank in the KGB, but this hardly made him a military man; rather, Putin was a master of dissimulation and skulduggery, and his first invasion of Ukraine relied much more on these traits than his second invasion did.

It was an open secret that Russia had instigated the war in 2014, but it was tricky to pin the tail of blame on the Russian donkey, so to speak, since the blindfold of Russian deception was being applied quite skilfully. This phase of the conflict was an intelligence officer's war: we may laugh out loud at the absurdity of Putin's claims that Russia was not involved in what he described as local uprisings in parts of Ukraine against Kyiv's authority, but at the time, these lies served a real purpose.

Was Russia actually at war with Ukraine? Putin wrong-footed the West by not admitting Russia's direct involvement – not because this was believable but because no sooner had war broken out than explanations of what was happening became stuck in a series of conflicting narratives. Russia was engaged in a mixture of activities: ducking and diving responsibility; calibrating the level of violence it was using to avoid all-out war; while seemingly playing along with attempts to contain the violence, such as through its participation in the OSCE mission. This allowed the Russian government to steal back Crimea, to devastate part of the Donbas and to create an open fissure in Ukraine's territory. Putin stayed in the game for eight years, keeping Ukraine wounded and its economy haemorrhaging as a result of the war and its resulting privations.

*   *   *

It started with the annexation of Crimea, a Russia special operation that was clearly rehearsed and given the 'go' order as Yanukovych lost his grip on power. The day after armed men raised Russia's flag over the Parliament building in Crimea, on 28 February, Russia's unmarked soldiers took control of the Crimean airports in Simferopol and Sevastopol. The speedy Russian operation caught Ukrainian forces off guard, and some of them surrendered while others even switched sides to Russia. On 4 March, Putin claimed at a press conference that the forces in Ukraine were not Russian but locals from Crimea.

On 16 March came the *pièce de résistance* of Putin's operation: a referendum was held to ask local residents: '1: Are you in favour of the reunification of Crimea with Russia as part of the Russian Federation? [or] 2: Are you in favour of restoring the 1992 constitution and the status of Crimea as part of Ukraine?' With an apparent 83 per cent turnout, 95.5 per cent of voters picked the first option. There were no international observers, and the mission I belonged to with the OSCE was not allowed to enter Crimea (the closest it got was to be based in Kherson, where some Crimean residents had fled).

By the end of March, the annexation was passed into Russian law. 'An attentive observer', wrote Alexander Salenko, would notice certain mysterious metaphysical parallels between the Crimean crisis and the process of the dissolution of the USSR which could be seen in the same referendum campaign, used both in the Soviet Union referendum on 17 March 1991 and in the Crimean referendum on 16 March 2014. It appears that history repeats itself and moves into the next round in the spiral.[3]

It is also worth recalling that in the December 1991 independence referendum, Crimea was the least enthusiastic region, with 54 per cent of residents supporting independence from the USSR, which had suggested that there were stronger pro-Russian sympathies than elsewhere in Ukraine. Regardless, the events of March 2014 still amounted to the theft of the century – annexations like this were virtually unheard of in modern times.

In the afterglow of the Crimean referendum, Putin delivered a triumphant speech in the Kremlin's Georgievsky Hall. In these opulent imperial-era surroundings, he conveyed once again his various manias around Ukraine, holding forth as to why the Soviet collapse was an underlying justification for the annexation:

> Millions of people went to bed in one country and awoke in different ones, overnight becoming ethnic minorities in former Union republics, while the Russian nation became one of the biggest, if not the biggest ethnic group in the world to be divided by borders. Russia found itself in a position it could not retreat from.

The Maidan protests twisted in Putin's narrative from being a popular rejection of Yanukovych into being an all-out rejection of life in Ukraine:

I understand why Ukrainian people wanted change. They have had enough of the authorities in power during the years of Ukraine's independence. Presidents, Prime Ministers and parliamentarians changed, but ... they milked the country, fought among themselves for power, assets and cash flows and did not ... wonder why it was that millions of Ukrainian citizens saw no prospects at home and went to other countries to work as day labourers.

To criticise nationalist forces in Ukraine he stuck in a dig at 'these ideological heirs of Bandera, Hitler's accomplice during World War Two...'

Of course, no Putin speech would be complete without another broadside at NATO expansion:

We have already heard declarations from Kyiv about Ukraine soon joining NATO. What would this have meant for Crimea and Sevastopol in the future? It would have meant that NATO's navy would be right there in this city of Russia's military glory, and this would create not an illusory but a perfectly real threat to the whole of southern Russia ... NATO remains a military alliance, and we are against having a military alliance making itself at home right in our backyard or in our historic territory. I simply cannot imagine that we would travel to Sevastopol to visit NATO sailors.

Pretext or not, the self-declared rationale, and the boost it delivered to Putin's domestic popularity at the time, were noteworthy. And why had Russian done this now? 'If you compress the spring all the way to its limit, it will snap back hard. You must always remember this.'4 Putin's patience with Ukraine's path since independence was over.

DONBAS 'PEOPLE'S REPUBLIC'

Life in the self-declared Donetsk People's Republic (DPR) was sur-real when I stayed there towards the end of 2014. We were billeted in a four-star hotel and told not to wander outside, unless on official monitoring patrols, in light of the death of an aid worker from a different organisation, who we were told had been killed by a stray shell while on a cigarette break a few blocks away.

Sure enough, we heard and felt the vibrations of outgoing artil-lery fire from close by. The sight of armed separatists wandering into the hotel for a coffee was all too common. And to compound the sense of lawlessness, I was once woken up in the dead of night by the sound of a shotgun blast, followed by a car screeching away on the street below.

We were the guests of the DPR authorities and their militias, who insisted on escorting at terrifying breakneck speeds our OSCE ve-hicles in their own gleaming new police cars when we drove in and out of town. It would be a while before the DPR and the Luhansk People's Republic (LPR) shifted the clocks to match Moscow time, and long before Putin decided that Russia would officially recog-nise both republics in 2022. And it was early enough in the conflict that you could still find Roshen chocolates in Donetsk City, which I thought odd since they were the 'President's brand', and weren't the separatists rejecting anything that traced back to Kyiv? Already, Donetsk City felt like a place trapped in a geopolitical twilight zone, no longer a de facto part of Ukraine, and not yet officially claimed by Russia. My colleagues 140 kilometres away in Luhansk City re-ported something very similar going on there.

After Russia seized its main prize with the annexation of Crimea in March 2014, securing its existing Black Sea Fleet naval base, at-tention switched east. This served Russia's goals since the seizure of

Crimea was a *fait accompli* achieved without any protracted fighting, whereas the international eye was drawn towards the Donbas war, where lives really were being lost.

The Russian government famously shrugged its shoulders, saying that the DPR and LPR were not of its making, and that any Russian soldiers serving were there on holiday – an argument so absurd that early on in the war it helped Russia to shut down the conversation. On one level at least, Putin was correct: an eccentric band of individuals had departed Russia with the idea of fomenting separatist uprisings again the Kyiv government, but they were certainly doing so with the Kremlin's support.

The most notorious 'Russian tourist' was the former military officer Igor Girkin, who played a key role in leading the Russian forces arriving in the Donbas and rallying the separatists. When his work was done and he returned to Russia, he became a media celebrity amongst Russian nationalists for comments such as 'I was the one who pulled the trigger of this war'.[5] With his pencil moustache and penchant for historical battle re-enactments, Girkin, also known as Igor Strelkov (his *nom de guerre*), was somewhere between a military fantasist and an ideologue.[6]

He was supported by propagandist Konstantin Malofeev, whose access to funding was useful to Girkin.[7] Malofeev's role in Ukraine's separatist uprisings was later spelled out by the EU when it issued the 21st-century equivalent of a 'wanted' poster for him, a sanctions listing, which offered insights into the murky world of the DPR:

Konstantin Valerevich MALOFEEV; Born on 03/07/1974 in Puschino; Mr Malofeev is closely linked to Ukrainian separatists in eastern Ukraine [*sic*] and Crimea. The Ukrainian Government has opened a criminal investigation into his alleged material and financial support to separatists. In addition, he gave a number of public statements supporting the annexation of Crimea and the incorporation of Ukraine into Russia and notably stated in June 2014 that, 'You can't incorporate the whole of Ukraine into Russia. The east [of Ukraine] maybe.' Therefore Mr Malofeev is acting in support of the destabilisation of eastern Ukraine.[8]

The limits of Russian territorial ambition at this time is an important matter. When war erupted in 2014, the amount of territory that would fall to the Russian-instigated separatists could not have been preordained. The origins of the DPR and the LPR trace back to this moment. After the annexation of Crimea, paramilitary groups supported by the Russian security services staged rallies in which they demanded secession in several eastern and southern Ukrainian cities. During April 2014, these paramilitaries began seizing regional administration and city hall buildings. In Donetsk City Hall on 7 April, the paramilitaries declared the 'Donetsk People's Republic'. People calling themselves 'Donbas militias' took over police departments in Kramatorsk and Sloviansk on 12 April and Makiivka, Yenakiieve and the port city of Mariupol on 13 April. To the north in the Luhansk region, the paramilitaries took over the regional government building in Luhansk City on 28 April and proclaimed the 'Luhansk People's Republic'. The people taking over the buildings and smashing windows looked like thugs in combat trousers with sports or leather jackets thrown over the top. The contrast with the well-armed uniformed professional soldiers who had swiftly seized the Crimean Peninsula was stark.

On 11 May, the DPR and LPR staged their own referendums and now declared themselves to be independent of Ukraine. Donetsk

City, which is the largest city in the Donbas, became the centre of the separatist movement.

In other cities the uprisings fizzled out. Mariupol, which became famous for the tragedy it endured in the 2022 war, was such a case. Separatist paramilitaries attempted to take control of army bases and the local Interior Ministry office in Mariupol, but they were fought off by troops loyal to Ukraine. Other Ukrainian cities like Kharkiv in the north-east and Odessa in the south also experienced separatist unrest. Odessa was the site of a confrontation at the city's Trade Union House in May 2014 that killed thirty-one people, in which pro-Russian activists burned to death when the building was set ablaze.[9] Putin referred back to this incident in 2022, suggesting that Russia needed to bring to justice those who started this fire.

Crucially, Mariupol, Kharkiv and Odessa all remained firmly under Ukrainian government control, which meant that the actual DPR and LPR lands were not especially big at all, even if they held the major cities of Donetsk and Luhansk. Unlike the slickly executed Crimea operation, the uprisings across east and southern Ukraine seemed haphazard and improvised, with the Russian security services having little apparent preplanning, and just grabbing what they could instead.

Igor Girkin propagated this impression when talking about his initial success in Donbas: 'If our unit hadn't crossed the border everything would have fizzled out like in Kharkiv, like in Odessa,' he later told Russia's *Zavtra* newspaper. Adding to his disappointment, 'Initially I assumed that the Crimea scenario would be repeated: Russia would enter … That was the best scenario. And the population wanted that. Nobody intended to fight for the Luhansk and Donetsk republics. Initially everybody was for Russia.'[10]

As example of this took place in the city of Sloviansk, which is in the Donetsk region. On 12 April the paramilitaries took over the local Interior Ministry building and a man called Vyacheslav Ponomarev proclaimed himself to be the new mayor. Ponomarev called for a curfew to begin, outlawed pro-Ukrainian political parties, and promptly called on the Russian government to dispatch a peacekeeping force. This never materialised. Girkin was either present or in the vicinity of Sloviansk at the time, and one can imagine how he must have seethed with disappointment when the proverbial Russian cavalry never came racing across the Donets basin to back up the separatists.[11] In his book *85 Days in Slavyansk* (the Russian spelling of Sloviansk), pro-Russian separatist Alexander Zhuchkovsky reflects on the local anti-Maidan movement: 'What happened in Donbas in 2014 was entirely due to the Russian population of the region ... It wasn't until months after the start of the uprising that the Russian Federation began to intervene.' Even then he felt betrayed and rued the 'Russian Federation's ignorance of its genuine supporters in Ukraine.'[12]

The lack of direct Russian involvement proved problematic to the local separatists. As the International Crisis Group NGO found in an interview in east Ukraine with a senior DPR leader, 'Our big attraction at the start was the belief we would lead them into the Russian Federation.'[13] In Russia's big cities, activists were recruited and funds raised for the Donbas, including at public booths, but for now, the DPR and LPR were not going to be recognised officially by Russia's government or annexed like Crimea had been.

Ukrainian perception of the People's Republics

To the Ukrainian government, the DPR and LPR were all 'terrorists'. Initially caught on the back foot by the outbreak of fighting, Ukraine moved to a war footing, declaring the start of its 'Anti-Terrorist Operation' (ATO) on 13 April 2014. The terminology reflected the attempted characterisation of those leading the anti-government forces as malcontents to be targeted. The decision to begin a counteroffensive was one that Kyiv's government had to take, in order to recover as much of its lost territory as it could, and to prevent the separatists from taking any more.

Initially, Ukraine's war effort was itself haphazard, a reflection of their lack of battle-readiness. One of my colleagues even saw a UN-emblazoned helicopter belonging to the Ukrainian military flying over the Donbas, which its crew had to press into active service right away, with no time available to remove the UN heraldry after it had returned from supporting a UN mission in a different continent (a role that Ukrainian air transporters often filled).

The amateur aspect to Ukraine's early fightback was clearly seen through the actions of a myriad of 'volunteer battalions' that manned the ramparts in the east. Some battalions were the armed wings of political movements that had been active in Kyiv's street protests, such as the Right Sector. Others, like Dnipro-1, were funded by oligarchs, in this case Ihor Kolomoyskyi. With these self-starting and often self-equipping bands of soldiers bolstering the ranks of pro-Kyiv forces, Ukraine triumphed in some areas and by July 2014 had restored government control over key cities in the Donetsk region, such as Kramatorsk and the aforementioned Sloviansk.

In some of these towns liberated by the Ukrainian military, I heard of families separated by feuds resulting from differing reactions to the separatists. In addition, there were countless families physically separated by the front line itself, with family members distributed between government and non-government-controlled areas. Sometimes, the front line cut right through villages and settlements. In one of the oddest developments, some pensioners in separatist areas were still trying to cross the front line to collect their pensions, as Ukrainian state services began to cease being administered in the rebel areas.

This brings up an important question: how should one characterise this phase of armed conflict? When it comes to the terminology of 'invasion', 'proxy war' and 'civil war', choosing one term is unwise. It was definitely an invasion; it involved proxies; but it also ignited some of Ukraine's existing fault lines. Even as Russian soldiers and volunteers crossed the border to foment chaos, there were local people who decided to take up arms against Ukraine's government. There were socio-economic and identity issues at stake in east Ukraine that had contributed to a local sense of alienation, and exploiting this was essential to Russia's proxy war approach.[14] However, it should be stressed there was no chance that Ukraine would have ever suffered a civil war without Russia's malign hand.

Was Ukraine at war with Russia or not? It depends on how rigidly these states of being need to be classified. Whereas '"peace" and "war" are conceived as opposites in the West,' wrote Adda Bozeman, referencing the instinct to classify for legal or moral purposes, 'this is quite in counterpart to non-Western mindsets in which those concepts interpenetrate'.[15] For Putin, the master of dissimulation, an ambiguous state of war was a comfortable place to be at this time.

MH17 and a world aghast

'If a plane crashes and impacts on the ground the spread of the debris clusters more closely, but if it comes apart in mid-air, the debris spreads far and wide.' This awful distinction had never occurred to me until it was explained by a member of the crash site recovery team in Donetsk City.

He was talking about the shooting down of the Malaysian Airlines flight MH17 on 17 July 2014, when its wreckage was strewn around the villages of Hrabove, Rozsypne and Petropavlivka in the Donetsk Oblast, covering an area of around fifty square kilometres and comprising six main debris sites. As the later investigation report into the tragedy conveyed:

> The wreckage that was found near the villages of Rozsypne and Petropavlivka shows that the cockpit and the front section of the aeroplane were the first to break off and crash. Initially the centre and tail sections of the fuselage remained intact and ended up a few kilometres further eastwards, near the village of Hrabove. The distribution of the wreckage across these three eastern crash sites shows that the end section of the fuselage, the wings and the tail section came down next, followed by the centre section, which came to rest upside down.[16]

To enable this investigation, the wreckage recovery mission began in November 2014. Smashed and twisted pieces of plane fuselage were taken to Kharkiv by train, and one of my first responsibilities was to join the MH17 patrol team as we escorted the investigators and debris removal personnel to the crash site to make sure they were granted access by the separatists who controlled this area.

In the immediate aftermath of the MH17 tragedy, claim and counterclaim passed between the Moscow and Kyiv governments. Russia fatuously claimed that MH17 had been downed by a Ukrainian warplane. The Russian state denied culpability and obfuscated the matter, despite it being evident that the separatists – with Russian help – were shooting down Ukrainian military aircraft just days before they downed MH17. For instance, the Ukrainian armed forces suffered their biggest loss of life to date in a single incident on 14 June when an IL-76 military transport was shot down by surface-to-air missiles fired from Luhansk, killing forty paratroopers and nine crew on board. On 16 July, a Ukrainian Sukhoi Su-25 jet was also shot down. Perhaps the separatists armed with surface-to-air weapons though they were on a winning streak in these days and became trigger-happy.

The subsequent investigation led by the Dutch Safety Board concluded that MH17 had been downed by a Russian-supplied and operated BUK surface-to-air missile system, which had then been sent back to Russia by road to try to remove proof of its presence in Ukraine.

What happened to the 298 people on board MH17 was horrendous. The Dutch lost 193 citizens – the plane had been en route from Amsterdam to Kuala Lumpur, hence the Dutch Safety Board taking a lead in the investigation. Its report, published years after the tragedy, explained that 'the occupants were barely able to comprehend their situation. There was hardly any time for a conscious response.'[17] Some of my OSCE colleagues, including our local staff and interpreters, recounted the horrendous scenes of human debris that they saw strewn across the fields in the immediate aftermath. My arrival in Donetsk came a little after the tragedy; the sight of strewn-out cabin luggage was more than disquieting enough to see.

The recovery of the debris allowed the crash investigators to re-construct what had happened to MH17. It also allowed the bereaved to visit the hangar in the Netherlands used for the partial fuselage reconstruction. I was told by an ex-police officer colleague that people who have lost a loved one in a violent incident can some-times instinctively want to visit the site of their passing, to see with their own eyes where the person spent their final moments. Since this site was in rebel-held east Ukraine, at least the partial reconstruction of the plane allowed for something akin to this.

It took five years for prosecutors to announce the culprits: three Russians, including Igor Girkin, Sergei Dubinsky and Oleg Pulatov, and one Ukrainian, Leonid Kharchenko. The Russians were said to be former Russian intelligence officers (Girkin from the FSB, Russia's domestic intelligence agency, and Pulatov from the GRU, Russia's military intelligence unit). Tellingly, the Ukrainian, Kharchenko, was an amateur with no prior military background.[18] Three apparently retired Russian professionals and an untrained local separatist – a telling combination, and a testament to how this war was being waged by the Kremlin's security agencies.

*   *   *

The MH17 tragedy had the impact of curtailing the use of aircraft over the war zone. Anyway, the use of Russian combat airpower in Ukraine to bomb the enemy into submission would have stretched Putin's deniability to breaking point, so there was no substantial war in the air.

Instead, military analysts said that Russia was waging a 'hybrid war', which meant a blend of brute force accompanied by subversion. Indeed, the unannounced 'little green men' arriving in Crimea and the paramilitaries in the Donbas, plus the rapid-fire online disinformation campaigns waged by Russian activists such as over the MH17, created the impression of a unique way of war.

While it may have seemed revolutionary at the time, the ground reality of the Donbas war did not look especially futuristic. Instead, it looked more like a twentieth-century industrialised conflict. In the bitterest of ironies, on the centenary of World War One's outbreak in 2014, trench lines and shellfire had returned to the edge of Europe, as the sides dug down into the earth and settled in for a long fight.

EARLY BATTLES AT THE START OF A LONG WAR

What does it take for Ukraine's military to be involved in high-intensity combat in locations close to the Russian border? This question resurfaces by implication whenever there is talk of the Ukrainian armed forces recapturing all of their country's lost lands, evicting the invaders from every inch lost to Russian aggression. Except the closer the Ukrainian military got to Russia's borders, the harder the task became, because the Russian military could always rush in more reinforcements, or just bomb Ukrainian forces from their own side of the border.

A version of these events unfolded the month after the MH17 tragedy, when Ukrainian armed forces were defeated at Ilovaisk, which is located thirty-seven kilometres east of Donetsk City and, as the crow flies, less than fifty kilometres from Russia. Starting from 10 August, a mixture of Ukrainian armed forces and volunteer battalions dug in around the suburbs of Ilovaisk city which, if they had secured these positions, could have cut off the DPR in Donetsk City from a crucial umbilical cord to Russia.

The Ukrainians moved into the city and street fighting began. The separatists retaliated with Russian military support, pounding the Ukrainians with heavy artillery fire. Ukrainian supporting units that were supposed to cover the rear of their colleagues inside Ilovaisk had to retreat, and Russia's proxies announced that they had recaptured Ilovaisk on 27 August. When the surrounded Ukrainian forces stuck in Ilovaisk tried to retreat, despite an apparent on-the-ground assurance from the separatists that they would be allowed to do so, they were shot like fish in a barrel. The Ukrainian military reported that 459 of its soldiers were killed and 478 injured in the Ilovaisk massacre.[19]

'Ilovaisk' became a byword for treachery amongst the Ukrainian military and public, and it is a battle that retains contemporary significance, showing just how hard it can be for Ukraine to fight back so close to Russia's borders. The defeat at Ilovaisk was demoralising for the Ukrainian leadership. A Ukrainian general involved in the battle was blunt: 'We could have handled the separatists, but we can't fight the Russian army.'[20] This became a regular feature of the war, with Russian army units stepping in to make sure the DPR and LPR never suffered a fatal defeat by the Ukrainians.

*   *   *

Another key battle took place in Donetsk Airport between May 2014 and February 2015. The airport turned into a gladiatorial arena, crumbling around the warriors as they clashed. Once it was no longer usable as an airport, it lost any strategic value, instead becoming a totemic location for both sides. According to a local journalist's account:

The separatists nicknamed the defenders of the airport 'cyborgs' to explain the tenacity of the defenders who stood fast against heavy artillery fire. 'The friendly neighbour' provided separatists with T-72 tanks, self-propelled mortars, grad Multiple Launch Rocket Systems [for the 'cyborgs' to endure]. In September 2014, the control tower became the symbol of its invincible defence ... Unable to recapture the airport, the insurgents decided to raze it to the ground. On 21 January, they detonated the second floor of the New Terminal, which served as the base of Ukrainian units ... On 22 January, the cyborgs were forced to withdraw from the rubble...[21]

It was an astonishing battle: so entrenched had both sides become in the airport that my OSCE colleagues even monitored troop rotations, as fresh forces from both sides replaced their exhausted colleagues and casualties were removed. Eventually, when the cyborgs lost their hold in the ruined airport, they retreated and redrew their front line along Pisky, Avdiivka and other nearby villages, amidst continuing artillery fire.

The so-called 'Father of the Cyborgs', known as Colonel Redut, was singled out for his role in coordinating the Ukrainian defence of the airport. According to the journalist Oleksandr Motornyi, 'Many units have been through the Donetsk airport, but there was never an appointed commander. It just became obvious that Redut was the best.' The Ukrainian Defence Ministry, in its morale-boosting myth-making, described him as 'Colonel of Special Forces with callsign "Redut" who was headed the defence of international airport "Donetsk"' and screened a film about his exploits.[22]

Ukraine's armed forces were already chalking up enduring myths of last stands, war heroes and desperate defences against the odds as early as the winter of 2014–15.

*　　*　　*

The city of Mariupol, which took on this mantle as the last redoubt in 2022, had its own near-miss with disaster in the first phase of the war. Its strategic appeal to the Russians was always clear, as a port city with access to the Sea of Azov, and a land bridge linking the Donbas to Crimea. Starting on 25 August 2014, residents helped fortify the approaches to the city after it entered Russian crosshairs. Mariupol suffered a devastating shelling attack on 24 January 2015, killing thirty people and injuring scores of others. But the real battle took place in the small village of Shyrokyne, just eleven kilometres from Mariupol, which became the scene of fighting between Ukrainian and Russian forces. In February 2015, the Ukrainian Azov battalion led the charge in the defence of Mariupol's outskirts.[23] For now, war had not come to Mariupol itself. Recalling this puts into context Russia's all-out bombardment of Mariupol in 2022, which killed thousands – the Russians wanted to capture it back in 2015 but never got close. So, seven years later, the Russians returned to complete their unfinished job.

TALKING AND FIGHTING

'What's the point of us shooting and proposing diplomacy at the time?' So asked Zelensky in the 2022 war.[24] The problem was that the Kremlin had turned this into an art form in the early years of the war in 2014 and 2015. An essential part of an intelligence officer's toolkit is to be able to say one thing and do another, which is how Russia approached the peace talks in 2014. They were always going to get off to a bad start in Ukraine because Russia officially denied that it was even a party to the fighting in the Donbas. Even if everybody knew otherwise, its denials meant that the Russian government was never going to place its sole signature next to a peace deal. Instead, Russia got the DPR and LPR leadership to sign the peace deals that emerged, and insisted Ukraine's government speak to the separatists to decide how to halt the shooting.

This did not stop the Russian government from looking over all diplomatic proceedings. The highest-level diplomatic push came in the guise of the 'Normandy Format' group, which first met on

6 June 2014. The symbolism of the seventieth anniversary of Operation Overlord and the D-Day landings set the stage for the German Chancellor and the Presidents of France, Russia and Ukraine to explore the possibility of settling the conflict. The diplomacy faced an uphill struggle: Russia sat at the top table of diplomatic efforts to manage the war, but did so only in the confidence that it would not be named as a party to the ongoing hostilities in any joint declarations that emerged.

Another contradiction was Germany's position. Yes, Germans were angry at Putin's Russia for instigating the war, but many in Germany's elite were unwilling to sacrifice profitable trade relations with Russia, notably in energy. There were also some deep emotional ties around post-Berlin Wall healing that resided in the era of Gorbachev and Helmut Kohl, admixed with some anti-US feelings driven by the Iraq war and the War on Terror. On 26 June, the EU finally signed its association agreement with Ukraine. Neither France nor Germany wanted the USA shipping arms to the Ukraine. The USA itself was not too keen to become involved in its own full-blown proxy war at this time.

This set the stage for the first significant diplomatic agreement on the war, known as the Minsk Protocol, facilitated by OSCE's mediation in Belarus. It was signed on 5 September 2014 by the OSCE, ex-Ukrainian President Kuchma representing Kyiv, Russia's ambassador to Kyiv, and representatives of the DPR and the LPR. Amongst its provisions were 'an immediate bilateral ceasefire'; 'monitoring and verification of the ceasefire by the OSCE'; a commitment 'to withdraw illegal armed groups and military equipment ... fighters and mercenaries from Ukraine'; and 'decentralisation of power [by Kyiv to the] "Particular Districts of Donetsk and Luhansk Oblasts"'. In an addendum a week later, further provisions were to 'pull heavy weaponry fifteen kilometres back on each side of the line of contact' and 'to ban flights by combat aircraft over the security zone'.[25]

'Minsk' became a byword for failed diplomacy. The Minsk Protocol codified the contradiction of Russia supporting the separatists while wriggling out of being officially named as a combatant party. Thus, the Minsk Protocol treated Ukraine and the separatists as the warring parties, thereby obscuring the war's true dynamics. In reality there was no real way round this conundrum: to have named Russia as an aggressor would have precluded Russian participation in the Normandy meetings and in the Minsk talks – but by being unable to name Russia, the deal was virtually impossible to implement.

This became clear during the winter of 2014–15 as the fighting intensified in Donetsk Airport, Ilovaisk and the outskirts of Mariupol. The Minsk deal appeared wrecked, so on 11 February 2015 an additional package of measures was negotiated (known as 'Minsk II'). This deal stipulated once again a ceasefire and a withdrawal of large-calibre weapons from the front line.

At the same time as the negotiations were taking place over the Minsk II deal, a battle was raging over the strategic rail hub town of Debaltseve. Located in a thin peninsula of Ukrainian government-controlled territory that jutted into rebel-held areas, Debaltseve had one side exposed to the DPR and the other to the LPR (meaning that Russian-backed forces could close in on it from all sides).

Elsewhere along the front line, Ukrainian forces were not holding back either. At the southern tip of the Donetsk region, the Azov Battalion advanced out of Mariupol, holding the DPR off, and creating a protective buffer around Mariupol.[26] Ukrainian delegates in Minsk signed the additional package of measures out of desperation, given their armed forces had just lost hold of Donetsk Airport and Debaltseve in quick succession. With Mariupol also threatened, they needed a reprieve. As the International Crisis Group reports, it caused a major stink of surrender in Ukraine:

> The fall of Debaltseve is the second major Ukrainian loss of troops and materiel in six months. After Ilovaisk, angry volunteer battalion commanders denounced government 'treason' and called for a march on Kyiv … Military professionals have long used terms like 'disastrous' and 'hopeless' to describe [Ukrainian] high command. The problems are ascribed to the general demoralisation, corruption and neglect of the defence establishment under previous Presidents, a process that reached its apogee under Yanukovych … Close observers agree that a direct confrontation between the Russian and Ukrainian armies would end in defeat for Kyiv.[27]

Had Russia intervened with its army in an all-out war at this point, maybe it could have beaten Ukraine. Instead, it carried on its ad-hoc military support and the front line became static. Concern around a possible major Russian offensive periodically resurfaced, such as in the weeks preceding 8 May 2015, the seventieth anniversary of Germany's defeat in World War Two, as the DPR and the LPR stated their intent to parade their military equipment.[28] In the event, summer 2015 passed without any major offensives – as did every subsequent summer up to 2021. The Donbas war zone remained an open sore in Ukraine's exposed flank, impervious to all remedies.

THE LANGUAGE OF WAR

'It's like borscht but it's cold,' I was told by a local colleague.

I wondered what trickery this was as I stared into my first ever bowl of okroshka, a cold white soup. The soup contained a multitude of raw vegetables, potatoes and eggs, and, like many Ukrainian dishes, was drenched in chopped dill.

I was glad for my introduction to the cold soup since, contrary to what one might assume before spending time in Ukraine, the summer gets uncomfortably hot, and a cold, rehydrating soup is a welcome thing on a busy day of patrolling.

There is always far more to a country than one assumes as an outsider, and even though I would always only ever be an outsider, I was already noticing how the advent of war was changing things.

Once blood has been spilled in a relationship there is sadly no going back. This was the Rubicon crossed by Russia in 2014, and Ukraine was dragged unwillingly along for the ride. Needless to say, the mutual recriminations between these countries only grew worse. Which is where the mention of dill has at least tangential relevance.

After 2014–15, some Russians began to call Ukrainians 'ukr' or 'ukry' (short for Ukrainians), but also 'krop' and 'ukropy', which sounds like the word for the Russian herb dill. It turns out that the other country to consume as much dill on its food as Ukraine is Russia.[29]

Less whimsical slurs were also directed by Russians at Ukrainians, notably calling them 'Banderas' – a nickname to humiliate patriotic Ukrainians by linking them with Stepan Bandera, who was associated with fighting the Russians and doing so by siding with Nazi Germany.

Bandera was born in Galicia when it belonged to Austria-Hungary. 'Bandera became more of a symbol than a person … a nationalist who regarded Russia as a principal enemy of Ukraine and was prepared to sacrifice all for the single goal of gaining independence from it.' He therefore sided with the Germans to fight the USSR. In one respect, Bandera was following the lineage of Bohdan Khmelnytsky and Ivan Mazepa, picking one side when Ukraine became trapped in the vice of a war of empires. But by picking the hated Nazis, Bandera secured an association for all time with the murder of Jews and Poles. The Germans didn't even treat Bandera well, jailing him at one point. But 'for Ukrainian nationalists, Bandera symbolised the Ukrainians who had fought for independence against the USSR'.[30] At the end of his presidency, Yushchenko bestowed the 'Hero of Ukraine' title on Bandera, and a Bandera statue was later unveiled in Lviv.

Bandera's legacy has remained controversial, and Russian propaganda now added such terms as 'Ukro-fascists' and 'Bandero-Nazi' to its growing vocabulary of denunciations of Ukraine. For as long as the war could not be brought to an end, Russian–Ukrainian relations only declined further and further into the gutter of demonisation, name-calling and prejudice.

Ukrainians also devised insulting names for Russians or those who were excessively sympathetic to Russia. For instance, Ukrainians who were usually older and nostalgic about the USSR were sometimes called 'Sovok', which derived from 'Soviet' but also sounded like 'scoop/shovel', hinting at what garbage the USSR used to be. Another term to refer to those with Russian sympathies was 'Kolorad', which referred to a black-and-orange St George ribbon that was a symbol of heroism in the USSR, but the slur now referred to the resemblance in colours between the ribbon and an insect from the USA, the Colorado beetle. Another name was 'vatniks', meaning body warmers in reference to a military-style padded jacket worn by the Soviet soldiers and workers and its derivative 'vata', meaning cotton wool. Apparently, cotton-filled jackets of this kind were heavy, ugly and uncomfortable and barely protected the wearer from the elements.

The mutual name-calling and recriminations invariably worsened once the fighting started, and Russian propagandists amplified their messaging to portray Russian speakers in Ukraine as being persecuted by the Ukrainian authorities. For instance, the Russians had a jibe based on a fictitious phone call:

'Hello, is this the SBU (Security Service of Ukraine)?'

'Yes. What do you have to report?'

'My neighbour speaks Russian!'

The evidence of persecution by Ukrainians of Russian speakers was thin, however. As a Ukrainian friend explained to me at the time, 'I'm a Russian speaker and my family have not been persecuted,' although her family resided outside of the Donbas, as did many Russian speakers.

It hinged more on the fact that many people in the Donbas did not support the Maidan Revolution, and a general sense that the Donbas communities were being asked to accept an interpretation of history and cultural symbols that they did not share, but that were second nature to Ukrainian nationalists. All of these issues could have been worked through peacefully over time if Ukraine had been left to its own devices, but Putin's Russia had instead cynically mobilised them as the way to start a war in Ukraine.

*　*　*

Russia's actions to wreck and steal parts of Ukraine did not go unchecked by the rest of the world. Russia was punished by Western sanctions and expulsion from the G8, the informal group of leading industrialised nations. 'We condemn the illegal referendum held in

Crimea in violation of Ukraine's constitution,' announced the now slimmed-down G7, to which Lavrov said that being kicked out was no big deal.[31] At the time, Russia's government seemed willing to take this punishment, revelling in its ostracism.

Russia also firmly considered the USA to be hypocritical in its condemnation of Russia, because of its own Iraq invasion, its Afghan occupation lasting well beyond Osama bin Laden's killing in 2011, and its Libya intervention of that year alongside the British and French air forces. Why should Russia not also enjoy great power privileges? For Putin and Russia to defy the West was worth its weight in gold alone. But back then, Russia was unwilling to escalate the war further, not wanting to turn 'a local proxy war into a general war between Russia and Ukraine', which would have 'destroyed the fiction that Russia was not involved', even if 'to create "Novorossiya", it would need to invade on a large scale, and it was not willing to do this at the time'.[32] At the time, Russia thought that Ukraine would agree to the terms of the Minsk deal, and that if it remained war-torn, Ukraine could not quickly be admitted into the EU or NATO. These calculations influenced the next phase of the war.

CHAPTER 7

HOME FRONTS AND FRONT LINES

A REFLECTION ON PHONEY WARS

POROSHENKO, CHOCOLATE KING

There are certain famous milestones that everybody easily recalls when it comes to Ukraine and Russia: 1991 and the end of the USSR, for instance; 2014 and Russia's 'little green men' who annexed Crimea is another; and 2022's invasion is an obvious entrant into the layperson's chronology. What about the long years between 2015 and 2021? Many outsiders would be harder pressed to recall what happened in this era.

During this time Ukraine was only intermittently in the global headlines. The Donbas war had rumbled on, but it did so over an increasingly static front line with no major changes in territorial holdings after February 2015. The suffering in Donbas was overtaken by the far bigger scale of human tragedy in Syria's civil war. Terrorist attacks conducted or inspired by the Islamic State group occurred globally, spreading their own brand of fear. Russia, too, became fixated with the Middle East, mounting its own military intervention in Syria's civil war starting in September 2015. Meanwhile, Russia's literal keyboard warriors tried to subvert the US election in 2016 via online disinformation.

The media gravitates to the drama of breaking events, and with Ukraine's war settling into a monotonous low rumble, there was little novelty to report on. Unless you were from Ukraine, or were there for work, studies or other personal reasons, Ukraine began to drift back into international obscurity, something I noticed with alarm.

Having left government service and departed Ukraine for London, I changed career and became a university lecturer. I still visited Ukraine in a private capacity for different projects, heading to Kyiv as a guest lecturer at the Sikorsky Polytechnic Institute, for instance, and as one of several speakers at a discussion in the Rada on resolving wars. It was a genuine privilege to enter the grand Rada building and to see Ukrainian parliamentarians like Musta-fa Nayyem attend the discussion. I also returned to the Donetsk region to advise a peace-building charity.[1]

In London, I spoke at an event hosted by the Ukrainian Insti-tute in Holland Park on internal displacement. It was always worth speaking about Ukraine, but a decreasing number of people seemed to be interested outside the Ukrainian diaspora and the experts in governments and think tanks. I struggled to convince the War Studies department at King's College London, where I taught, that Ukraine mattered much at all. I had become a Ukraine bore, I re-alised, and eventually I too drifted away to work on other projects.

Yet in this period, which spanned Petro Poroshenko's presiden-cy (June 2014–May 2019), Ukraine experienced much that proved vitally important for what came after, notably in its evolution as a country at war. On the home front, a strange schism developed between the war zone in the east and the rest of Ukraine, which remained unscathed by the violence. The moth-eaten map of Ukraine, divided between the majority of government-controlled lands, the small sliver of Russian/separatist-controlled lands and the lost peninsula of Crimea, was a continuous reality.

The fighting in the Donbas waxed and waned in intensity, but it never fully ended. Ukrainians experienced the sensations of numbness and sorrow as a regular stream of its soldiers were killed and injured in the Donbas war zone. Physical rehabilitation of the injured, the sorrow of the bereaved, and the psychological toll facing veterans were ever-present realities. And yet as life carried on in the big cities untroubled by bombs and bullets, some Ukrainians became inured to what was happening on the front line.

Once, in central Kyiv, in front of the pristine blue and white walls of St Michael's monastery, I wandered around a public exhibition comprising burned-out cars, tanks and truck-mounted multiple launch rocket systems. The exhibition was there to educate Ukrainians living in the peaceful capital city of the grim realities unfolding out of their eyeshot, 750 kilometres east. This sense of distance strengthened some fringe voices in Ukraine. Right-wing activists, political parties and militias formed a minority voice in Ukraine, but it was a voice that could bellow whenever it channelled its outrage at Russia's predation of Ukrainian lands. And its voice on these issues never broke, after the ranks of the right-wing were swelled by combat veterans who had rotated in and out of the front line. Many of them had initially done so as part of the volunteer battalions, with names like the 'Right Sector' and the 'Azov Battalion'. Some of the volunteer battalions formed during Euromaidan had attracted real thugs who brawled with the Berkut police during the violence in Maidan Square. These were the revolutionary shock troops of the Euromaidan, and now, many volunteer battalions headed off to fight the Donbas war.

Russian propaganda seized on the role these groups had played in the protests that had deposed Yanukovych in order to fallaciously paint the entire Euromaidan process, and Kyiv's new politics, as being implacably against Russia and Russian speakers in Ukraine.

This was not accurate. Ukraine's Defence Ministry and Interior Ministry were working hard to mainstream some of the volunteer battalions by integrating them into the police or military. There were sound operational reasons for doing so, since in the early stages of the war, volunteer battalion soldiers had operated separately to the regular army in the Donbas, hampering cooperation. They were a mixed bag. Some battalions, like Dnipro-1, were funded by businessman and were more professional. Some volunteers were true amateurs, heading to the front lines having kitted themselves out in outdoor stores and spray-painted their civilian vans in a rudimentary camouflage pattern. Others included ill-disciplined ruffians, such as the 'Tornado battalion', which had to be disbanded by the Interior Ministry after it engaged in kidnappings, torture and extortion – and when its members were taken to court, they scuffled with the police.[2]

Wars attract all sorts; a minority of the Ukrainians who headed off to fight the separatists in the Donbas of their own volition were unruly, to say the least, but the volunteer battalions had been essential in helping Ukrainian troops to hold the line in the early days of the war.

The biggest impacts of the Donbas war on the rest of Ukraine involved the millions of internally displaced persons, along with the economic impact of the rupture in relations with Russia, which had been a major trading partner before the war.

The effects of the Donbas war were especially felt by communities in other regions hosting the millions of internally displaced persons (estimated at 1.36 million people in 2018).[3] Schemes, some of which were funded by external donors like the EU, helped to rehouse these displaced people in so-called 'modular homes' in cities across Ukraine. In some cases, the financial support these people received to try to restart their lives left those in their host communities bitter. Why were the former Donbas residents getting handouts? This rubbed some Ukrainians up the wrong way – everyone was struggling financially. To put this into perspective, in 2015, an entry-level salary for enlisted volunteer soldiers was 2,340 hryvnia per month, according to data from Ukraine's Defence Ministry. This was 20 per cent lower than wages earned by construction workers.[4] For the families of a soldier on the front line, and indeed for all ordinary Ukrainians, times were tough. Making matters worse, the hryvnia had lost a lot of value, leaving all but the oligarchs poorly off.

* * *

Petro Poroshenko was one such oligarch. Born in the Odessa Oblast in 1965, the Roshen chocolate brand that he owned, and his media company holdings, had built his wealth. Although he undertook his military service during the waning days of the Soviet Union, his dominant life experiences were of the privatisation that took hold in Ukraine in the 1990s, with Roshen founded in 1996.

His presidency represented the great hopes of Euromaidan for Ukraine's entry into European structures; Poroshenko duly obliged by finally signing the EU's association agreement. He was also expected by the supporters of Euromaidan to deliver results on the anti-corruption drive and the general reform process of public services in Ukraine that still bore the influences of the Soviet era. On top of this, Poroshenko needed to keep Ukraine's importance high on the international agenda in Brussels, London, Washington and other global capital cities of influence for fear of his country being forgotten by the West. It was a collection of issues tasting far more bitter than the average box of tasty Roshen chocolates; although Poroshenko approached these policy challenges with gusto, his presidency faced uphill struggles in every major issue, not least when the Panama Papers leak in April 2016 revealed that instead of placing his businesses in a trust before becoming the President, he had actually moved his assets into an offshore holding company in the British Virgin Islands, Cyprus and other locations that were revealed in the leaks.[5]

These stories cast doubt on Poroshenko's suitability as the embodiment of Euromaidan's spirit. But he was also Ukraine's first ever wartime President, and the Donbas situation never let up. It may have seemed like a phoney war to those who only took real notice of Ukraine in 2022, but during the long preceding years, the Donbas war had been a continual drain on Ukraine's ability to stabilise and to modernise itself; like a plughole that could never be fully closed, draining a little more of the country with every passing year, even as the forces of Ukrainian patriotism were on the rise.

'TEMPORARILY OCCUPIED TERRITORIES'

As the inaugural 'Minister for the Reintegration of the Temporarily Occupied Territories', he had been put in charge of a most optimistically named government ministry.[6] Tall, urbane and humane in his articulation of the situation in Ukraine's lost east, Vadym Chernysh spoke about the difficulties of the war with candour. There were humanitarian issues to deal with involving those who had fled the war zone and those who had chosen to remain. There was also a negotiation process to participate in, held in Minsk with international mediators, in which Ukrainian officials like Chernysh met the representatives of the DPR and LPR separatists to try to get the ceasefire to hold, while dealing with the myriad of issues afflicting the divided populations of Donetsk and Luhansk.

But the Minsk talks were going nowhere and were trapped in a kind of Groundhog Day. One reason was that all sides kept on fighting. Another reason was that back in Kyiv, the question of how to deal with the Russian-backed territories had become a political hot potato. For Chernysh, completing the remit contained in his new job title had become mission impossible.

The Minsk deal was effectively unimplementable for Ukraine's government. Poroshenko could not persuade the Rada to support the Minsk deal, because its provisions would have allowed local elections in Donetsk and Luhansk, tantamount to a surrender bill in the eyes of Ukraine's political right, who feared that the rebel republics would become de facto Russian dependencies. A visceral illustration of the bind Kyiv found itself in over the Donbas war came on 31 August 2015, courtesy of a hand grenade that was thrown outside the Rada building during a demonstration against the debate that was taking place in the chamber within. Parliamentarians were considering legislation that would have given autonomy to the territories held by pro-Russian separatists. This was the worst violence in Kyiv since the Euromaidan itself. A member of Ukraine's National Guard was killed by the grenade and other people were injured.[7] The mooted 'autonomy for the east' bill would never be passed.

In some quarters in Ukraine, xenophobia towards the Donbas residents rose as they were considered 'fifth columnists' who 'might as well move to Russia and leave us be' (to paraphrase some of the worst views bouncing around at the time). This even led some members of Ukraine's ruling coalition to lobby to freeze the conflict on Ukraine's terms, because if the Minsk settlement was fully implemented then Ukraine would have to bear the costs of rebuilding the Donbas, despite Russia keeping its influence there through the autonomy that the DPR and LPR would need to be granted as per the Minsk deal terms. Some Ukrainian politicians took a hard line and even suggested sealing off the DPR and LPR lands entirely, giving up on their return and leaving them to fester under Russia's neglectful influence. The International Crisis Group, an NGO that studies armed conflicts, quoted an astonishing range of views from Ukrainian hardliners: 'People in the separatist areas are totally brainwashed. They still live in the Soviet Union'; 'Maybe, just maybe, they will one day come to their senses, and they will return to us, but until then we should close them off'; and a Ukrainian officer who was originally from the Donbas being the bluntest of all: 'Let the people who want to be Russian go to Russia; we will help them leave. In the meantime, the separatist districts should be fenced off, and Russia left to support them.'[8]

Unresolved wars attract all manner of external actors offering behind-the-scenes roadmaps and solutions, some of which can be self-serving for the interests of said outside actors. One astonishing secret plan originated from Donald Trump's campaign team to broker a deal that would have conceded the Donbas to Russia to end the war, selling out the Ukrainian government in the process.

Details appeared in the Mueller Report: 'Trump's stated position on Ukraine [was] that the Europeans should take primary responsibility for any assistance to Ukraine, that there should be improved U.S.–Russia relations, and that he did not want to start World War

III over that region.' Which is why, on 2 August 2016, Paul Manafort and his long-time business associate Konstantin Kilimnik ('who the FBI assesses to have ties to Russian intelligence') discussed a 'backdoor' way for Russia to take over bits of east Ukraine. The plan would involve 'creating an autonomous republic in its more industrialised eastern region of Donbas [in which] Russia would assist in withdrawing the military, and Donbas would become an autonomous region within Ukraine with its own Prime Minister.' Astonishingly, Yanukovych would be brought back as 'an ideal candidate as Prime Minister' to 'facilitate the reintegration of the region into Ukraine with the support of the US and Russian Presidents'. The plan seems to have excited Manafort enough to explore it once Trump was in power, since in early 2018, Manafort commissioned a polling firm to ask opinions on Yanukovych's possible role in resolving the Donbas war.[9]

This idea, or any other peace plan, never got off the ground. The war, and east Ukraine's misery, dragged on. On one level this was great for Russia, because it allowed Putin to heap blame onto Kyiv for the unresolved war.[10] Creating another frozen conflict was in line with Russia's strategy of keeping its armed forces on the soil of lands that it believed it should dominate. But Russia also purposefully stalled the Minsk deal, offering no assurances on how it would disarm the large and well-supplied DPR and LPR forces. Russia's government also washed its hands of culpability. After the February 2015 Minsk agreement was signed, Putin's spokesman Dmitry Peskov said that Russia was a guarantor but it was not directly concerned. 'We simply can't [implement the Minsk agreement] physically because Russia is not a participant in the conflict.'[11]

As if to prove this point, the Russian army had cleverly inserted into the war zone – in an official and unarmed capacity – a fully uniformed colonel-general and his Russian army staff, with Ukraine's full permission, ostensibly to keep a check over the separatists. Alongside a Ukrainian general who shadowed his work, this Russian colonel-general participated in the Joint Centre for Control and Coordination (JCCC), in which unarmed Ukrainian and Russian officers sat together in a room filled with maps, apparently in a bid to nip any escalation in the bud by phoning up units involved in inadvertent flare-ups at the front line. The JCCC was set up in June 2014, its origins shrouded in mystery, and it was one of the war's oddities.*[12]

The Russians knew what they were doing: years before in a different war in Moldova, Russia had established a JCC to send in their officers to keep an eye on the separatist Transnistria war (this Joint Control Commission included Russian, Moldovan and Transnistrian representatives located in that war's buffer zone).[13] Now, in Ukraine, as I saw with my own eyes in 2015 at the JCCC, the Russian colonel-general assigned to the job was in daily face-to-face contact with the DPR and LPR, keeping a direct eye on Russia's proxies. They made for a curious sight: I recall the fearsome, squat figure of Russian Colonel-General Lentsov flanked by a skinny man from the DPR in an ill-fitting camouflage outfit, and another man from the LPR dressed in a plain white roll-neck jumper, who looked no older than an adolescent. The JCCC carried on right until the Russians finally abandoned it in 2017.

As Russia settled in for a long war, so did the Ukrainian army. The Ukrainian government said that 69,000 of its troops were assigned to its Anti-Terror Operation (ATO), although not all of them were based on the 500-kilometre front line.[14] Over these long years

---

*   The JCCC 'was established to facilitate bilateral dialogue between Ukraine's Ministry of Defence and military representatives of the Russian Federation', according to the OSCE.

of war, Ukraine fortified its physical front line, and the ATO was eventually replaced by the Joint Forces Operation (JFO) in 2018. Aside from the acronym change, so beloved of militaries the world over, there was a big shift as the lead organisation in the security effort switched from the Security Service of Ukraine (SBU) to the military. It is a good job that Ukraine took this step in light of later events, since the 'ATO' moniker had been chosen to serve the initial purpose of trying to root out the law-breaking separatist militias. But with Russia's regular army poised just over the border and always ready to intervene, it made a great deal of sense for Ukraine to dig in for a long war that could, one day, escalate.

For the residents of the Donbas, a surprising number refused to flee and carried on living close to the contact line. When I asked a Donbas-native colleague of mine why this was, her personal view, albeit speaking for some Donbas residents rather than all of them, was striking:

Our perception of death in the Donbas is a bit distorted because of our industrial past and dangers faced by our miners as well as our present situation of danger caused by the war. That is why so many people stayed in tiny villages smack on the Line of Contact for eight years. That is why now [in May 2022] with the front line semi-circling Kramatorsk and Sloviansk just twenty to thirty kilometres away, 25–30 per cent of the population refuses to be evacuated. We learned not to be afraid of death because of where we worked. We lived with the sudden violent deaths of young people in our everyday lives for three or four generations and our self-preservation failed as a result. Kharkiv, Dnipro and Zaporizhzhia do not have that. Or should I rather say, the temperature of their frog boiling in a kettle is far lower than that in Donbas.[15]

For people who carried on living close to the Donbas war zone, crossing the front line as it existed between 2014 and 2021 could be a regular undertaking. Some people crossed the front line because their family or property was on the other side to where they lived, or because they wanted to buy goods at a cheaper price on the other side of the front line. The Ukrainian government introduced a permit system for Donbas residents to apply for a special pass to cross the front line. During this time there were five approved crossing points (four in the Donetsk Oblast and a fifth in Luhansk Oblast). Huge volumes of traffic clogged up these crossing points on a daily basis, with people queuing on foot and in cars to cross. The application system to apply for a crossing pass was cumbersome and prone to corruption, since passes could also be found on the black market to jump the official waiting list. For locals in the Donbas, the delays, frustrations and hazards of crossing the line became a feature of their everyday lives, especially in the long years during which the fighting lost some its early bite but carried on intermittently nonetheless.[16]

*   *   *

The guns never truly fell silent for long enough to begin serious talks to end the war and to bring peace to the Donbas. In moments of despair, Poroshenko called for a peacekeeping mission to be deployed by the UN or EU.[17] To no avail, of course, since Russia would hardly countenance a UN mission, while the EU's perceived role in the 2013–14 crisis ruled it out as a neutral platform. Meanwhile, the Minsk process remained a sticking plaster placed over gaping wounds, barely helping to stem the blood flow.

The longer the war persisted, the trickier it was to reunify parts of Ukraine bisected by the front line, and for Kyiv's government to repair its relationship with the people of the Donbas. War always exacerbates xenophobia and this was true on all sides in Ukraine. A 'national dialogue' process between Kyiv and the Donbas regions was under way, but it would take years to reverse the ill-feeling stoked by the war.[18] The 'temporarily' in the term 'Temporarily Occupied Territories' was proving rather more aspirational a description than a statement of reality.

REFORMING UKRAINE

Reform of a country wholesale is always going be harder when its economy is in trouble. As a headline indicator, the Ukrainian economy's gross domestic product had contracted by -10.8 per cent in 2014 and -9.77 per cent in 2015, before showing a glimmer of hope with growth of 2.44 per cent in 2016, 2.36 per cent in 2017, 3.49 per cent in 2018 and 3.2 per cent in 2019.

Unsurprisingly, the war had hammered Ukraine's trade with Russia, which had previously spanned the gamut of monolithic gas and energy contracts all the way to the small enterprises that came naturally to cross-border links between the populations. Ukraine's exports to Russia took time to drop off from a post-independence peak of US$19.82 billion in 2011, US$17.63 billion in 2012 and US$15.08 billion in 2013 to a steeper decline of US$9.8 billion in 2014, US$4.83 billion in 2015 and US$3.59 billion in 2016. Always running a negative trade balance with Russia, Ukraine imported a declining but still large amount of goods and services from its former imperial overlord, counted at a peak of US$29.13 in 2011, US$27.24 billion in 2012 and US$23.24 in 2013, almost halving to

US$12.68 in 2014 and dropping to just US$5.15 in 2015.[19] Perhaps it was surprising that any trade persisted at all, but the Ukrainian economy had deep links to its neighbour.

Another headline trend conveyed concerns over Ukraine's health as a country: persistent population decline. The overall population of Ukraine had declined dramatically since independence due to a combination of large emigration and low birth rates, dropping from over 50 million in the early 1990s to 44 million in the 2010s. This trend was already under way when the war started in 2014, and greater numbers of young, educated, talented and multilingual graduates were finding work overseas in other countries, bolstering the already well-established Ukrainian diaspora communities in Canada, Poland, Israel and the USA, each of which host substantial numbers of people of Ukrainian extraction. The biggest number of Ukrainians living abroad remained the Russian Federation, of course, which added yet another dimension to the complexity of fighting and cutting ties with a neighbouring country.

To keep its economy afloat, Ukraine had repeatedly turned to the International Monetary Fund for help. Already in 2008 and 2010 respectively, Ukraine had received US$16.4 billion and US$15.15 billion of assistance (of which US$4.5 billion and US$1.89 billion was earmarked for initial immediate disbursement). And then war hit: in 2014 the IMF offered another US$17.01 billion (US$3.19 billion to be dispersed immediately) and in 2015 US$17.5 billion (US$5 billion to be dispersed immediately).[20] IMF bailouts included a 'stand-by arrangement' for 'financing to help overcome balance of payment problems in economic crisis'; 'stand-by credit' for 'financial assistance with short-term balance of payment needs'; and an 'extended fund facility' for 'serious medium-term balance of payment problems due to structural weakness'.

Year	Amount	Type	Initial immediate disbursement
1995	$1.96 billion	One-Year Stand-By Credit and Systemic Transformation Facility	
1996	$867 million	Nine-Month Stand-By Credit	
1997	$542 million	One-Year Stand-By Credit	$49 million
1998	$2.2 billion	Three-Year Extended Fund Facility	$257 million
2004	$605 million	Twelve-Month Stand-By Arrangement	
2008	$16.4 billion	Two-Year Stand-By Arrangement	$4.5 billion
2010	$15.15 billion	29-Month Stand-By Arrangement	$1.89 billion
2014	$17.01 billion	Two-Year Stand-By Arrangement	$3.19 billion
2015	$17.5 billion	Four-Year Extended Fund Facility	$5 billion
2018	$3.9 billion	Fourteen-Month Stand-By Arrangement	$1.4 billion
2020	$5 billion	Eighteen-Month Stand-By Arrangement	$2.1 billion
2022	$1.4 billion	Rapid Financing Instrument	

Table 1: IMF Ukraine bailout list

All in all, Ukraine's economy was on a drip-feed of foreign help from which it could not unplug. Ukraine badly needed friends around the world to offer its economy a softer landing from the shrinking size of its trade with Russia, and to assist with the growing needs of its defence budget. Expertise in Poroshenko's government came from Ukraine's diaspora via Ukrainian Finance Minister Natalie Jaresko, who held this post between 2014 and 2016. Born in Illinois to parents who were Ukrainian immigrants to the USA, Jaresko held senior finance roles in the US government and private sector before taking up Ukrainian citizenship in 2014 to serve as Finance Minister. Officials like Jaresko who could naturally speak the West's language of donor support were vital to getting continual economic assistance.

Ukraine also commissioned studies to assist with its defence re-structuring, bringing in a team from the RAND Corporation, the US think tank, to author a study that was 'undertaken in response to a request by the presidential administration of Ukraine and in participation with the National Security and Defence Council and sponsored by Ukraine Investment Alliance', and that was entitled 'Security Sector Reform in Ukraine'. Amongst its findings were that 'decision making is often taken to the highest levels, overwhelming senior officials' and that 'organisations designed to coordinate ministries and agencies are weak or ineffective'. When Ukraine's military performed well in 2022, it was not only down to weapons and training by NATO but to policy analysis guiding the restructuring of its military command.

Year	Foreign Military Financing	Ukraine Security Assistance Initiative
2014	$6,103,000	
2015	$47,000,000	
2016	$85,000,000	$226,500,000
2017	$99,000,000	$148,600,000
2018	$95,000,000	$195,500,000
2019	$115,000,000	$214,800,000
2020	$115,000,000	$256,700,000
2021	$115,000,000	$275,000,000
2022	$322,000,000 (obligated)	$300,000,000

Table 2: US to Ukraine defence trade and defence assistance, 2014–2022[21]

DOMESTIC REFORM: DEVOLUTION

At the core of Ukraine's reform efforts, however, away from the highlights of macroeconomic help and building a more capable army, was the less attention-grabbing nitty-gritty of domestic reform. This was no less important in helping Ukraine to move beyond its various Soviet-era structures.

All over Ukraine's oblasts, administrative reform was taking place at different speeds. There was one big theme that tied together the strands of the domestic reform process: decentralisation. It was hardly the most thrilling spectator sport to monitor this process, but it was an important part of Ukraine's efforts to modernise the country along European lines.

As a study of the process explained, 'Before the Euromaidan protests, state power in Ukraine was highly concentrated ... the enormous imbalance between the power of the centre and that of municipalities was a fundamental obstacle to the creation of a sustainable, functioning state.' What was being attempted was the 'devolution and delegation of power from the national to the municipal level', in other words amalgamating some small municipalities and giving them greater administrative and financial powers, for instance around taxation and the fostering of local business activity.[22] Incidentally, the Russian Federation under Putin had done precisely the opposite, eroding local administrations in favour of lumping decision-making power in Moscow. In Russia the ruling party lorded it over the regional political assemblies, with incumbent governors effectively appointed by the President's office.

Ukraine was also undergoing a serious reform effort against corruption in public life. To the anti-corruption activists inside and outside of government, at times this task must have made them feel like King Canute, pushing against the irrepressible tide of corrupt practices. The priority areas were 'customs, deregulation, privatisation, de-monopolisation and the reform of public administration', with defence spending being 'particularly opaque', according to a 2018 study of the efforts. 'Corruption schemes remain untouched in some parts of the energy sector. An overhaul of the civil service is also essential', while 'reforms of the law enforcement agencies are proceeding slowly, if at all' and 'it is too early to say whether judicial reform will lead to improvements in the functioning of the courts because of the deep underlying culture of corruption in the judicial system'. The National Anti-Corruption Bureau was created, but facing vested interests with influence over the judiciary, its work was difficult.[23]

To make this all the more tangible, I noted that Kyiv briefly had two police forces. I once watched as the new police officers arrived in a gleaming patrol car, dismounted and headed up the steps past the bar I was sitting at to find the owner. The complaint: to turn the music down since it was disturbing the neighbours. The police officers were incredibly polite, both male and female and, dare I say, looking rather dapper in their brand-new dark blue uniforms. Crucially, they didn't ask for a bribe. They were nothing like the older police force that was being phased out, which to my foreign eyes seemed a decade prior to have consisted of some very untrustworthy-looking officers, with heavyset middle-aged men leading truncheon-twirling younger officers.

Indeed, prior to 2015, policing was carried out by the Interior Ministry, who also operated the feared Berkut special police unit that had unleashed deadly violence against the Euromaidan protesters. The Berkut had already been disbanded. And, with the launch of a new national police force, a big step was taken to make the police more trustworthy. The media blitz surrounding the new police force in the capital was a clear early step in a reform process away from Ukraine's Soviet-era administrative foundations. This kind of wholesale, ambitious reform would have been hard at the best of times, but these were not such times, and doing so while a war was under way made the task at once harder and more urgent.

If nothing else, the administrative reform was yet another method through which those Ukrainians who believed in the process wanted to differentiate their country from Russia's old-fashioned ways.

PUTIN'S WAR ADDICTION

'In the whole range of human activities, war most closely resembles a game of cards.' So it was and will always be, in the estimation of the legendary Prussian general and philosopher of war Carl Von Clausewitz.[24] Clausewitz fought for his native Prussia against the revolutionary army of Napoleon Bonaparte, but Prussia was defeated by France in 1806. So, Clausewitz moved to Russia to assist the army of Tsar Alexander I, since Russia was now also at war against France, and Clausewitz wanted to carry on the struggle against French revolutionary supremacy in Europe. Now with Russia, Clausewitz participated at the Battle of Borodino in 1812, famed for its depiction in Leo Tolstoy's novel *War and Peace*.

In Clausewitz's own writing, published posthumously as *On War*, he credited his Corsican adversary with the rarest kind of military genius that is required to see past the fog of war (which Clausewitz called 'friction'), forcing victories on the most chaotic of battlefields. Clausewitz developed an influential philosophy of war that identified timelessly pertinent factors governing the clash of arms. Momentum was one such factor:

> By looking at each engagement as part of a series, at least insofar as events are predictable, the commander is always on the high road to his goal. The forces gather momentum, and intentions and actions develop with a vigour that is commensurate with the occasion, and impervious to outside influences.[25]

This was the high road that the Russian war machine was on, with each successive military victory, whether it was a partial or delayed success, building more momentum and feeding Putin's war addiction. In addition to Putin, several of the key civilian and military officials who orchestrated the 2022 invasion of Ukraine were present for these earlier successes (Lavrov became Foreign Minister in 2004; Sergei Shoigu, the Defence Minister, and Valery Gerasimov, the Chief of the General Staff, were appointed to their roles in 2012). After the war to punish Georgia in 2008 and the limited Ukraine intervention in 2014, it was Russia's bombastic entry into the Syrian civil war in 2015 that convinced Putin and his long-serving officials of their apparent military genius and the prowess of their armed forces.

Russia's intervention in Syria was significant for Ukraine: for several years, the Kremlin's military eye was primarily trained on events far away from Europe. Although the Kremlin's wrecking job was hardly finished in Ukraine, just eighteen months after the Crimea annexation, Russia switched its focus to Syria. This time it was no secret: Putin was bombastic about sending in the Russian air force, navy, military advisors and contractors to prop up the regime of Bashar al-Assad. The aim was to prevent the West from achieving another regime change, after the USA decreed that Assad should step down following his brutal repression of a rebellion that had sprung up in the wake of the Arab Spring democracy protests.

Russia's military gamble in Syria did not come out of nowhere. During the Cold War, Syria was a client state of the Soviet Union. For instance, in 1957 a Soviet warship deployed to Latakia to help Syria during a Cold War crisis. The Assad dynasty, which has ruled Syria since 1971 when Bahar's father Hafez al-Assad came to power, continued to rely on Russian support after the Cold War.

When civil war erupted in Syria in 2011, Russia supported Bashar al-Assad with diplomatic cover at the UN. Russia offered a vital diplomatic reprieve for Assad after 21 August 2013, the day Syria's regime used chemical weapons in Ghouta, a rebel-held suburb of

Damascus.[26] Obama declared a red line in order to reinforce the taboo against using chemical weapons. But the Russians changed the game, offering the USA the chance to act jointly to remove all stocks of chemical weapons from Syria, with oversight by the UN body the Organisation for the Prohibition of Chemical Weapons. By accepting Russia's offer, Obama never followed through to defend his red line, buying Assad more time to crush the rebels.

This arm's length Russian approach worked for a while, but by 2015, Assad's army was on the back foot. Now, Russia went to war on behalf of Assad's beleaguered military. In September 2015, Russia deployed a sizeable naval and air task force to Latakia. Russia joined the rogues' gallery of Assad's wartime allies, including the Iranian-backed armed group Hezbollah. Russia's air force masterminded an especially brutal aerial bombing campaign over the rebel-held enclave of Aleppo in northern Syria in late 2016, including bombing civilians and hospitals, and the military tide began to turn in favour of the Assad regime.

Russia's intervention benefited from a sustained disinformation effort. Russia argued that Assad's regime provided a bulwark against the jihadists affiliated to groups like al-Qaeda and ISIS, and that *all* the rebel groups it had been striking with its airpower were 'terrorists'. Russia brokered short-lived 'cessations of hostilities' and 'humanitarian corridors' on behalf of the Assad regime that served only to assist Russia's war aims. And, as the war progressed, Russia convened the diplomatic 'Astana Process' involving several of the major belligerents (Iran, Turkey, Syria and presided over by Russian diplomats) to hash out 'spheres of influence' that chopped up Syrian lands. The Astana Process notably excluded the anti-Assad rebels, the USA and other Western countries, and left the parallel UN 'Geneva Process' of peace-building talks to wither in insignificance.

As the years went by, Assad's rule stabilised, his army regained control of more of Syria, other actors were marginalised, and Russia could announce itself as the overlord of this outcome.

This was galling for the governments in Washington and London to watch, having floundered in their own invasions of Iraq and Afghanistan. Unlike the hubristic USA, which had deployed a massive ground army boosted by coalition forces to depose regimes and try to rebuild these countries from scratch under democratic governments, only to be met by years of insurgency and different degrees of strategic defeat in each war, Russia seemed to have avoided these traps. Russia sensibly limited the scale of its ambition in Syria, avoiding the escalation trap of feeding in ever more forces simply to prop up Assad's regime, which would likely have led to Putin's gamble yielding poor returns for him.

There were setbacks along the way, like the crash in December 2016 of a Russian TU-154 Tupolev military transport aircraft into the Black Sea on its way to Syria, which killed all ninety-two people on board including members of the Red Army choir and of the military orchestra. There were also absurd moments of triumph for Russia, such as when the Mariinsky Symphony Orchestra from St Petersburg played a concert amidst the ruins of the ancient Roman Empire city of Palmyra. The message was clear: Russia's military had boldly defended this symbol of civilisation from the vanquished horde of ISIS terrorists who, a year earlier, had filmed beheading videos in Palmyra.[27]

Russia had forced its way back into the top table of Middle Eastern influence, securing the lasting allegiance of the Assad regime, grass-roots popularity with Assad's loyal subjects, and access to the naval base at Tartus and the airbase at Hmeimim (which, as of 2021, it was still expanding). A deal was struck between Moscow and

Damascus in 2017, permitting Russia to have sovereign jurisdiction over the Tartus base and to use it free of charge for forty-nine years. It took several years for his Syria intervention to bear fruit, but Putin appeared to have ultimately increased Russia's winnings at the gambling table of war. Clausewitz's famous dictum that 'war is only a continuation of state policy by other means' remained at the beating heart of Putin's foreign policy, rivalled in importance perhaps only by Russia's role as a major energy exporter.

Around this time, Russia's entertainment industry was doing its best to boost the cult of fascination around its military and its security services. In popular TV serials like *Foundry* (2008–14), *The Sleeping Ones* (2017–18) and *Nevskiy* (2016–), plot lines typically glorified the work of Russian security operatives. The spy characters tended to be professional and physically fit superhumans who had mastered everything from medicine to rocket science. Many of the criminal characters they confounded were foreigners from the former USSR or from the Russian Federation's national minorities. These totally unrealistic shows were swallowed up by some Russians as representing intelligence capabilities that Russia actually possessed. Overall, the nationalistic side of Russia developed in the 2010s on the basis of pride in real and fictional triumphs for its security forces.

*   *   *

Ukrainians had watched events in Syria and Russia's renewed militaristic pride with alarm and detachment. Poroshenko likened Russia's actions in Syria to its actions in Donbas, and later warned that Putin's 'neo-imperial aggression' had spread because the West was unwilling to stop Russia. Ukraine's increasingly frozen war was losing column inches in the international media to the scorching catastrophe taking place in Syria. Russia's intervention there had increased the number of refugees leaving Syria, with many bound for European countries, keeping Western attention focused on the Middle East – just as it had always been since 9/11.

Security along the borders of eastern Europe was lower down the priority list for them, even if it most certainly was not all quiet on the eastern front at this time and Ukraine's war with Russia continually threatened to escalate.

Ukraine even introduced martial law for thirty days in late 2018 to cover ten of its regions after a naval clash in the Sea of Azov on 25 November 2018. The incident involved Russia attacking two Ukrainian patrol vessels and a Ukrainian tugboat as they travelled to Mariupol via the Kerch Strait (which links the Sea of Azov and the Black Sea). Russia took prisoner twenty-four crew members, and claimed it was defending its territorial waters around Crimea. Poroshenko was expectedly livid, even if the Ukrainian prisoners were later released.

Then, in a highly symbolic move, on 10 December 2018, the Rada passed a law that terminated the 1997 Friendship, Cooperation and Partnership Treaty with Russia. Ukraine was now using more direct language to paint Russia as the aggressor state. There was no sense of complacency in Ukraine, only foreboding, as to Russia's next move.

When the Kremlin's military eye finally looked away from the Middle East and re-focused on Ukraine, Petro Poroshenko would be long gone from power. And the scene would be set for a showdown in Ukraine that would eclipse all that had come before it.

CHAPTER 8

ZELENSKY'S DESTINY

A REFLECTION ON HEROES AND ANTIHEROES

ACTING THE PART

'It was as if Charlie Chaplin had morphed into Winston Churchill,' wrote the US magazine *Time*, referring to the changing faces of Volodymyr Zelensky. This was a metamorphosis he underwent in less than four years, from a light-hearted TV actor to a wartime leader. Ukrainians knew him as the fictional character Vasily Petrovich Goloborodko in the TV satire *Servant of the People*, playing a scrupulous teacher whose accidental rant about the evils of corruption in Ukraine is filmed, goes viral and leads to him becoming the real President. The show ran from 2015 to 2019, and its popularity captured the post-Euromaidan zeitgeist around stamping out corruption.

When Zelensky made a real bid for the presidency, he named his political party after his TV show. In the 21 April 2019 presidential run-off, Zelensky thrashed the incumbent Poroshenko by securing 73 per cent of the vote. The fact that life had imitated art was not the real story here; rather, it was that the arrival of a telegenic political outsider had, rather like Obama in 2008 or Macron in 2017, given a fresh face to their nation's politics. Democracies need periodic injections of fresh blood to remain vibrant and this was Zelensky's appeal. That said, Zelensky's presidency was still backed by an oligarch, Igor Kolomoisky, who had a majority ownership of the channel that broadcast Zelensky's show, so it was not a total break with Ukraine's past. In other ways Zelensky's rise was precedent-setting, not least in moving Ukrainian politics into an authentically post-Soviet generation.

This was alarming to the Kremlin. While Poroshenko wasn't loved by Putin, at least he was from a generation with real memories of the USSR, and he carried himself as a fat cat business baron to boot. Zelensky was comparatively incomprehensible to Russia: he directly embodied the principles of the Euromaidan, was born of bookish Jewish parents but had become an entertainer and, having been born in 1978, he would not recall too much of the USSR. Zelensky was also the fourth Ukrainian President that Putin had seen in office during his long stretch in the presidency and as Prime Minister, and the first total political amateur. Putin probably thought that he would eat Zelensky for breakfast.

Sure enough, in his initial presentation of Ukraine's policies towards Russia, Zelensky came across as rather naive. He was full of youthful enthusiasm, but devoid of the wisdom that can come from age and from dealing professionally with matters of real gravitas. It is unlikely that learning lines for his TV shows, and perfecting his comedic timing, was any kind of preparation for the Donbas war. Which is why, when Zelensky entered office in May 2019 voicing his hope that the war could be brought to an end, it was Putin who probably laughed the hardest.

Upon taking office, Zelensky tried to ease Kyiv's relations with

Moscow through exchanges of prisoners of war. This generated a brief respite, but Zelensky soon found that like his predecessor, his government had little political space to strike a deal with Russia that could bring the Donbas war to an end without surrendering east Ukraine to Russian influence.[1] Zelensky may have been a breath of fresh air to the Ukrainian electorate, but Russia was still going to try to suffocate him by removing as much political oxygen as it could.

US wartime aid

To the wider world, Zelensky first came to international attention after his infamous telephone call with President Trump on 25 July 2019 was leaked. During the call, Zelensky thanks Trump for 'your great support in the area of defence. We are ready to continue to cooperate for the next steps. Specifically, we are almost ready to buy more Javelins [portable anti-tank weapons] from the United States for defence purposes.'

At which point Trump responds, 'I would like you to do us a favour though because our country has been through a lot and Ukraine knows a lot about it.' Later in the call Trump asks a question that incriminated him in a breach of the use of office of the President of the USA.

> There's a lot of talk about Biden's son, that Biden stopped the prosecution and a lot of people want to find out about that so whatever you can do with the Attorney General would be great. Biden went around bragging that he stopped the prosecution so if you can look into it…[2]

Trump was referring to Hunter Biden's personal business interests in a Ukrainian gas company that he wanted Zelensky to investigate, insinuating that US defence support was now contingent upon Ukraine digging up dirt on a Trump political rival. This was such a serious misuse of his office that Trump was impeached over his conduct regarding Ukraine.

Details of the call were leaked by a White House-based US army officer, Alexander Vindman, who worked on the National Security Council (NSC) and was listening to it live as part of his White House job. In a further twist, Vindman happened to have been born in Kyiv, one of the million-plus US citizens with Ukrainian origins or ancestry. In his NSC role covering Europe, he personally attended Zelensky's inauguration as part of a US delegation. His act of publicising Trump's call to Zelensky made Vindman a minor celebrity in parts of the USA, resulting in such appearances as a cameo on the sitcom *Curb Your Enthusiasm*, where in the fictional script he berates the star Larry David after overhearing an incriminating phone call.

Most people heard this story and were aghast at yet another indictment on Trump's evident lack of scruple, but for Ukraine the crucial part of the story was the way it evidenced the continued difficulty it faced in securing enough US defence assistance. When the war first broke out in 2014, the US under the Obama administration was hesitant to sell Ukraine lethal military equipment, and the Ukraine war never really occupied a prime position of foreign policy concern in Washington DC at the time.

Senator John McCain was the most vocal big-name proponent in Washington DC for a greater US role in helping Ukraine, and he happened to visit Dnipro alongside Senator Tom Cotton while I was based there in 2015. McCain and Cotton visited the base of the Dnipro-1 battalion, who had been locked in combat since the start of the war with Russian and separatist forces. Footage of the visit shows McCain in conversation with Dnipro-1 personnel, watching footage of Russian troops in east Ukraine and offering words of inspiration to Ukrainian soldiers.[3] As a Ukrainian quipped to me around the time of McCain's visit, he was in town to say, "'America is behind you" – but he never specified how far away the Americans were'. To be fair to McCain, he was furious at the lightweight response to Putin's war by the West and was scathing of the Normandy Format diplomacy: 'The German Chancellor [Merkel] and the President of France [Hollande] legitimised the ... dismemberment of a country in Europe.' Of the negligible level of US military assistance being given to Ukraine, all he could say was, 'I'm ashamed of my country.'[4]

Obama, who was in office for the first three years of Ukraine's Donbas war, was unmoved by the cause, while Trump's sympathies with Russia were well known, leaving Ukraine with a level of US support that was far from decisive, either in defensive or in diplomatic terms, at this time.

The two pledges

Zelensky's presidency can be divided into two obvious parts – before and after 24 February 2022. In his first few years of holding office, he faced uphill struggles in both of his big campaign pledges: resolving the Donbas war and fighting corruption. Regarding corruption, the vested interests were pitted very much against reform, and in October 2020, the Constitutional Court curbed the powers of the National Agency for Prevention of Corruption. This prompted criticism from the US embassy in Kyiv. Zelensky clashed with the court, which eventually restated the agency's powers, but tensions persisted between Zelensky and the chairman of the court, Oleksandr Tupytskyi, who was suspended and later dismissed by Zelensky in 2021.

There were faltering attempts to end the Donbas war, but it was akin to approaching a Gordian knot. Zelensky called for dialogue, stating that 'we will not be able to end the war without direct talks with Russia'.[5] But the fundamental problem was still that Russia had little incentive to end the war and Ukraine had little leverage to force such an outcome.

In June 2019, Zelensky reappointed the now octogenarian former President Kuchma to once again represent the Ukrainian government at the working-level peace talks. As a septuagenarian, Kuchma had represented Ukraine in the original Minsk talks and had later stepped away from the demanding job due to his age. (As I recalled from my time with the OSCE, it was hardly an enjoyable experience hearing DPR bosses like Denis Pushilin, a man half Kuchma's age, berating all and sundry on behalf of his separatist republic, when everyone in the room knew Russia was pulling the DPR's strings.)

Whenever Zelensky and his negotiators made any headway talking with the DPR and LPR, they also immediately incurred the wrath of Ukraine's own hardliners, who shot down any putative deal as a surrender bill. At one point, the Azov battalion berated Zelensky for making progress with a deal that would have seen Kyiv respect elections in the DPR and LPR if Russian troops left.

Towards the end of 2019, there was a decision to resurrect the Normandy Format talks involving Ukraine, Russia, France and Germany, which had petered out three years beforehand. This resulted in Zelensky's first face-to-face meeting with Putin in Paris, with France's Macron and Germany's Merkel sitting between the Ukrainian and Russian leaders, which, predictably, led nowhere substantial. As before, the USA was not party to these talks, and all the talks could produce was agreement on a prisoner swap, which duly took place around the time of Orthodox Easter. Re-watching the footage from the Paris talks now, it is striking just how youthful the besuited Zelensky looks, sitting round the same table as his arch-enemy, Putin, and how far away he looks from the hardened and military-fatigued Zelensky seen by the world in 2022.

*   *   *

In 2020, the coronavirus pandemic began to ravage the world, sparing neither Ukraine nor Russia. This had the impact of bringing much in-person diplomatic activity to an end, and the next Normandy Format talks in April were virtual. Importantly, this meant that Zelensky and Putin never again met in person, as Putin in particular hunkered down in apparent isolation in Russia.

There was a ceasefire agreed to by all sides on 27 July 2020, which for a while dampened down the amount of shooting, but it came apart by the end of the year.[6] This left Zelensky facing the same problem: how do you end a war when you have little leverage but every desire to do so? At this stage, there were snatches and indications of the leader he would later become, for instance in his visits to the Donbas war zone to see the latest developments for himself and present commendations to Ukrainian soldiers in April 2021, although having turned just forty-one before assuming the presidency, some on-the-job training would be expected as he got accustomed to the role of wartime leader. During this time, NATO nations such as the USA, UK and Canada were providing training to Ukraine's army, helping its army's tactics and doctrine, but there was no indication when the storm would break, even as the air thickened and the tension began to mount in 2021, Zelensky's third year in office.

'MOTHER RUSSIA, TAKE DONBAS HOME!'

So intoned Margarita Simonyan live on stage in Donetsk City, capital of the DPR, one year and one month before the all-out Russian invasion, on 28 January 2021. Simonyan was a big name in Russian media: as editor in chief of the RT news channel, her words reflected Russian state sympathies. She had made the short trip from Russia to Donetsk City to make a direct emotional appeal by urging the full annexation of the Donbas at an event called the Russia Donbas Forum, which was held in the DPR-controlled Donetsk City. The event was also attended by a Russian senator (Kazbek Taysaev), as well as the DPR and LPR leadership.[7] Putin was not there, and his press secretary later distanced the Kremlin from the event, saying that integrating the Donbas into Russia was not a policy worth pursuing (that is, until a year later, when his boss decided on precisely the opposite policy). Nevertheless, the Russia Donbas Forum served as a public demonstration of the ideological appeal to some in Russia's elite of taking these lands into Russia.

Why was the Russia Donbas Forum held? By 2021, some of the residents and backers of the DPR and LPR felt that they had been abandoned, left to exist in a geopolitical twilight zone in which they were not recognised officially by Russia, while at the same time being ostracised and laid siege to by the Ukrainian army (or so it would have felt to them).

For instance, on the Russian social media site VKontakte, Russian nationalist blogger Alexander Zhuchkovsky offered his account of the situation in the DPR early in the war:

People survive. There's a crisis in Russia too, but our crisis [in the DPR] has totally different criteria … The conditions are wartime. People are reduced to the limit … something to eat, something to wear for the cold … They mostly live on savings. Of course, some government offices are working, but the pay there is on average 5,000–7,000 roubles [$65–$90] a month.

To the wider world, the DPR, the LPR and indeed the Donbas was the back end of nowhere. But it was an unresolved matter to its residents and, increasingly, to the Kremlin, that pro-Russian forces had taken control of these territories but had received only limited Russian support. To the Kremlin, however, the woes of DPR and LPR residents were secondary to how the unresolved Donbas war could be exploited to further antagonise Ukraine.

*   *   *

Knowing what we now know, it is impossible to view the events of 2020 and 2021 in any other terms than as a ticking clock, counting down with each passing month to Russia's all-out invasion. It is also clear that there was a remarkable number of warning signs in this period that Russia was about to shift gears and refuse to accept the status quo in Ukraine, and in some cases, hindsight is hardly needed.

At the start of 2020, Putin reshuffled his Cabinet and replaced his former point person on Ukraine, Vladislav Surkov, with another official, Dmitry Kozak, who in 2003 had tried to broker a lasting deal between Moldova and Transnistria (the deal failed, but Kozak at least had credentials in repressing Moscow's will vis-à-vis breakaway republics). Now free from office, Kozak's predecessor gave an alarming public interview in February 2020 in which he suggested that Ukraine would only respond to being restrained by force. 'Relations with Ukraine were never simple, even when Ukraine was part of Russia. Ukraine has always been troublesome for the imperial and Soviet bureaucracy,' Surkov was quoted as saying, before delivering his ominous soundbite: 'Forceful coercion for brotherly relations, this is the only method that has historically proven effective when it comes to Ukraine. I do not think that any other will be invented.'[8]

That same month, Putin himself suggested to the Russian media site TASS that Russia and Ukraine should merge. In Putin's words, 'Any integration of Russia and Ukraine, along with their capacities and competitive advantages would spell the emergence of a rival, a global rival for both Europe and the world. No one wants this. That's why they'll do anything to tear us apart.'[9] 'They', in this usage, being the West and all the outside powers who in Putin's view wanted to keep Russia and Ukraine apart (but there was never any mention by Putin of the ordinary people *in* Ukraine who wanted this, too).

Words were soon accompanied by Russian deeds when there was a dress rehearsal for amassing Russian forces along Ukraine's borders.

Beginning in late March and lasting into April 2021, Russia moved an intimidatingly large number of its military personnel and equipment into Crimea and into its western regions bordering Ukraine, notably Rostov and Voronezh. An estimated 100,000 Russian personnel had been assembled for what was explained as a snap military exercise. Russia was either involved in a show of strength or was preparing an invasion, and the uncertainty over its intentions persisted until late April, when it declared the end of its exercise and withdrew some of these troops.

This massing of troops was followed by the Russian military's 'Zapad' (Russian for 'West') exercises in September 2021, which were staged in both Russia and Belarus, including in the Russian western enclave of Kaliningrad on the Baltic Coast. This followed on from previous Zapad exercises in 2017 and 2013 but only served to heighten concern that Russia was preparing for major military action.

Belarus

Events that unfolded in neighbouring Belarus provided yet another portent of Ukraine's impending doom. Ukraine had for a long time been concerned by the close association between its northern neighbour and the Russian Federation. The activities of Russian forces in Belarus had long been a worry for Ukraine, which kept its ear to the ground for any signs of Russia extending its security presence in the eastern European region including through joint military drills. Ukraine was petrified that Russia might build a permanent military base in Belarus.

There was certainly something murky going on between Russia and Belarus. In a curious incident in July 2020, the authorities in Minsk arrested thirty-three military contractors from the Russian private military company the Wagner Group. This included nine who had Ukrainian passports, so the Ukrainian government asked for them to be extradited to Ukraine. The Prosecutor General's office cited the Wagner Group's past role in the Donbas war. All but one of those arrested were eventually sent back to Russia (the remaining individual held Belarusian citizenship). The incident indicated some kind of Russian meddling in Belarus.

When Belarus's long-time dictator Lukashenko decided to run for a sixth term in office in a presidential election held on 9 August 2020, he faced mass street protests from a citizenry that was sick of his rule. Lukashenko was inevitably declared the winner, but the protesters complained that the vote had been rigged, while his main opponent, Sviatlana Tsikhanouskaya, declared that she ought to have won. Lukashenko's regime kicked into survival mode as the Belarus security forces violently suppressed the protests, beating and arresting scores of protesters and forcing Tsikhanouskaya to flee the country.

Europe's self-styled 'last dictator' had clung to power but in doing so became more dependent on Putin's Russia, something that Lukashenko had tried to stave off. He had been in power since 1994 and was the only President many Belarusians had ever known. With his imposing frame and blunt, brutish manner, Lukashenko had until now kept Putin at least somewhat off his back, but no more. As Belarus came under Western sanctions for the violence meted out by its security forces against the unarmed protesters, Lukashenko had no choice but to look to Russia for financial salvation and for diplomatic recognition.

If Ukraine had become the disobedient, independent-minded sibling in Putin's eyes, Belarus was still able to be disciplined by the firm hand of Moscow's power, pliant in part because it was run by a leader who was a throwback to the USSR. For Ukraine, its northern border now seemed less secure than ever before as Russia tightened its influence over Belarus.

Afghanistan

In the summer of 2021, the Russian intelligence services still seemed to be at their devious best due to their alleged complicity in stoking the manufactured migrant crisis at the Poland–Belarus border, in which they flew in migrants and refugees from African and Middle Eastern countries with the promise of helping them to enter the EU and duly tried to push them over the border into Poland. Russian and Belarusian authorities worked together to create this migrant crisis in an effort to harass the EU. So far so hybrid, as tactics go. So, what changed in Russia's calculus, to shift from harassments and intrigue to all-out industrial war?

Perhaps the US and NATO rout in Afghanistan decisively shifted Putin's thinking. After a twenty-year campaign, in the summer of 2021 NATO left in a panic after the Afghan army it had equipped and trained for two decades fell apart in the face of a Taliban offensive. When the final US planes left Kabul, some did so with desperate Afghans literally clinging to their wheels. These people, some of whom had pinned their fate on the US-backed government in Kabul, saw no future after the Western departure. It was a humiliating start to Biden's foreign policy. Even the USSR had abandoned its doomed ten-year occupation of Afghanistan in a more orderly fashion back in 1989. Russians would not have been surprised that the US and its NATO allies had failed in Afghanistan, but their read-across to Ukraine assumed that NATO would falter here, too.

A narrative of Western ineptitude and division, stretching from the EU to NATO, seemed to have gained currency in the Kremlin during 2021, emboldening Putin to take the riskiest military gamble of his long leadership.

* * *

Starting in October 2021, Russia again massed its armed forces in its western regions abutting Ukraine, in Crimea and in Belarus.

Dmitry Medvedev (now Russia's Deputy Chairman of the Security Council) published his own open letter denouncing the validity of the Ukrainian state, including a baffling line that was evidently lost in translation: 'A goat competed with a wolf, only a skin like a goat survived.'*[10]

In both ideological and material terms, the signs were increasingly ominous. Nevertheless, as befitted Russia's autocratically run government machine, no wider case was being made in a prominent way to whip the Russian people into a frenzy for war. Worse, some people in Ukraine had been lulled into a false sense of regularity by the low-intensity Donbas war and the fact it had unfolded at an arm's length away from cities like Lviv and Kyiv and even Kharkiv and Poltava, which were further east but had been largely out of harm's way since 2014. Neither the Russian nor the Ukrainian people were poised and ready for what was about to happen. When the moment of truth came, it was at once a moment of shock and surprise and not a surprise at all.

From late 2021, events were in free fall, and they plummeted right until they smashed into the bottom of a deep and dark precipice.

BEATING THE DRUMS OF WAR

Intelligence assessment is an imperfect art, and as intelligence professionals the world over know, reading the runes from a collation of fragmentary information, derived from imagery intelligence, intercepted communications, from the chatter of human agents and

---

*   Medvedev continues, 'The eternal and main question arises: what to do in this situation? But nothing. Wait for the emergence of a sane leadership in Ukraine, which is aimed not at a total confrontation with Russia on the brink of war, not at organising moronic "Crimean platforms" created to fool the population of the country and pump up their muscles before the elections, but at building equal and mutually beneficial relations with Russia. That's just with such a leadership of Ukraine and it is worth dealing with. Russia knows how to wait. We are patient people.' It turns out that there was not much of a wait at all until Russia began its invasion.

from sifting through vast amounts of open-source information, never equates to crystal ball-gazing. Moreover, when it comes to military affairs, counting tanks can never convey strategic intent. Nevertheless, the vast US intelligence machine, and that of its close allies in the UK, was about to have a field day by accurately predicting the fact of Russia's coming invasion.

Whether this mattered or not in the long run is debatable; nothing the USA said or threatened in advance ultimately deterred Russia from taking the road to full-scale war. But it certainly helped to drown out the beating drums of war coming from Russia by stealing control of the narrative leading up to the invasion. Rather than Russia's threats to Ukraine leading news cycles around the world, US warnings of imminent Russian aggression became the story.

After the debacle of the mangled and incorrect intelligence reporting that had been used by their political masters to justify the invasion of Iraq in March 2003, the American and British intelligence agencies were out to redeem their reputations this time round by successfully interpreting Russia's intent as it amassed troops around Ukraine. Following the debacle in Afghanistan in the summer of 2021, when the NATO-trained and NATO-equipped Afghan National Army capitulated against the Taliban as the US announced it would leave the country, the US and its allies involved in Afghanistan wanted to believe, but dared not to, that Ukraine's army would stand and fight if the Russians came in numbers over the border. These legacies of Western war-making since 9/11 – as well as the immense intelligence collection and analysis machinery of the USA and its NATO allies – informed the hair-trigger warnings of a Russian invasion of Ukraine that were issued by the USA starting in the autumn of 2021.

'Pootin', as Joe Biden tended to pronounce his name, would have a 'heavy price to pay' if Russia invaded Ukraine. 'We made it clear to President Putin that if he makes any more moves, goes into Ukraine, we will have severe sanctions. We will increase our presence in Europe with our NATO allies, and it'll just be a heavy price to pay for it,' said Biden on New Year's Eve. Already in November the USA had dispatched Bill Burns, the CIA head who had once served as US ambassador to Russia, to Moscow to convey US concerns. Biden had held virtual meetings with Putin in early December 2021 during which, as the White House statement conveyed, 'President Biden reiterated his support for Ukraine's sovereignty and territorial integrity and called for de-escalation and a return to diplomacy'.[11]

Then, on 17 December 2021, the Russian government gave the American government a surprising document. According to the Russian Ministry of Foreign Affairs,

> During the December 15 2021 meeting at the Russian Foreign Ministry, the US party [ambassador] received a draft treaty between the Russian Federation and the United States of America on security guarantees and an agreement on measures to ensure the security of the Russian Federation and member states of the NATO.[12]

This document showed that Ukraine was both a pawn in a wider geopolitical game being played by Russia and an objective in its own right.

The draft treaty, leaving spaces for signatures 'for the United States of America' and 'for the Russian Federation', presented a number of demands for the USA:

1. 'The Parties ... shall not implement security measures adopted by each Party individually or in the framework of an international

organisation, military alliance or coalition that could undermine core security interests of the other Party';

2. 'The Parties shall not use the territories of other States with a view to preparing or carrying out an armed attack against the other Party or other actions affecting core security interests of the other Party' [which was ironic, given that this was precisely how Russia was using Belarus's territory, to prepare an attack on Ukraine];

3. 'The United States of America shall undertake to prevent further eastward expansion of the North Atlantic Treaty Organization and deny accession to the alliance to the States of the former Union of Soviet Socialist Republics';

4. 'The United States of America shall not establish military bases in the territory of the States of the former Union of Soviet Socialist Republics that are not members of the North Atlantic Treaty Organization, use their infrastructure for any military activities or develop bilateral military cooperation with them';

5. 'The Parties shall undertake not to deploy ground-launched intermediate-range and shorter-range missiles outside their national territories, as well as in the areas of their national territories, from which such weapons can attack targets in the national territory of the other party';

6. 'The Parties shall refrain from deploying nuclear weapons outside their national territories and return such weapons already deployed outside their national territories'.

The Russian Ministry of Foreign Affairs issued a separate proposed agreement between Russia and NATO that covered similar ground: again, 'the principles of cooperation, equal and indivisible security' were mentioned. The 'NATO–Russia Council' was mentioned as a forum for hashing things out, while in a nod to the Cold War that was seemingly oblivious to technological advancements, 'telephone hotlines shall be established to maintain emergency contacts between the Parties'. The desire for 'improving mechanisms to prevent incidents on and over the high seas (primarily in the Baltics and the Black Sea region)' was cited.

Naturally, Russia asked that 'all member States of the North Atlantic Treaty Organization commit themselves to refrain from any further enlargement of NATO, including the accession of Ukraine as well as other States'. In addition, 'the Parties that are member States of the North Atlantic Treaty Organization shall not conduct any military activity on the territory of Ukraine as well as other States in the eastern Europe, in the south Caucasus and in central Asia'.

What should we make of this?

It is easy to dismiss everything the Russian Federation says as disinformation, pretext and, more generally, as deceitful hogwash. Certainly, the list of Russian demands was so far-reaching that the Kremlin could never have assumed they would be agreed to by the USA and NATO. Perhaps the Kremlin thought they could be the basis for a negotiation in which Russia was invited to have a say and a direct stake in Europe's security, or perhaps these demands were merely issued to buy time before the invasion of Ukraine. Trust was low between the USA, NATO and Russia, and a meaningful negotiation highly unlikely. Nevertheless, the consistency in some Russian demands was evident, and CIA director Bill Burns, who had lived in Russia as US ambassador, had years ago warned Washington that Ukrainian membership in NATO was a red line for Russia.[13] Now, Russia had spelled out its red lines once again and it was incumbent on the US government to respond.

Sure enough, in January 2022 the USA responded. In the words of Secretary of State Antony Blinken, the written US response to Russian demands 'sets out a serious diplomatic path forward should Russia choose it'. The USA was not interested in agreeing to a moratorium on further NATO expansion, instead proposing talks on arms control and transparency of military deployments in Europe. Blinken went on, 'The document we've delivered includes the concerns of the United States and our allies and partners about Russia's actions that undermine security, a principled and pragmatic evaluation of the concerns that Russia has raised, and our own proposals for areas where we may be able to find common ground.'[14]

In January, as the US–Russia negotiation stalled, US intelligence warnings became more pessimistic, including an accurate prediction of the 'distinct possibility' Russia might invade Ukraine the following month.[15] Russia continually denied it was planning to attack. As the US began to predict a possible Russian move accurately and threatened huge economic sanctions if Russia invaded, the quick-fire publication of US intelligence was unprecedented. What used to be the preserve of the secret intelligence community, gathered for the eyes of the US government only to inform its decision-making, was now publicised to shine a spotlight on Russia's malcontent towards Ukraine. The US, however, resisted imposing pre-emptive economic sanctions on Russia, something Zelensky called for.[16] This was probably the correct decision by the US: it is unconvincing to think that pre-emptive sanctions would have had any other outcome than allowing Putin to claim some kind of victimhood at the hands of the US government and invade Ukraine anyway.

*　*　*

The next piece in Moscow's strategy was the now legendary bilateral meeting between Putin and China's President Xi Jinping at the opening ceremony of the Beijing Winter Olympics on 4 February 2022. Whether or not Putin exchanged words with Xi about an invasion of Ukraine, the most astonishing thing to emerge from this meeting was a joint government declaration that listed both countries' grievances with the West, saw Russia back China over Taiwan, and promised a 'friendship without limits' (although a glaring omission was any mention of Ukraine; instead, China backed Russia's objections to the further expansion of NATO). In the translation on the Kremlin website, the document was portentously titled 'Joint Statement of the Russian Federation and the People's Republic of China on the International Relations Entering a New Era and the Global Sustainable Development'.[17] This was a clear act of signalling by Putin that no matter the sanctions threatened by the USA, Russia now had other options in the global marketplace.

Like a slow-motion car crash, war was now just weeks away. It crept up on everyone, from the thousands of Russian soldiers freezing in their billets and their parked vehicles in Belarus over the winter, who were not told by Putin that they were about to go to war, to the Ukrainian soldiers tensely manning their redoubts in the Donbas as they had done for eight years; and to those in the wider world such as the French government who thought the USA and UK to be alarmist and dismissed their repeated warnings. Even Zelensky didn't seem to take it seriously in public: not until the last minute did he really believe that Russia would escalate the existing Donbas war into a full-blown invasion, despite his rising to the challenge.

This returns us to the moment presented in the opening pages of this book, of Zelensky taking to the stage in Munich on 19 February to sound the warning and to ask for help, all the while trying to remain cool in front of the cameras and avoid provoking the Russians by offering them a pretext, lest they use his words to start the invasion. 'To really help Ukraine, it is not necessary to constantly talk only about the dates of the probable invasion. We will defend our land on February 16, March 1 and December 31.'[18]

This was understandable on one level: Zelensky did not want to instil total panic in his country, even as certain international airlines cancelled their flight services to Ukraine pre-emptively, the images of MH17 reduced to a twisted heap of metal debris in the Donbas no doubt playing in the minds of the airline bosses. Biden later said, 'I know a lot of people thought I was maybe exaggerating [the imminence of Russia's invasion], but I knew … There was no doubt. And Zelensky didn't want to hear it, nor did a lot of people.'[19] All doubt was soon extinguished. In the next chapter, the early part of the invasion is recounted. Before doing so, it is essential to revisit an important question.

WAS THE INVASION STOPPABLE?

An obsession can be a dangerous thing. Putin had consistently voiced Russia's opposition to Ukraine's possible candidacy in NATO's continuing expansion from at least 2005. Consistency in this instance was not a virtue, and far from it. Dictatorships have the inbuilt tendency of precluding new pairs of eyes from re-examining old issues because the same person hogs the leadership. Over two decades, Putin's views of Ukraine became warped. His experience of dealing with Ukraine moved from the apparent pliability of Kuchma to the next-generation objectionability of Yushchenko, to the return of pliability with Yanukovych, to the obstinacy of Poroshenko, and now to yet another new generation with

Zelensky. All the while it was still Putin, seeing Ukraine oscillate like a pendulum swinging between Russia and the West but now slipping from his grasp.

But why mount a massive invasion now? Why not eight years before, or at any other time? What was it that sent Putin over the edge, and was there anything that anyone could have done about it? Lest we consider Ukraine's suffering the invasion as inevitable, these are questions worth posing.

Some Russian supporters asked similar questions. On the Russian social media site VKontakte, Russian nationalist activist and blogger Alexander Zhuchkovsky voiced his feeling that the DPR and LPR had been abandoned by Russia back in 2014–15, and wondered aloud, 'Why now?'

> There have been discussions about why Russia did not start a war against Ukraine eight years ago, but only now. The easiest and most popular explanation: they weren't ready … [But the better explanation is] hopelessness. There was no other way out than a pre-emptive attack. But you need to understand that this hopelessness itself arose because of the non-attack eight years ago, when 'they were not ready.' It would seem a vicious circle, but no. The unpreparedness of a state or an individual for something is often an abstraction, an excuse. Readiness … is determined not by resources, but by goal setting and motivation.[20]

For Zhuchkovsky, Russia was finally getting round to what it should have done at the start of the first Donbas war, but the delay showed the Donbas to be incidental to Putin's calculus.

Amidst all of the bogus justifications picked from the gutter by Putin about 'fascists' and 'Nazis' in Kyiv, there were also important geopolitical issues at stake for Russia, in Putin's estimation.

However, it is first worth addressing the terminology of these justifications. How could Ukraine be fascist? When Lavrov later tried to explain, he tied himself in knots and invoked the deserved ire of Israel by comparing Zelensky to Hitler, who also had 'semitic roots' according to Lavrov. This 'fascist' justification was likely a rallying call for the Russian public and the Russian soldiers of the front line to have something with which to smear their enemy as they rode into battle. The accusation of being a 'fascist' was a red herring when it came to the war's driving causes, not least since all sides routinely denounced each other in this way. Ukrainian shops were known to sell toilet rolls with mugshots of Putin sporting a Hitler moustache on them, and routinely also called the Russians 'fascists' once the invasion began, reflecting the hideous absurdity that a Russian regime so obsessed with Hitler's invasion of the USSR in 1941 had become the murderous invaders themselves.

As objectionable as Russian slurs were against Ukraine, the possible future admission of Ukraine into NATO was a more tangible issue with actual geopolitical ramifications. In 2014, Russian invasion was triggered by the ousting of Yanukovych, which in turn arose from protests around Kyiv's future association with the EU. This time it was NATO, but there were no immediate signs of Ukraine's admission into the alliance that Russia could say it was retaliating against in 2022.

What progress had NATO made in its courtship with Ukraine, by now twelve years after the Bucharest half-way house offer? According to the NATO website:

Since the NATO Summit in Warsaw in July 2016, NATO's practical support for Ukraine is set out in the Comprehensive Assistance Package (CAP) for Ukraine. | June 2017, Ukrainian Parliament adopted legislation reinstating membership in NATO as a strategic foreign and security policy objective. | In 2019, a corresponding amendment to Ukraine's Constitution entered into force. | June 2020, Ukraine became the sixth Enhanced Opportunity Partner (EOP). | In September 2020, President Volodymyr Zelenskyy approved Ukraine's new National Security Strategy, which provides for the development of the distinctive partnership with NATO with the aim of membership in NATO.[21]

Moves were still afoot, and while none of them signalled Ukraine's imminent NATO membership, they may have looked very different outside NATO and Ukraine.

Could these moves have been misinterpreted by Russia as a slippery slope to Ukraine's entry into NATO? Each move would have fed into the paranoia in Putin's regime. For instance, on 12 June 2020, Ukraine was made into an Enhanced Opportunities Partner by NATO, and this status granted Ukraine access to further military exercises and equipment programmes provided by NATO, although it did not confer a commitment to future full Ukrainian membership. For its part, Ukraine was still reforming its military apparatus to meet NATO's standards for future membership. For instance, a new division of military command was enacted in Ukraine's armed forces leadership as the role of Chief of the General Staff was split from the role of Commander of the Armed Forces to match the normal NATO arrangement. These and other bureaucratic and technical standards were being met but hardly amounted to an immediate membership announcement. Ukraine joined a motley collection of five other EOP NATO countries (Australia, Finland, Georgia, Jordan, Sweden), two of which – Finland and Sweden

– have since joined NATO in 2022 in response to Russia's invasion. Most alarming to Russia were the amendments made to the Ukrainian constitution in 2019 to include the following under Article 102: 'The President of Ukraine is a guarantor of the implementation of the strategic course of the state for gaining full-fledged membership of Ukraine in the European Union and the North Atlantic Treaty Organization.'[22]

This coincided with a more favourable US presidential administration, with Trump replaced by Biden in January 2021. Biden announced a US$125 million military aid package for Ukraine on 1 March 2021 which declared 'the US commitment to providing defensive lethal weapons to enable Ukraine to more effectively defend itself against Russian aggression' with the ultimate aim of boosting Ukraine's 'Euro-Atlantic aspirations in support of a secure, prosperous, democratic, and free Ukraine'.[23] Once again, this would have only fuelled the paranoia of Putin's regime.

As ever, we must distinguish between a *provocation*, which implies something that necessitates a response, and *motivation*, which refers to the reasons one finds convincing for taking action. In no way can Putin argue that the NATO–Kyiv dialogue was a provocation to Russia. But it was a motivation because NATO would encroach on Russia's perceived post-imperial sphere of influence if Ukraine were to ever join. Even if NATO's courtship of Ukraine was unlikely to deliver full membership of the alliance any time soon, moves were afoot that could have been interpreted as suggesting otherwise, hence the pre-emptive rationale behind Russia's attack (in Putin's mind, at least).

* * *

As the just war scholar Michael Walzer wrote many years ago with the unjust US war in Vietnam in his mind, the moral case for military intervention is a delicate matter. Walzer was no pacifist, but his standards were high and his exposition well worth revisiting from his book *Just and Unjust Wars*.

'For as long as men and women have talked about war, they have talked about it in terms of right and wrong,' wrote Walzer. He reminds us that our primary perceptions of international aggression are analogical to domestic crimes, which makes the international world accessible through notions of crime, punishment, self-defence and law. The 'Munich principle' accepts the loss or erosion of independence for the sake of survival of individuals who would otherwise perish in a war to defend against aggression. Putin's justification for war tried to play with the Munich principle, as well as playing with the notion of self-determination for the secessionist DPR and LPR. As Walzer wrote, 'States can be invaded and wars justly begun to assert secessionist movements (once they have demonstrated their representative character, to balance prior interventions of other powers; and to rescue people threatened with massacre).'[24] This is what Putin asserted in relation to the DPR and the LPR's 'will of the people'; NATO and the US meddling in Ukraine; and for Putin's baseless allegations of the Ukrainian army responses to the Donbas War. In every instance there was no moral case for war, and to the extent we can discern with the available information, no imminent threat to Russia of NATO forces being deployed to Ukraine, or of Ukraine joining NATO any time soon. Based on Walzer's tests, Russia's invasion was most certainly unjust.

Before we get too comfortable with this judgement, there are still awkward questions around NATO expansion to consider. Russia had been written out of the script when it came to security affairs in its neighbourhood, and Andrey Kortunov, head of the Russian International Affairs Council, said just before the war began, 'This is a bargaining position – [the Kremlin] is trying to get some degree of partial acceptance' of the points it raised in its December 2021 demands to the US and to NATO.[25] Experienced Western experts held similar interpretations, for instance the former US ambassador to NATO Robert Hunter, who served in the post between 1993 and 1998. Putin was undoubtedly out to bully Ukraine but was also 'seeking a major role for Russia in European security, given that the last two decades the US and NATO have sought to subordinate Russian influence in Europe'.

As war beckoned, Russia's demands to discuss future NATO expansion were ignored. Would it not have been wiser to seriously negotiate with Putin over the NATO point in an attempt to avert the war in the critical months of December 2021 and January 2022? The US Secretary of State Antony Blinken, who played a key role in the response to Russia's demands, said at the time that 'we will leave no stone unturned to see if we can prevent a war'.[26] Was this right? Was there ever a serious discussion with Russia about Ukraine and NATO expansion as the clock ticked down?

The brand-new German Chancellor Olaf Scholz, on a visit to Moscow, jibed that it would take longer for Ukraine to join NATO than Putin would remain in power. But this was a weak reassurance to Russia and NATO unabashedly said that its door was open to Ukraine. Zelensky himself said that Ukraine would not be deterred from pursuing NATO membership. NATO Secretary General Jens Stoltenberg was apoplectic in his defence of the open door and Ukraine's right to gaze at it, even if walking through was not as yet a prospect. Any notion of a formal treaty declaration or constitutional amendment by Ukraine that it would agree not to join NATO in the future was dismissed out of hand by Kyiv, Washington and Brussels. NATO was adamant in its defence of a principle – its open door to Ukraine – that NATO had no immediate desire to follow up on. This was a hell of a paradox.

As the crisis brewed, a pair of interesting articles appeared in the journal of the International Institute for Strategic Studies, *Survival*. Former NATO ambassador Robert Hunter offered a considered view based on his decades of experience regarding NATO expansion:

> In the 1990s, NATO did indicate that any European country emerging from the wreckage of the Soviet Union could seek to join. But it also made clear that not all applicants would necessarily be accepted as NATO members. Overall, this NATO position is more than a little disingenuous, since the chance for most formally eligible countries remains remote. There is one overarching requirement for NATO membership – unanimous approval of existing allies – and it is difficult to attain. From the beginning, it has been evident that NATO made the freedom of choice declaration without any intention of admitting aspirants as a matter of right, but now has been trapped by its own verbiage. [27]

Later in the issue, another fascinating historical view was provided by the UK's final ambassador to the USSR, Sir Rodric Braithwaite. It read like a no-holds-barred retrospective:

> Since 1991, Western diplomacy in eastern Europe has been by turns arrogant and incompetent. The initial enlargement of NATO to include the Baltic states, the Czech Republic, Hungary and Poland was probably unavoidable, both politically and morally ... But the Americans

and their allies continued to mutter pieties about the Ukrainians' right to choose their own alliances, while simultaneously announcing that they have no intention of sending combat troops to defend Ukraine should it need them. That is an unserious position, and risks setting up the wretched Ukrainians for yet another betrayal.[28]

In the months ahead, for all the war enthusiasm voiced by Western commentators of all stripes for Ukraine to deliver the Russians a bloody nose and to defend their land, the question of whether the war could *really* have been averted fell away. Simply publicising an accurate day-by-day image intelligence picture of the Russian troop build-up while threatening to sanction Russia was never going to be enough to head off a war, no matter how much the US government may have convinced itself otherwise. Selling out the Ukrainians was also not a morally feasible option. But it would take some gall not to look back with serious regret when, early into the invasion, Zelensky changed his tune on NATO membership. On 15 March 2022, he told the UK-led Joint Expeditionary Force that 'Ukraine is not a member of NATO … We have heard for years that the doors were open, but we also heard that we could not join. It's a truth and it must be recognised.'[29]

Of course, even if Ukraine had forsworn NATO membership, the question of whether Ukraine could join the EU – an issue that partly animated Russia's 2014 invasion – would have remained open. It was never as easy as a neutrality pledge stopping Russian action, and it may have left Ukraine even more open to Russian predation further down the line. Putin's Russia was a serially deceitful interlocutor, after all. There are no easy answers, but the NATO open door and its role in the longer-term causes of this war is not an open and shut case, either.

* * *

'Nations see themselves as the centre of the universe,' wrote Ken Booth in *Strategy in Ethnocentrism*. 'They interpret the actions of adversaries or potential adversaries in terms of their own problems and vulnerabilities ... The idea that one person's security is often another person's insecurity is a simple point to accept intellectually but rarely informs the thinking of strategists.'[30] These are words worth reflecting on as we bring the chapter on the events immediately preceding the invasion to a close.

No amount of Russian disinformation could turn Russia's hatred of NATO expansion into a moral justification of war. The Russian protestation that NATO expansion endangered its security was far-fetched and self-serving, but the complaint that NATO and indeed EU expansion curtailed Russia's sphere of historical and cultural influence is clearer. The more Westernised the former satellite states and SSRs became, the more strategic influence would flow from Washington, London and Brussels, and less from Moscow. Well, tough luck, you may say: Russia has more than enough space without needing to influence others, and sovereign governments should be free to choose who they ally and partner with. Sadly, the unforgiving world of geopolitics doesn't allow for these luxuries in a way that is detached from balances of power. By decreeing Putin's Russia to have no right to influence in eastern Europe, we must also understand that Putin felt this was Russia's entitlement and was showing a willingness to use force to back this vision.

By this logic, was there grim satisfaction in some Western corners that Putin was about to make an immense strategic error by manoeuvring his country into the position of being an unashamed aggressor? And that, this time, unlike in 2014 with his stealthier invasion of Ukraine, Putin might be trapped? Regardless, it would be Ukraine and not NATO that would now face the wrath and the death and the destruction of Russia's war machine. Ukrainian lives were being placed en masse on the altar of sacrifice in a wider disagreement over whose principles – the West's or Russia's – should prevail in Russia's former imperial lands. If Ukraine was ever to be a beneficiary in this struggle, it must first endure loss and pain.

CHAPTER 9

WAR OF CONQUEST

A REFLECTION ON DESTRUCTION

SURROUNDED AND INVADED

Orcs all around and ready to pounce – 'orcs', the foot-soldier monsters from *The Lord of the Rings*, was a name adopted by some Ukrainians to slur the invaders. And now the horde came in force. Unlike in 2014, when Russian soldiers came in smaller numbers, this time there was no pretence of stealth. In 2022, all the tools of conventional war were unleashed by Russia: mechanised infantry battalions; main battle tanks; helicopter-borne assault troops; artillery bombardments; naval blockades, airstrikes; cruise missiles; just hell on earth.

It was hardly a true surprise attack since Russia's military build-up was so obvious, but it was a shock to the senses nonetheless. The opening days were chaotic. In Ukraine, heartbreak, anguish, anger, panic, resignation and resolve all mixed together in a tidal wave of emotions that swept the country. Russian bombs rained down on civilians and soldiers alike, often with little regard for the distinction, and many Ukrainians understandably fled. Cars clogged the main roads and packed trains headed westward, with Lviv being the sanctuary destination for many, a gateway to Poland and the EU. Families were split apart as children and the vulnerable left while others stayed put and joined territorial defence units. For the Ukrainian military it was action stations, but so too for many Ukrainian civilians.

In the opening days of the invasion it became abundantly clear that Kyiv was Russia's main target and Zelensky was on Putin's kill-list. As Zelensky later recounted to the media, he was told by his military that Russian forces were entering Kyiv to hunt him down at the start of the invasion. And so the legend was born: the US government got in touch with an offer to spirit Zelensky out of Kyiv so he could establish a government in exile, but his widely repeated response was 'I need ammunition, not a ride'.[1] Confirming whether Zelensky delivered this line with these exact words has been difficult, with one suggestion being that the phraseology originated from a US official briefed on the call; regardless, it was a great global headline and it set the tone for his wartime leadership.[2]

What is beyond doubt is that Zelensky remained in Ukraine to rally his nation. Within hours of Putin's 'special military operation' kicking into gear, Zelensky delivered a literal call to arms: 'We will give weapons to anyone who wants to defend the country. Be ready to support Ukraine in the squares of our cities.'[3] He then severed Ukraine's diplomatic relations with Russia and began to work the video calls with leaders from around the world, urgently asking for as much help as they could offer.

The reason for his urgency was clear as missiles slammed into Ukraine's cities. Kyiv's suburbs, as in many Ukrainian cities, were dominated by tall grey concrete tower blocks, dozens of them pointing to the sky in synchronicity as if standing to attention. Now, Russian missiles struck them at random, killing innocents inside and imposing a lasting grief on their loved ones outside. Into Kyiv's basements and metro stations the people poured, descending from the highest residences to seek subterranean shelter.

'Friends! For safety's sake, stay at home or in shelters as much as possible!' So came the announcement of Kyiv's mayor since 2014, the former heavyweight boxer Vitali Klitschko. 'Do not go out and do not go to the city. Leave home just to go to the shelter. We are defending our city!' he tweeted, forty-eight hours after the invasion began.[4]

His brother, fellow boxing veteran Wladimir Klitschko, summed up the feelings of millions of his compatriots: 'Putin makes it clear that he wants to destroy the Ukrainian state and the sovereignty of its people. Words are followed by missiles and tanks. Destruction and death come upon us. That's it, blood will mix with tears.'

Wladimir added a telling line: 'The Ukrainian people are strong. And will remain true to themselves in this terrible ordeal. A people longing for sovereignty and peace. *A people who consider the Russian people their brothers*. It knows that they basically do not want this war.'[5] Brothers – you might ask, how could a Ukrainian invoke such a word on the very day the invasion began? Even as Russian munitions struck their terrifying opening blows, Ukrainians like Wladimir Klitschko knew there was a fratricidal element to the war – just a trace perhaps, but enough to make all of the death and destruction even more heart-breaking and bewildering. Some Russians had no idea why their country had suddenly gone to war with its neighbour. Millions of Ukrainians live in Russia and many Russian and Ukrainian families are linked, making the fratricidal aspect of the war abundantly clear. Courageous Russian anti-war protesters tried to make their voices heard but were hounded and jailed by Putin's security state, leaving the dominant narratives in Russia the state-propagated ones. Ukraine had enjoyed 362 months and counting as a sovereign and free state at the moment the invasion began; now, Russia's military was trying to abrogate this sovereignty as the bullying older sibling.

Z

There is nothing shaped like the Latin 'Z' character in the Cyrillic alphabet (Cyrillic has 'з' for this sound). But 'Z' was the symbol emblazoned on Russia's military vehicles in Ukraine. Crude 'Z' shapes were painted on or affixed with gaffer tape to Russian vehicles to mark them as being on the same side. Merchandise and propaganda billboards back home in Russia used the 'Z' to convey support for the war. Why 'Z'? Perhaps it related to the periodic 'Zapad' (meaning 'West') military exercises Russia staged with Belarus, but this was still spelled 'запад'. Perhaps it was an allusion to the 'Z' in 'Zelensky' as spelled in English or perhaps it was a sideways 'N' to allude to the crackpot Kremlin slur of Zelensky's government being 'Nazis' – such were the disjointed narratives Russia was pushing out to justify its invasion to its soldiers and domestic populace.

A key figure in these justifications was the Orthodox Patriarch Kirill of Moscow, who sanctified the invasion as waged in defence of the Orthodox Slavic world. This Russian accusation was a spiritual one, to avert the Ukrainian secularisation that was taking place in the name of joining the US-led 'Western liberal empire'. The Kremlin and its key influencers like Kirill assembled an absurd set of narratives to provide an ideological edge to the invasion. Under this shroud of official and spiritual sanction, Russia attacked.

Starting on 24 February, Russian troops advanced along four main axis of attack: in the south, pouring out of Crimea, they headed toward Kherson in one direction and Mariupol in another; in the north, Kharkiv was one target and Kyiv the main prize for Russian conquest. Curiously, in these early days of the invasion, there was little emphasis on capturing further territory in the Donbas itself, the location of Russia's fictional *casus belli*, aside from limited supporting operations in Luhansk Oblast.[*6]

Urban warfare

Gazing at a map of the start of the invasion, a many-tentacled beast seemed to envelop Ukraine as various arrows indicated the lines of Russia's advance. The clearest barometer of military progress for either side would now be the control of Ukraine's cities. This point is worth dwelling on to make better sense of the patterns of fighting and human suffering that followed.

Why had cities become the focal point of the war? The initial Russian war aim was regime change at the barrel of a gun, and this elevated Kyiv's importance as a military objective at the invasion's start. More fundamentally, Ukraine's topography and its dominant patterns of civic life also elevated urban centres as crucial objectives of war. Aside from the Carpathian Mountains in the south-west, which did not feature at all in the ground war, much of Ukraine's expanse is relatively flat and its arable land is essential to its seasonal farming. However, only a minority of Ukrainians live rurally. Urbanisation prior to the invasion was around 70 per cent. According to a World Bank study of Ukraine's cities, 'Ukraine's urban system

---

[*] As assessed by the Institute of War in the opening month of the invasion: 'Main effort – Kyiv (comprised of three subordinate supporting efforts); Supporting effort 1 – Kharkiv; Supporting effort 1a – Luhansk Oblast; Supporting effort 2 – Mariupol and Donetsk Oblast; and Supporting effort 3 – Kherson and advances westward.'

is mainly composed of a large number of small towns and cities but most of the urban population lives in cities with more than 100,000 inhabitants.'[7] Of these cities, the top ten in terms of pre-war population, listed in descending order from the largest, were Kyiv, Kharkiv, Odessa, Dnipro, Donetsk, Zaporizhzhia, Lviv, Kryvyi Rih, Mykolaiv and Mariupol (with Luhansk in eleventh place).

In other words, Russia had invaded a place where control of the cities equated to control of the country. There were no commanding heights or natural resource fields to conquer that alone could compete with the importance of controlling Ukraine's cities. Parking tanks in empty farming fields could disrupt food supplies but it could not alone defeat Ukraine.

Consequently, Russian bombardments focused heavily on urban targets, whether delivered by its artillery or airstrikes or missiles. When they struck, Russia's Defence Ministry claimed it was hitting Ukraine's military infrastructure, but the reality of civilian deaths suggested otherwise.

Mayor Klitschko reported on the aftermath of one such attack on 18 March: 'Friends! Dear Kyivans! The enemy continues to attack the capital. In the morning, a residential area in the Podolsk district was shelled by orcs. One person died, nineteen were injured, including four children. Six houses, kindergartens and a school were damaged.'[8] The awful toll on civilians continued to mount.

In these opening weeks of the war, Kyiv's fate initially hung in the balance. If the capital city fell to the Russian invaders, it was likely that Putin could have announced victory right away. Of course, it did not pan out that way at all.

---

* Also of interest is that 'at the fall of the Soviet Union the West was mainly rural while the East had largely urbanized', indicating the amount of Soviet investment to industrialise and urbanise east Ukraine in particular.

SAVING KYIV AND CREATING A LEGEND

Gamblers go for big wins: Putin had ordered Russia's military to storm Kyiv, depose Ukraine's leadership and install a puppet regime that was subservient to Moscow. Ever the intelligence officer and no general himself, Putin wanted to keep secret the invasion date and ordered his army to begin from a cold start – quite literally for the tens of thousands of troops billeted over the winter in freezing, spartan camps in Belarus and western Russia. No advance warning was given to them that they should prepare to invade Ukraine on a given date. Putin's approach to mission command seemed better suited to launching a covert special forces raid in which handfuls of elite soldiers are kept on high readiness before being given a secret mission and a sudden 'go' order. This approach applied itself awkwardly to a huge invasion force staffed by a mixture of conscript and regular soldiers.

Moreover, by invading Ukraine from so many different directions, none of Russia's individual lines of advance seemed to be coordinated with the others. It was as if Putin had simply said on the morning of the invasion to each of his field commanders, 'First man to Kyiv wins,' and briefed them no further. Problems crept into Russia's invasion right from the get-go.

A spearhead of Russian forces reached Obolon, a neighbourhood in Kyiv's northern outskirts, in just two days of the invasion's launch. Russian military vehicles were filmed in Obolon's streets through the windows of terrified residents, but these lightly equipped Russian forces could not conquer the capital alone. Rather, these were probing attacks ahead of the arrival of a large Russian column, which was still driving down the main roads from Belarus, capturing the iconic town of Chernobyl along the way. So, to speed up their assault on Kyiv, the Russian military attempted yet another daring shortcut.

The town of Hostomel is in Kyiv's north-western outskirts and it houses Antonov Airport, which was used for cargo flights. In the first two days of the invasion, elite Russian forces mounted an airborne raid deep into enemy territory to seize this airstrip intact. The airstrip could then have been used to fly in reinforcements and supplies for Russia's assault on Kyiv. The VDV (the acronym for Russia's air assault troops) took a starring role in this ambitious operation, but it had seemingly been dreamed up by a scriptwriter rather than by a professional military planning staff. Russian gunships strafed Hostomel from the air and VDV troops arrived at the airport in helicopters as planned, but a fierce battle raged as Ukrainian troops counterattacked and pushed the Russians to the outskirts of the airport.

The VDV took heavy casualties in the battle for Hostomel.[9] Surviving VDV troops could have recited without irony these famous lines from Alfred Tennyson's poem 'The Charge of the Light Brigade', written about the 1850s Crimean war: 'Not though the soldier knew / Someone had blundered. / Theirs not to make reply, / Theirs not to reason why, / Theirs but to do and die.'

And what a strategic blunder the start of Russia's invasion was. First the VDV and then countless more Russian soldiers and officers from mechanised units advanced along the approach to Kyiv. They were fought to a standstill by Ukrainian defenders in the vicinity of a triumvirate of cities, Bucha, Irpin and Hostomel, which formed a shield to Kyiv.

The indomitable will of Ukrainians to defend their homeland and their inspirational political leadership under Zelensky were big factors in their tactical successes. The will to fight cannot win battles, however, and a number of other battle-boosting factors improved the effectiveness of Ukraine's forces in combat.

First, years of training delivered by British, American, Canadian and other military instructors had helped Ukrainian soldiers and officers practise NATO methods of operations since 2014. Typically, NATO armies place an emphasis on decentralised command structures and empowering the initiative of junior officers, the converse being the Soviet-era stereotype of an overly centralised command structure in which the initiative of junior officers is not well fostered. Ukraine's armed forces were still perceptibly shedding their Soviet legacy. Their most senior soldier in 2022, Chief of the General Staff Serhiy Shaptala, was Ukraine's first ever senior general to have begun his soldiering career *after* the USSR's demise. Lieutenant General Shaptala was born in 1973 and joined Ukraine's army in the 1990s, whereas his immediate predecessor, Serhiy Korniychuk, was born in 1965 and joined the old Soviet Red Army in 1982. This is not a comment on the latter's commitment to Ukraine, only an important marker of the passage of time.

The second reason for the Ukrainian military's prowess related to foreign-supplied weapons. Ukraine's arsenal was still mainly based on Soviet and Russian equipment but was also now being supplemented by other weapons. The US and UK rushed in some last-minute military supplies in the weeks prior to the invasion, with plane loads of man-portable anti-tank missiles and missile launchers arriving.[10] These weapons, light enough to be carried by individual soldiers as they hunted enemy vehicles in forests and in ruined cityscapes, included the US Javelin and the UK NLAW (Next Generation Light Anti-Armour Weapon). Such weapons proved potent against Russia's armoured personnel carriers (APCs) and T-72 main battle tanks (MBTs), which comprised a bedrock of the invasion force.

Separately, Ukraine had inked a deal with Turkey's government to purchase armed drones. Several of these Turkish-made *Bayraktar* TB2 medium-altitude unmanned aerial vehicles (UAVs) were already in Ukraine's arsenal before the invasion. In October 2021, Ukrainian Foreign Minister Dmytro Kuleba and Turkish Foreign Minister Mevlüt Çavuşoğlu agreed to build a factory in Ukraine to manufacture more Turkish armed UAVs.[11] While there may not have been time to outfit the factory before the invasion, the TB2 drone proved effective in destroying Russian armoured vehicles, targeting them from high in the sky as they were stuck in slow-moving convoys. These and several other technical and tactical military factors helped Ukrainian soldiers to even the odds against the invading Russians.

* * *

By mid-March, three weeks into the invasion, a dichotomy had arisen in Russia's military progress. In Ukraine's more sparsely populated and less defended south, Russia's troops had made swift progress in their advance, but in the north, Russian troops were stuck at the gates of Kyiv and Kharkiv, not daring to enter in force and mainly bombarding from a distance. When Russian military vehicles did drive into these cities they were hunted by Ukrainian forces armed with Western-supplied anti-tank missiles. Kharkiv, Ukraine's second city, experienced a botched air assault in which Russian paratroopers landed and fought intense street battles, but never managed to capture the city.[12] Ukraine's armed forces were exploiting the defender's advantage in cities like Kharkiv, exploiting their knowledge of the terrain and their occupation of the high ground to destroy the advancing Russian troops before they could dig in. The Russians therefore resorted to bombing the city from a distance.

Kyiv was always going to be a tough prospect for Russian forces to fully encircle and assault. Kyiv's pre-war population of 2.8 million was nearly twice that of Kharkiv and three times that of Odessa, the next largest Ukrainian cities. Kyiv had some natural defensive properties as a sprawling city divided by the Dnieper River and its tributaries.[13] The iconic locations of the Verkhovna Rada, Maidan Square, Khreshchatyk Street and St Sophia Cathedral are on the western side of the Dnieper. No doubt Kyiv's defenders had planned numerous scenarios in case Russian troops entered the city in force to capture these symbolic sites. Mayor Klitschko reflected on the tank traps littering the streets: 'I can't recognise my own city, with all the emptiness, barricades and blocks.'[14]

The battle for the control of Kyiv never came. So stuck had the Russian column become at the city's outskirts that Putin, ever the gambler, cut his losses. And these were significant losses indeed. By late March, Western governments estimated Russia had lost twenty battalion tactical groups (BTGs) out of a total of between 115 and 120 that were deployed at the start of the invasion.[15] The BTG was the Russian army's chief fighting formation, with each BTG numbering 800 personnel at full strength alongside dozens of their armoured vehicles, and trained for manoeuvre warfare (i.e. taking the initiative and attacking).

No major set-piece battles awaited. Kursk, a city in Russia famed for being the site of the greatest tank battle of all time, was 220 kilometres away from Kharkiv, known for its tank factories of old. But no tank battles of even a hundredth the scale of Kursk in 1943 now took place. The Ukrainians had funnelled the Russians into smaller pockets before pouncing. The Russians had seemingly funnelled themselves by invading with so many different lines of attack, with no apparent supreme commander to coordinate these advances.

The reasons for Russia's early military failures were legion: overly optimistic campaign planning by the Russian General Staff; poor logistics in support of stretched supply lines; poor morale and lack of readiness amongst Russian soldiers; a lack of close air support to cover Russia's ground advances; and a lack of cyber and electronic warfare support to disable and confuse Ukraine's defenders. It seemed like an analogue invasion in a digitally enabled age. Putin had seemingly concocted no more sophisticated a battlefield strategy than to roll his army into Kyiv and Kharkiv and to watch the Ukrainians fall to their knees. No proper accounting was made of enemy morale, tactics and the impact of the provision of outside weapons, let alone an honest assessment of the effectiveness of Russia's armed forces.

On 24 March, the one-month anniversary of the invasion, Russia's Defence Ministry ordered an embarrassing about-face. Russian Colonel-General Sergei Rudskoy declared 'Phase One' of the invasion complete since 'the combat potential of the Ukrainian armed forces has been significantly reduced', although this claim was clearly nonsense given how doggedly Ukraine was fighting back. Colonel-General Rudskoy also admitted in this briefing that 1,351 Russian personnel had been killed and 3,825 injured. Ukraine's military gave a figure at the time that was ten times higher and the true figure was likely in between these claims. Regardless, Russia's huge losses of men and materiel put a stop to their march to Kyiv. Rudskoy now said, 'Our forces and means will concentrate on the main thing – the complete liberation of Donbas.'[16] It would be several weeks until Russia reconstituted its battered forces in the Donbas to begin 'Phase Two' of its offensive.

As Russia's land forces redeployed, an embarrassing disaster struck its navy on 18 April. The pride of Russia's Black Sea Fleet, the guided missile cruiser *Moskva*, was hit by Ukrainian shore-based anti-ship missiles.*[17] Images of the listing ship made their way online, becoming a visual metaphor for the creaking Russian war machine. The *Moskva* eventually sank, sending an unspecified number of its crew to a watery grave, providing a symbolic coda to this phase of Russia's invasion.

Having successfully defended its two biggest cities, Kyiv and Kharkiv, and having sunk a Russian flagship, Ukraine's armed forces created a legend, one that touched all kinds of treasured emotions and well-known story arcs. To fight for freedom against the odds. To resist wherever possible the jackboot of tyranny. To triumph against authoritarians and barbarians alike.

If only it were that simple.

CRAWLING ACROSS THE DONBAS

To explain the twists and turns of this war, a rudimentary education in the difference between a 'plan' and a 'strategy' is useful. A plan is something typically put together in peacetime, whether simple or complex, and it involves breaking down the component parts of the task at hand for completing a goal. We have work plans, exercise plans, holiday plans, complex plans for giant engineering projects, and so on – whenever we have a task requiring forethought, we draw up a plan. A mere *plan*, however, is little use in wartime. Enter

---

* According to the IISS naval and aerospace experts Nick Childs and Douglas Barrie, '*Moskva* had several layers of defensive armament. But these defences, as well as their supporting sensors and combat systems, were all elderly and the extent to which they had been maintained and were operational is uncertain.'

the notion of *strategy*, which differs in crucial aspects: strategic be-haviour involves confounding a deadly opponent who is trying to kill and humiliate you and to block your goals.[18]

Strategists old and new, from the Prussian soldier-philosopher Clausewitz to modern theorists of war, are at pains to explain the difference between peacetime and wartime activities. Several modern strategy writers express this point in different ways, like Edward Luttwak[19] and Lawrence Freedman.[20] The late Professor Colin Gray is cited here thanks to the pithy title of his article, 'Why Strategy is Difficult', a truism the Kremlin was being reacquainted with days into the invasion.[21]

'Strategy is the application of common sense to the conduct of war. The difficulty lies in the execution,' writes Gray. Why is this? 'Strategy is neither policy nor armed combat; rather it is the bridge between them.' Using this distinction we can locate Russia's chosen policy ends (regime change at first; occupation of Ukrainian land; and forcing Kyiv to accept Moscow's superiority). We can locate Russia's violent tools (land invasion, artillery, air and missile attacks against Ukraine's military and infrastructure, terrorising its civil-ians, and so on). The 'strategy' is how violence is wielded to advance these goals.

Gray carries on: 'Strategy is perilously complex by nature. Every element or dimension can impact all others.' Since strategy involves the application of organised violence to further political ends in the face of setbacks, enemy action and the fog of war, it is 'extraordi-narily difficult, perhaps impossible, to train strategists' because 'no educational system puts in what nature leaves out'. As such, 'Com-petence shown by rising politicians or soldiers in their particular trade is not proof of an aptitude for strategy. The strategist has to be expert in using the threat or use of force for policy ends, not in thinking up desirable policy ends or fighting skilfully.'

Vladimir Putin had a problem: he was no strategic military genius. Sure, he had presided over a run of past wartime victories – often at huge costs in lives – in Chechnya, Georgia, Crimea and Syria, but the all-out invasion of Ukraine was a magnitude of military ambition beyond anything he had attempted before. Putin began casting around for blame. Were Russia's military difficulties in Ukraine the fault of Defence Minister Sergei Shoigu? Curiously enough, despite a penchant for military uniforms, Shoigu had never been a military professional and was previously Russia's Civilian Emergencies Minister. Was it the fault of Chief of the General Staff General Gerasimov? For a decade he had presided over Russia's military operations, but the Ukrainian invasion plan of 2022 had seemingly been influenced by other former spies, including Nikolai Patrushev, favoured by Putin in his inner clique of decision-makers, likely eclipsing the advice of the professional military men like Gerasimov – or perhaps Gerasimov became carried away after too long in post and had ceased applying the common sense mentioned by Gray.

A shake-up was in order. In April, Putin appointed General Aleksandr Dvornikov the supreme commander of the invasion force, based on his reputation for leading the Russian task force in Syria to a successful start to that campaign back in 2015–16. Before Dvornikov's appointment in Ukraine, Russia's invasion forces had no single supreme battlefield mastermind, only a 100-mile screwdriver operated in Moscow, which delayed decision-making and eroded coordination between the invading elements.[22]

By the start of May, a dozen Russian generals had already been killed in the field, and Putin now relieved of their command senior figures who had lived to tell the tale of the invasion's botched start. Lieutenant General Serhiy Kisel of the 1st Guards Tank Army was fired for failing to capture Kharkiv, as was the Black Sea Fleet commander Vice-Admiral Igor Osipov, under whose watch the *Moskva* sank.[23] By June, rumours abounded that Dvornikov had also been replaced. Would these changes in personnel and strategy change Russia's military fortunes?

*   *   *

Russia's renewed offensive in the Donbas got off to such a slow start in April and May that one could easily have been deceived into thinking that Ukraine was heading to an all-out victory. Since the Ukrainians had been fighting in the Donbas for eight years their positions were well dug in, comprising concrete fortifications as well as trenches and defensive positions in small villages from which they had held the line since 2014–15. As Russia reconstituted its battered combat battalions, the first major battle in the Donbas would be fought at the southern tip of the Donetsk Oblast.

The southern port city of Mariupol had been coveted by Russia since 2015 since it offered a land bridge between occupied Crimea and the Donbas. This time, Russian forces advanced to Mariupol from its western side, but they still met a granite wall of Ukrainian defence.

The Ukrainians refused to give up for three long months, and the Russian military responded with a horrifying amount of shelling that levelled Mariupol, killed scores of its residents and forced the remaining defenders to hunker down in Mariupol's most defensible redoubt: the huge Azovstal steel plant. Here, Ukrainians including those from the Azov Battalion used the steel plant's subterranean tunnels to prepare defensive positions. As Zelensky confirmed, Ukrainian aircraft had maintained daring resupply efforts to their surrounded comrades trapped in the steel plant: 'Heroic pilots, who knew it was difficult, knew how to fly to Azovstal and bring them medicine, food, water, pick up the bodies of the wounded, it is almost impossible.' Zelensky added sombrely, 'We lost a lot of pilots there.'[24]

From inside the steel plant, Ukrainian commanders filmed harrowing video messages to convey their will to fight and the increasingly desperate conditions they were trapped in. Many of the Ukrainian troops were wounded, some seriously, and as the Russians tightened the noose around the steel plant, something had to give. This was old-fashioned siege warfare and on 20 May, Russian forces finally broke the defence. The remaining Ukrainian defenders surrendered and the Russians took them as prisoners, shipping them to prison facilities in the DPR. The siege of Mariupol bought time for Ukrainian forces elsewhere to prepare their defences, but its final outcome now galvanised the Russian offensive.

*　　*　　*

The complete conquest of the Luhansk and Donetsk Oblasts was the next Russian war aim. Here, the nature of the urbanisation in the Donbas is important to note: the separatist republics were centred around the cities of Donetsk and Luhansk and together with Mariupol were the three largest Donbas cities. The remaining cities were smaller, such as Severodonetsk in Luhansk Oblast, Kramatorsk and Sloviansk in Donetsk Oblast, each of which used to have around 100,000–150,000 inhabitants. Some of these cities had witnessed battles in 2014, but now, one by one, they fell to a ponderous and mercilessly destructive Russian advance. Gone were the days of the 'thunder runs' (US military slang for a swift attack on something held by the enemy) into Kyiv. Now, the Russian army purposefully slowed itself to a crawl, advancing under the cover of its artillery support, pounding specific locations one by one along the front line.

The Russian advance was a horrible spectacle to behold. It brought to mind the merciless advice of Niccolò Machiavelli, who advised his titular *Prince* on brutality in military conquests:

> There is no surer way of keeping possession than by devastation. Whoever becomes master of a city accustomed to freedom, and does not destroy it, may expect to be destroyed himself, because, when there is a rebellion, such activity justifies itself by calling on the name of liberty, and its ancient institutions, never forgotten ... [The] new ruler must determine all the injuries that he will need to inflict. He must inflict them once and for all, and not have to renew them every day.[25]

Machiavelli may have recognised what was happening in the Donbas. There was little left of Mariupol, Severodonetsk and the other locations at which Russia directed its big guns.[26] Resistance was being obliterated in a manner reminiscent of how the Russian military had assaulted the Chechen capital of Grozny two decades prior. In the Chechen example, after utterly devastating Grozny, Putin had orchestrated a reconstruction effort of the ruined city on the basis of funding local vassals.[27] It remained to be seen whether the Russian government could repeat this trick in Ukraine and beat off the Ukrainian counterattacks that would come.

In summing up the shift from trying to capture Kyiv and Kharkiv to fighting in the Donbas, Putin had been forced to abide by an important strategic tenet: shrink your strategic goals instead of sticking doggedly to impossible ones. Those who were willing Putin's invasion to fail derided the shift in goals as an embarrassing exercise in saving face – it was certainly this, but shifting to less ambitious aims had, in the short term, rescued Russia's war effort. As I wrote at the time in the *Wall Street Journal*:

> Goal moderation can be a sensible way to stay in the fight on more advantageous terms [...] Putin will be desperate to emerge from the war with something to show for it to counter internal critics who see this as a botched invasion. If he moderates his strategic goals, there are two logical outcomes of Russia's campaign: Either Russia will 'butcher and bolt' by withdrawing on terms at least partly favourable to some Russian objectives, or its forces will remain and bisect a greater portion of Ukraine.[28]

Prediction in matters of war is a fool's game, and the Russia–Ukraine war could take any number of turns in the future. At the time of writing, Russia's hyper-destructive crawl across the Donbas has conquered Luhansk and is turning its guns on Donetsk. At the time of reading, a different reality will present itself. Before drawing the narrative of this book to a close, we must consider one last vitally important feature of the invasion's beginnings.

WAR CRIMES MEAN NO PEACE TALKS

'Ukraine is a crime scene,' said the chief prosecutor of the International Criminal Court, Karim Khan, after he visited Bucha to see for himself the human toll of Russia's short occupation on Kyiv's outskirts. The graves were still being dug for the people of Bucha who lost their lives to both long-range bombardments and alleged short-range executions. A 42-member ICC team had arrived with forensic investigators, sent from their headquarters in the Hague, to 'advance our investigations into crimes falling into the jurisdiction of the International Criminal Court and provide support to Ukrainian national authorities', according to Kahn.[29] When asked if the chain of command could be cited as a defence by Russian service personnel involved in alleged atrocities, Kahn responded firmly. 'Nuremberg established it; superior orders is not a defence', he said of the culpability of Russian soldiers involved in the killings, from the lowest-ranked all the way to their commanding officers and political masters.[30] Sure enough, Ukraine began legal proceedings against a 21-year-old captured Russian soldier, Vadim Shishimarin, who admitted his guilt in shooting a 62-year-old Ukrainian civilian in the invasion's early days.[31]

Meanwhile, counterclaims voiced by Russian officials asserted that the images and footage of atrocities in Bucha and elsewhere had been faked. Russia's ambassador to the UK, Andrei Kelin, when asked in a BBC interview about certain specific incidents in which Russian soldiers were alleged to have murdered civilians in Ukraine, retorted by citing a different matter, claiming without evidence that the Ukrainian armed forces had been shelling the residents of the Donbas for eight years, as if finding some kind of false equivalence to justify his country's invasion.[32] The Russian state was certainly not going to give up its service personnel willingly to face foreign trials.

As with the prior MH17 trial and its naming of Russian suspects still at large, like Igor Girkin for the role in shooting down the Malaysia airliner in 2014, this was the problem: unless putting a prisoner of war on trial, like Vadim Shishimarin in May 2022, how would Ukrainian authorities or the Hague get their hands on those guilty in absentia? This would be a matter of importance in the post-war phase, whenever that phase came, and it would shape relations with Russia for a long time to come. Moreover, the pursuit of conflict justice could also affect the prospects for peace talks, which, rather surprisingly, had got under way within four days of the start of the invasion.

*   *   *

In Ukrainian parlance, liberated territories referred to places such as Bucha, occupied by Russia at the start of the 24 February 2022 invasion and from which Russian forces had since withdrawn. Occupied territories referred on one hand to places captured by Russian forces after 24 February 2022 that were still being held and on the other hand to territories occupied by Russian forces and their proxies since 2014, meaning the original DPR and LPR, which covered less than half the Donbas and Crimea. Finally, there was an unknowable amount of further territory that Russia still coveted control of.

Occupation and liberation. Garrisoning and withdrawing. This was the currency in which peace talks would ultimately be trading. In some places, currency was quite literally the issue at play, since the Ukraine's hryvnia had already been replaced by Russia's rouble in some occupied territories. Kherson, the southern city close to Crimea, had been captured early on in the 2022 invasion. Russian forces fought for control of the Antonovskiy Bridge, which crossed the Dnieper River and served as a gateway to the whole Kherson Oblast, and eventually used the bridge crossing to surround Kherson city in early March. By May, there was talk of the rouble being introduced in Kherson, and the Ukrainian mayor had been replaced with Russian administrators.[33]

Elsewhere in southern Ukraine, in the partially occupied Zaporizhzhia Oblast, Zaporizhzhia city itself remained in Ukrainian government control but Russia had captured the Zaporizhzhia nuclear power plant located on the south side of the Dnieper River. Russian officials even suggested that the nuclear plant, which was the largest in Europe, and that was now operated by Ukrainian staff in Russian captivity, would supply power to Russia and not Ukraine.[34] Such was the map of control in July 2022, before Ukrainian counterattacks to regain lost territory had got under way.

Zelensky often repeated a mantra: Ukraine would never willingly trade any of its land away. This created a dilemma: did Ukraine want to push the Russian presence back to the so-called 23 February 2022 line, representing the old front line that ran across the Donetsk and Luhansk Oblasts to demarcate the original territories of the DPR and LPR? This would be nearly impossible to redraw, since it was in places rather arbitrary, bisecting villages and reflecting the swing of offensives and retreats back in 2014–15. Or did Ukraine want to return to the pre-2014 line? In this case, Ukraine would regain control of the whole Donbas region, as well as Crimea, restoring its 1991 borders.

Putin, initially confident he could impose a victor's peace on Ukraine, had dispatched his chief negotiator Vladimir Medinsky (whom we first encountered in Chapter 1) to meet Ukrainian officials on 28 February. The Russian side suggested Minsk as the location for the talks, but the Ukrainian side demurred, given the association between Minsk and the past failed peace deals, and the role of Belarus's authorities as abetters of the Russian invasion. The Ukrainian government assembled a high-powered delegation for the talks, including presidential advisor Mykhailo Podolyak and Defence Minister Oleksii Reznikov, who met Medinsky's team in Belarus's south-east Gomel region, close to where the Russia–Belarus–Ukraine borders meet. At this first meeting, Medinsky's delegation denigrated Zelensky's government as illegitimate.

However, in later rounds of the talks and as battlefield fortunes faltered, Russia's delegation walked back from its maximalist demand of regime change. The second round of talks in Belarus on 3 March yielded a flawed agreement on humanitarian corridors for civilians to leave besieged Ukrainian cities, although Ukraine had to reject a Russian suggestion for evacuation routes to Russia and Belarus before evacuations could begin – even then, some evacuations were conducted under Russian bombing. The third round was held on 7 March, again in Belarus, and the talks moved online for later rounds.[35] At this time, Leonid Slutsky of the Russian side said, 'If we compare the positions of both delegations at the start of the talks and now, we see significant progress.'[36] And in Mykhailo Podolyak's words, 'There are fundamental contradictions but there is certainly room for compromise.'[37]

Although there was still much fighting to be done before there could be any kind of deal, the very fact of direct bilateral talks was noteworthy. In some wars, it can take years for the opposing sides to want to meet face to face and, even then, an entire global industry of international peace mediation exists in bodies such as the UN and the OSCE to offer an impartial middle-person linkage. In the most severe cases of bitterness and extreme distrust between the warring sides, the mediators can operate so-called 'proximity talks' in which delegations from either side are parked in nearby rooms so that they do not have to see each other, and the impartial mediators usher messages between them. (The UN 'Geneva Process' talks in the Syrian civil war operated on such a basis, to keep the Assad regime apart from the anti-Assad rebels during the talks.)

Even if the governments of Ukraine and Russia were willing to meet face to face right away, it would require international mediation to move the talks forward. Turkey stepped in: Foreign Minister Mevlüt Çavuşoğlu brought to Turkey's Antalya region the Russian Foreign Minister Lavrov and his Ukrainian counterpart Kuleba on 10 March. The opening of Turkish-mediated talks will be recalled for Lavrov's baffling claim that while Russia is not planning to attack any other countries, Russia 'did not attack Ukraine either'.[38] Lavrov's words reminded everyone of the propensity of senior Russian officials to engage in barefaced lying. These were still one-sided talks in which the Russian side wanted the violent punishments it was inflicting on Ukraine to translate into concessions. Kremlin spokesman Dmitry Peskov said that Russia's war could stop 'in a moment', but only if Kyiv ceased its military operations; amended its constitution to forswear future NATO membership and state its neutrality; accepted Crimea as Russian territory; and recognised the DPR and LPR as independent states. It all seemed to be an exercise in futility since Zelensky was ruling out at this time any territorial concessions to Russia.[39]

Everything still hinged on events on the battlefield, not on the talks. The former would dictate the latter, but the parallel pursuit of talks alongside the fighting was already an important facet of this war.

QUESTIONING THE LEGEND

A legend is a difficult thing to live up to. Surely we should all root for Ukraine's valiant armed forces to repeat their triumphant counteroffensives at the start of the war by repelling the Russian orcs from every inch of illegally occupied territory? Even if stuck in a war of attrition, should we keep feeding the Ukrainian war machine so that it can hold the Russians at bay? And, given what a shambolic and immoral mess Putin's invasion has been, wouldn't just deserts be served if his regime crumbled at home under the pressures of the war?

After all, Russian history shows similar chain reactions: in 1905, when Tsar Nicholas II's navy was sunk by Japan's navy at Tsushima Strait, catalysing discontent at home that led to a failed revolt against the Tsar; in 1917, when Nicholas II led the Russian army to defeat in the Great War and then lost the entire Romanov Dynasty to revolution; and more recently, in 1989, when the Soviet Union's defeat in Afghanistan played a role in weakening the Gorbachev regime and further eroded the already crumbling edifice of the USSR.

One must never rule out any outcome and it will be for future writers to reflect on what is yet to come. Those certain of any particular outcome should perhaps think again as to the sheer variety of outcomes that could result. For instance, a veritable army of Twitter-housed armchair pundits egg the Ukrainian military on and try to 'cancel' people who suggest that there may one day be a negotiated outcome by shaming them as 'appeasers'. However, the shifting fortunes of the war, and the Putin regime's determination to exit the war with something to show for it, suggest that a disappointment awaits those yearning for total Ukrainian victory.

In his *Time* interview, Zelensky was asked if he regretted his choice to remain in Kyiv and lead his country so valiantly in the face of such terror. 'Not for a second,' responded Zelensky, before wisely caveating that he has no idea how the war will end or what his place in history will ultimately be.[40] Who knows who has it inside of themselves to make a stand when the time comes? Will they buckle under the pressure? Run away, perhaps? Or will they stand and fight? We all like to think we would do the right thing if the time came to make a stand. But Zelensky, if he stays in power, may one day have to make difficult decisions on behalf of Ukraine and consequently may see his lustre vanish in the eyes of some people. It is too early to say how history will judge him. But the transition from hero to antihero can be a swift one.

Dare you question the legend of Ukrainian heroism and the moral clarity of Ukraine's war against the Russian invader? But dare you also question the beastly durability of Russia's armed forces? This is a story still in full swing, and the final roll calls of heroes and antiheroes may yet take years to reveal themselves.

CHAPTER 10

ROAD TO RUIN

A REFLECTION ON HOPE

SURVIVING BLEAK TIMES

Whatever else it ushers in, war always brings an abundance of loss and ruin.

In the first Donbas war that lasted from March 2014 until February 2022, an estimated 14,200 people lost their lives. This included 3,404 civilians (the majority of whom, 3,039 in all, including those on the downed MH-17 flight, were killed in the most active phase of the war in 2014–15, before the situation settled into a still-deadly semi-dormancy).[1] Ukraine suffered nearly 5,000 military fatalities, the remainder being from the Russian-backed armed groups. And this was *before* Russia's all-out invasion.

In 2022, the UN High Commissioner for Human Rights reported 11,544 civilian casualties in Ukraine, with 5,024 people killed and 6,520 injured between 24 February and 12 July. Many children featured amongst the casualties and, said the UN, 'most of the civilian casualties recorded were caused by the use of explosive weapons with a wide impact area, including shelling from heavy artillery and multiple launch rocket systems, and missile and air strikes'.[2] In other words, their streets and homes and evacuation routes had been pounded by indiscriminate shell fire. The true death toll was likely higher than the UN was able to record. And it should never go without saying: behind each life lost or shattered are dreams ended and futures stolen by the cruel hand of Russia's war.

The war has also been a catastrophe for thousands of Russian families learning of their lost or seriously injured sons, husbands and fathers. The human stories of those helping to care for injured and traumatised veterans will, for years to come, play out in parallel on both sides of the Russian–Ukrainian border, wherever that border may one day be drawn at such a cost in lives.

I shudder to think what the rising death toll may amount to by the time the war ends. The dead bodies I saw on the streets of Kramatorsk, when I was present in that Donbas city during a cluster bomb attack on 10 February 2015, always remind me that abstract talk of strategy and geopolitical contest translates to a very human reality. On that day the Russian side attempted to destroy the local Ukrainian military HQ at Kramatorsk airfield, but the horrible inaccuracy of their missiles also left eight civilians dead, some killed metres from where my colleagues and I happened to be standing. Their bodies lay next to windows shattered and branches scythed from trees by the explosions, while a pair of rocket fins were left protruding from the ground outside No. 42 Lenin Street and No. 37 Kramatorsk Boulevard.[3] I lived in Kramatorsk back then, and I was heartbroken to learn of Russia's next missile strike on the city, on 8 April 2022, this time targeting the railway station and killing fifty-nine civilians. Children were amongst them, and surely some of these people were trying to get away from the war zone that day. Ultimately, war is a ghastly affair. Through this ghastliness, our most basic human instincts must be activated when we think about Ukraine, asking ourselves why it came to this.

FOR UKRAINE

Just as the Orange Revolution in 2004 proved to be a precursor to the more violent Revolution of Dignity a decade later, so too had Russia's hybrid war of 2014 proven a nasty dress rehearsal for its invasion eight years later. With the benefit of this historical overview, we can see how Ukraine's vulnerability to Russian aggression grew over this time, with Putin's mania heightening every time Ukraine tried to solidify relations with the West.

The longer span of Ukraine's history shows how its leaders often had to pick one side when opposing empires faced off over Ukrainian territory. Consider the widely varying stories of Bohdan Khmelnytsky, the Zaporozhian Cossack leader who sided with the Russian Empire against the Polish–Lithuanian Commonwealth in the seventeenth century, and who picked the winning side in this contest. Of Ivan Mazepa, a later Zaporozhian Hetman who picked the losing side when he chose the Swedes and Poles against the Russian Empire in the eighteenth century. Of Stepan Bandera, the controversial figure who tried to side with Nazi Germany against the USSR in the twentieth century...

The characters are less significant than the broad historical pattern, of Ukraine caught in the middle of rival behemoths and picking a side. This remains true today. In the past thirty years, Ukraine was slowly surrounded by an expanding NATO on one side and a resurgently imperialistic Russia on the other side. The yearnings of leaders like Yushchenko, Poroshenko and Zelensky for Ukraine's entry into NATO is understandable in light of this, but the degree to which the path was ever really open is questionable. At times in years gone by, Western ideologues and geopolitical mavens have indeed ushered Ukraine to join, but the political realities of NATO membership have precluded entry. Now, Russia has played the ultimate veto of all-out war, and the prospects of eventual Ukrainian membership of NATO feels remote, since a new member state cannot be admitted in the midst of waging an armed conflict.

'NATO Article 5 in the Donbas' – imagine for one moment that, somehow, Ukraine's military strike such terrifying counterblows against the invading and occupying Russians that Moscow has to withdraw its forces; that Ukraine rebuilds with Western help; restores intact its borders of 1991; and eventually joins the NATO alliance as a reward for its sterling war effort against the Russians. Now, with Ukraine a member of the alliance, NATO's Article 5 collective defence intervention would be triggered if there was ever renewed fighting in the Donbas, right on Russia's doorstep. Sounds fanciful, doesn't it? Even with the passage of years or decades, such eventualities seem unrealistic. Sweden and Finland may have joined NATO in 2022, and as they did so, Putin distinguished Ukraine as a different and special case. In Putin's words, unlike Sweden and Finland, Ukraine is used as a platform for activities to destabilise Russia itself. Even if his claim is dismissed as nonsense, it is reasonable to posit that Putin wants to make blocking Ukraine's entry into NATO a generational undertaking handed down to future Russian rulers.

Ukraine's membership into the EU, conversely, received a boost in June 2022 when it was granted candidacy status. Ukraine, alongside tiny Moldova, which itself has been destabilised by Russia's invasion, received the good news from the President of the European Council Charles Michel. This was a big success for Zelensky after he relaunched Ukraine's bid to join the EU soon after Russia's invasion began. Sympathy for Ukraine was running high in Brussels, with

EU states such as Poland receiving scores of refugees, and much of the EU (aside from hold-outs like Hungary) trying to shut off energy purchases from Russia. The time was clearly right for a grand gesture by Brussels that promised Ukraine a hopeful future and that admonished Russia for its brutality.

However, French President Emmanuel Macron's comments in Strasbourg in May poured cold water over what EU candidacy status for Ukraine means. 'We all know perfectly well that the process to allow [Ukraine] to join would take several years indeed, probably several decades,' he said, adding, 'That is the truth, unless we decide to lower the standards for accession. And rethink the unity of our Europe.'[4] Dutch Prime Minister Mark Rutte said that he was reassured of the viability of candidacy status for Ukraine only after the European Commission drew up 'a tough assessment' that was 'brutally honest with Ukraine' about the reforms it still needed to enact to join the EU.[5] All of this was being asked of a country in wartime.

EU membership for Ukraine was still only a small light at the end of a long tunnel.

A premonition of permanent division

There are two big implications arising from these developments. First, a pledge of Ukrainian 'neutrality' that satisfies Russia is impossible to imagine. Ukraine's imperative to align with the West has been hastened by the invasion, by the need to receive Western funds for rebuilding Ukraine, and many more reasons besides. So, Russia will never be happy with Ukraine's path under Zelensky, or any leader like him.

Second, assuming the Ukraine of the future tilts towards the West, will it do so territorially intact? What will be left of Ukraine? A whole country, the outlines of which were traced at the moment of independence in December 1991? Or a moth-eaten country with an even larger set of 'temporarily occupied territories' to contend with? Only time will tell, and some parts of occupied Ukraine would now require considerable efforts to fully reintegrate into the rest of the country even if they returned to Kyiv's control, not least due to the sheer number of Russian passports and amount of propaganda pumped into the DPR, LPR and Crimea over many years, and the recent privations experienced by places like occupied Kherson.

Partition – another pattern in Ukraine's long history – may again rear its head. To be clear, I am not calling for partition, only pointing out that it may become a de facto reality. Zelensky and the Ukrainian armed forces will fight hard to prevent this. But if they are anything less than totally successful, the implications are worth considering. There is an instructive precedent in an example from elsewhere in Europe that is worth citing as one possible, albeit chilling, vision of Ukraine's future.

Divided Cyprus may end up offering a more instructive analogy to Ukraine than any number of mentions of World War Two heroics of 'standing alone' during a 'finest hour'.* Notwithstanding the island geography of Cyprus as a mismatch for Ukraine's vaster inland expanse, and all that has changed in forty-eight years, do bear with the analogy to discover its worth.

Turkey invaded Cyprus in 1974 to preclude the call by some Greeks and Greek Cypriots for 'Enosis', or unification between Cyprus and Greece. Calls for Enosis heightened after Cyprus gained independence from the British Empire in 1960, fostering paranoia in Turkey over losing Cyprus to its bitter rival, Greece. Turkey's

---

* The 1940–41 comparison is likely to get stuck at the 'lend lease' stage, since, while financial aid and weaponry is being provided from afar, there are no Allies to enter the fray late in the day and fight shoulder to shoulder with Ukraine.

invading army, however, made only partial military gains, pushing the front line to about a third of the island. Since then, the government in Ankara has sustained the 'Turkish Republic of Northern Cyprus' despite the reluctance of other countries to recognise the 'TRNC' (which may remind you of the DPR and LPR). Indeed, back when I worked at the UK Foreign Office as a junior desk officer on the Cyprus issue, we used inverted commas when referencing the 'TRNC', lest we accidentally suggest it had been officially recognised. Turkish military bases remain in the 'TRNC' to this day and the buffer zone with the Republic of Cyprus is policed by UN peacekeepers. A UN 'Special Representative of the Secretary General' keeps the dialogue going between the two parts of Cyprus. This division is astonishing to behold – it runs right through Nicosia at one point, with abandoned shops and houses a grim exhibit to the people who fled the fighting in 1974. Intriguingly, this division did not stop the Republic of Cyprus from joining the European Union in 2004. Over time, divided Cyprus evolved into a lasting feature on Europe's political map and has faded from many active memories as a seemingly unresolvable conflict.

Division is a horrifying prospect for Ukraine. Russia's armed forces may well want to make another attempt at sacking Kyiv, but if they cannot, they may seek as a compensation prize a stretch of occupied land from the Donbas to Crimea, transforming this into a permanent division. Would this preclude the rest of western and central Ukraine from entering the EU itself? Would cities like Lviv, Ivano-Frankivsk and Kyiv become cosmopolitan hubs of European reconstruction funds and tourism, while Donetsk, Luhansk and Mariupol remain in Russia's bosom? Ukraine would become an equivalent of divided Germany for the twenty-first century, the focus of a new Cold War between the West and Russia.

I hope this is not the case. It is a bleak prognosis for Ukraine, which is no stranger to past divisions. If you think such an outcome unlikely, please be warned that the history of wars of identity waged at the twilight of empires suggests otherwise.

As a closing thought on Ukraine's future, there is a bitter irony at play in fighting to exorcise the malign hand of post-Soviet Russian interference, but doing so in the name of restoring Ukraine's 1991 border, which itself is a Soviet inheritance. The border of the old Ukrainian Soviet Socialist Republic does not look very different from the 'intact Ukraine' that would be restored if Russia is kicked out entirely. It is more likely that a new Ukraine one day emerges, with its national character and its borders hardened and reshaped by the war. Perhaps only then can the transcendence from Ukraine's imperial past be completed.

FOR RUSSIA

Vladimir Putin thinks that Russian-speaking parts of Ukraine belong to a Moscow-centred Slavic civilisation state, and that Ukraine as a whole must pledge fealty in perpetuity to Russia – but will his successors think the same? Putin may one day experience a Stalin-like demise in which his death is hidden for some time, as successors square off against each other for the spoils of the empire. Or perhaps Putin will organise a managed transition to another veteran of Russia's security services, who continues waging both the war in Ukraine and the wider struggle against the phantom 'liberal hegemony' that Russia sees being imposed by the USA and its allies. As Putin enters his seventieth year at the time of writing – just four years shy of Stalin's age at death – the world wonders how long he will last.

It is easy to point and laugh at how many times Putin has

blundered in Ukraine, losing Russia's sway of influence in the outcome of the Orange Revolution before regaining it under Yanukovych in 2010, only to lose it all again when the Maidan Revolution of Dignity reset the political clock in Kyiv. And indeed, it is easy to tut at Putin's failure to force the Ukrainian government into implementing the Minsk peace deals of 2014 and 2015 at the barrel of a gun, just as one may also consider the 2022 invasion to be a botched job that can lead only to Russia's ruin.

Not so fast. Before getting too complacent in these narratives, we must also look at the parallel track of the US approach to managing NATO expansion in the late 1990s and 2000s, and how this also blundered when it came to Ukraine. NATO expansion may well have 'saved' numerous former Soviet satellite states by plucking them away from the Russian sphere of influence, and it may now have also 'saved' Sweden and Finland – but these successes were ultimately purchased at Ukraine's expense. Ukraine's territory is where Russia has drawn its blood-drenched red line over NATO's eastward expansion, and Ukrainians are the people who are dying not only for their own freedom and sovereignty but also for the right of NATO to expand right onto Russia's borders. Long after Putin, the Russian security state may continue to interpret the expansion of NATO as synonymous with the expansion of Western hegemony at the expense of Russia's say over Europe's future. The only say Russia used to have involved selling copious amounts of gas to European countries, and this may now have also ended.

The expansion of NATO has certainly influenced the evolution of Russian nationalism and given it endless, often baseless excuses to define the terms of Putin's challenge to Ukraine and to the West. Putin's Russia is now mounting an open civilisational revolt against Western-led hegemonic uniformity.

Even if you don't agree with a single word that I've written in the preceding paragraphs, Putin's followers subscribe to a version of these narratives, so please take note of them. Seeing the same events through different eyes remains the hardest task in human affairs, whether these are of matters mundane or profound. We tend to interpret major world events through our own values, sensibilities, and cherished subjective interpretations of history. Universality is a dangerous thing to subscribe to if you want to understand the world's biggest disputes and their myriad complexities.

In 1991, Russia lost the empire of the USSR, but it was not a defeated power. At that time, Russia's future as a European security actor and its identity as the nuclear-armed territorially largest country in the world were issues that were largely left to hang. Now, they have returned with a vengeance.

Regardless of Putin's ultimate fate, the war in Ukraine is shaping Russia in profound ways. It is more cut off from the Western world in particular than at any point since the Cold War due to the withering range of sanctions that have been imposed to punish Russia for the invasion. Major Russian banks have had their assets frozen and been thrown off the Swift international payments system, preventing their customers from making international transactions. Global brands have withdrawn from Russia in their hundreds, leaving Russians without access to iPhones, Big Macs and foreign-made cars. Russia's domestic manufacturing sector has to contend with shortages of key components that it can no longer source from international supply chains it is now denied access to, with Russian cars for instance no longer being fitted with airbags and other features because the materials are unavailable.

And yet, while the World Bank predicts that Russia's economy will shrink by 11.2 per cent in 2022, they also predict that Ukraine's economy will shrink by a massive 45 per cent due to the devastation wrought by a war that is almost entirely being waged on Ukrainian soil. Attrition through economic warfare is very much a part of the wider war, and it is something that some in Russia's population are grimly attuned to, having been raised on tales of Russia's Second World War hardships.

There is rising Russian domestic support for the 'SVO' (the Russian acronym for 'special military operation). According to a group of independent sociologists, since the start of the invasion domestic support amongst those Russians polled has risen from 59 per cent to 64 per cent and opposition has more than halved from 22 per cent to 9 per cent. Another survey, by the state-owned All-Russian Centre for the Study of Public Opinion, found support at 72 per cent by the end of May 2022, with responders varyingly thinking that the war was being waged to 'save Russia from NATO', to 'achieve peace', for the 'destruction of military equipment and forces', or to 'expand Russia's territory'.[6]

To bewildered outsiders looking at these polling results, the Russian people are obviously trapped in a police state that brainwashes them while locking up any dissidents. The number of people who have fled Russia in disgust at the war and in reaction to the sanctions imposed on their country is noteworthy. At the same time, a gritty wartime patriotism has descended for some Russians in the name of supporting their troops out in the field and those returning home alive while honouring the dead. Russians are acutely aware that their armies have historically suffered immense losses even when striving shambolically towards a victory. This domestic support in parts of Russian society for the war may not waver.

Why did Putin do it? Why launch an invasion that has turned his country into an international pariah and already killed thousands of its service personnel? With this war, Putin did not want to rebuild the USSR but to reunite the lands of Ancient Rus, the civilisational space that Putin feels has been turned against itself by the USA's use of NATO as a vanguard for injecting the nefarious temptations of geopolitical Westernisation into the region. Imperial legacies and geopolitics became entwined in Putin's mistaken belief that subduing Ukraine would be easy – but since it has proved anything but a cakewalk, the Russian war machine has settled in for a long struggle.

Gambling on war once again, Putin will either build his 'greater Russia' in Europe, uniting Belarus with occupied Ukraine to forge a new line of resistance against Western influences in Russia's backyard (this would be an imperial inheritance to be bequeathed to his anointed successor), or he will end up exhausted, defeated, deposed, dead; his corpse not lying in state but vanishing into the same memories as history's greatest criminals.

Alarmingly, the dichotomous terms of this gamble may have been attractive to the man who gave the order to invade on 24 February 2022.

FOR THE WEST

What do we mean by the West, beyond the obviousness of the USA, Canada and western Europe? We also mean the powerful structures they dominate, from NATO to the EU; and by extension, countries far and wide such as Australia and Japan that tend to align with the West when it makes a moral stand on matters of global importance. We also tend to refer to democracy as the governing systems of Western and Western-aligned countries as the key differentiator from the autocracies they compete against.

The war has clearly strengthened NATO through the admission

of Finland and Sweden as members, adding their small but formidable armed forces to the alliance. NATO has also seriously increased its military presence in eastern Europe, adding new deployments in 2022 to the garrisons it first sent to the Baltic states, Poland and Romania back in 2016 in response to Russia's first invasion of Ukraine. This time, with fears of a major war spilling over into NATO territory, the defence of NATO member state airspaces and borders has become a huge undertaking. It is unlikely that we will see an end to major NATO deployments to deter Russia along the alliance's eastern flank any time soon.

By June, NATO Secretary General Stoltenberg was doing his part to prepare Western publics for a long struggle against Russia in which ordinary citizens would have to cope with rising everyday energy costs as a result of the economic impact of the war:

> Our economic sanctions ... on parts of Russian industry, on the financial sectors, also have global ramifications for the energy markets. And therefore Europeans, NATO allies, the United States, partners, they pay a price. There's no way to deny that. But that price is much lower than the price we will pay if Putin gets his way by using military force against an independent nation. It is about the price we have to pay for freedom.[7]

This kind of rhetoric may not remain convincing for everyone. It is clear there is no uniformity in how 'the West' has responded to the Russia–Ukraine war. Germany is a case in point. When the invasion began, Germany came under pressure from its Western allies to drop the Nord Stream 2 pipeline project that would have allowed Russia to export additional quantities of gas through the Baltic Sea, therefore circumnavigating Poland and Ukraine. It took Germany an inordinate amount of time to agree, and only after a bitter debate involving German business interests that had come to rely on cheap exports of Russian energy. Olaf Sholtz had just been elected as German Chancellor, and he was slow off the mark in making a firm stand against Russia's aggression. Eventually, Germany agreed not only to axe Nord Stream 2 but to wean itself off importing Russian gas, to a big increase in its defence budget, and to providing some military equipment to Ukraine. This may be one of the war's enduring legacies for the West: that Germany has experienced a paradigm shift, shaking loose its key post-1945 assumption that it should avoid re-militarisation, and also shedding its post-1991 assumption around the importance of maintaining a friendship with Russia.

The EU is also experiencing a paradigm shift in terms of its energy policies. The EU has decided to end the majority of imports of Russian oil and gas – but Hungary was a hold-out, meaning that the ban on Russian energy would be partial, at the time of writing. Viktor Orbán had just been re-elected for a fourth term in office, and rather than a simple Putin sympathiser, his brand of Hungarian nationalism had made him a contrarian when it came to the edicts emerging from Brussels. It should be pointed out that although now forgotten due to the concerns of wartime, Poland's government had also been locked in a dispute with Brussels over the writ of EU law. The 'Western club' is not a single bloc and is never greater than the sum of its parts.

Well, that's just democracy for you – so one might say, while reflecting on how preferable this is as a political system, even in its most imperfect guises, when one considers the Russian or Belarus counterpoint of Presidents with a job for life from which to project their deadly manias.

* * *

The most energetic backers of Ukraine in its war with Russia – and indeed, the countries most likely to extrapolate from the war a wider morality play around the 'democratic world versus authoritarians' – were the British and American governments, who were also the most energetic providers of weapons to Ukraine. They were joined by ex-Warsaw Pact states such as Poland and the former SSRs in the Baltics, each scarred in their own ways by past Russian imperialism, forging a powerful band of countries willing to fully back Ukraine's war effort in the immediate wake of the invasion.

The invasion has offered each of these countries a clear culminating point for their accumulated grievances against Putin's Russia. Take the UK, for example, whose governing elite were apoplectic towards the Russian state over the barbarous attempt by Russian intelligence officers to kill the Russian defector Sergei Skripal in a UK city in 2018; over Russia's brutal bombing of Syria that began in 2015; over the MH17 tragedy in 2014; and so on, so long was the list of grievances. The USA, and Biden's Democrat Party in particular, was also aggrieved with Russia's government over the attempted hack of the election in 2016, as detailed in the Mueller Report, and with Russia's general rule-breaking around the world.

None of this is to minimise the sympathy and solidarity felt in London and Washington with Ukraine's plight as felt for its own sake; it is only to point out that Anglo-American leadership of an anti-Putin global coalition did not come out of nowhere. Quite the opposite, in fact, since some of the successes of the US and UK intelligence communities in calling out Russia's planned invasion came from their accumulated wisdom of being outfoxed by Russian deception in recent years and learning from these past experiences.

Moreover, the Russian invasion of Ukraine happened to begin not long after the twentieth anniversary of 9/11 and the recent US and NATO withdrawal from Afghanistan. The time was certainly ripe for a fresh Enemy Number One. There is no conspiracy theory here, just a statement of factual observation, that in the waning years of the threat of militarised terrorism, and with the end of nation-building missions abroad, there was now a major new military mission closer to home in Europe.

While it was unfair to say that there were Western governments out there wanting 'to fight Russia until the last Ukrainian', there was an awkward collision of wider interests at play. France's Macron became an 'appeaser' for suggesting dialogue with Russia to end the war, since the only conceivable line of policy was to back Ukraine to a decisive victory – a fight to the death, in other words, said Macron's critics in other Western countries. Ukraine's government said that the country wanted to fight, and it should be helped to do so, so ran the argument against forcing Ukraine towards a peace deal in which it ceded territory to halt the fighting, not least since Russia would certainly renege on such a deal anyway.

It was an awful debate. No matter the Ukrainian voices wilfully calling for Western arms to defend their country against Russia, Ukraine was now heavily dependent on everything from Western munitions to Western macroeconomic support to keep its war effort going. The basis of its struggle against Russia was still Ukrainian agency. But through its dependencies on outsiders, Ukraine itself began to fade into the outline of a pawn once again.

FOR THE WORLD

Kenya's ambassador to the UN in New York, Martin Kimani, delivered an unforgettable speech on 22 February:

We believe that all states formed from empires that have collapsed or retreated have many peoples in them yearning for integration with peoples in neighbouring states. This is normal and understandable. After all, who does not want to be joined to their brethren and to make common purpose with them? However ... we must complete our recovery from the embers of dead empires in a way that does not plunge us back into new forms of domination and oppression.

Perhaps Kimani could be criticised for suggesting that countries must live for ever with borders given to them by empires. More generally, his speech demonstrated just how sensitive a nerve the theme of wars of conquest had touched upon around the world, especially those wars born from the many imperial collapses of recent history.

Even if they were unmoved by the principles at stake, other countries came to feel the bitter economic ripples of Russia's invasion through disruptions to global energy markets resulting from the widespread sanctions on Russian oil and gas exports. And, as Russia conquered stretches of Ukraine's coastline, including ports like Mariupol and Berdiansk, it imposed a naval blockade on the export of Ukraine's wheat. Countries as far afield as Egypt and Indonesia that relied on importing Ukraine's food exports found their supplies disrupted.

Mild-mannered Singapore, never offending anyone, delivered a burst of strong sanctions against Russia soon after the invasion. Japan, pacifist and calm since its own imperial project ended in atomic disaster in 1945, opted to freeze most of its relations with Russia and employ its economic statecraft to a hitherto unseen extent to pull out of joint projects and to phase out its Russian energy imports.

Other countries had more ambiguous reactions. China (1.4 billion people), India (1.38 billion), Indonesia (274 million), Pakistan

(221 million) and Brazil (215 million) collectively represent five of the top ten most populous countries and, at 3.5 billion people, represent just under half the world's population. While individuals in some of these countries were appalled by the Russian invasion, their governments have done everything from backing Russia (China) to continuing to buy its arms (India) to arguing that Russia should not be kicked out of global bodies (Brazil).

India and China were getting a bargain as the price of Russian energy dropped. India was buying more Russian crude than ever, and by April this had reached 700,000 barrels a day. China was also buying copious amounts of Russian energy and sales of gas have risen with the expansion of the 'Power of Siberia' pipelines that connected the two countries. Overall, Russia earned $24 billion USD from its energy exports to China and India in the three months following the invasion.[8] Even if there was insane volatility in the pricing of oil and gas, the 'world' had not turned its back on Russia.

* * *

This was not solely the result of Russian disinformation – some people in far-flung places just did not especially care for the fate of Ukraine, seeing the conflict as a local matter in Europe, while also residually placing some blame on the USA for the handling of NATO expansion. By invading Ukraine, Putin's grand strategic bet was placed on the world becoming less unipolar (i.e. US-dominated) and more multipolar (meaning countries like Brazil, Russia, India, China and South Africa, the BRICS, gaining greater shares of the global power relative to the West than ever before). Lavrov often waxed lyrical about this global trend as bringing an end to the long era of global western European and North American dominion.

The world was indeed a more open field than at any time since 1991. Whether this bet on the world's multipolar character would backfire or not was one of the bigger questions opened by the invasion. Moreover, the situation in which no countries had actually come out in support of Russia's invasion (only turned a blind eye and carried on trading with it, in the cases of India and China) was still enough to create space for the Russian invasion of Ukraine.

It created the economic space detailed above, ensuring that money still flowed into the profits of Gazprom and other Russian state-run energy companies. It created political space by ensuing that the UN Security Council could never gang up on Russia as long as its new best friend China abstained from any UN motions that tried to condemn Russia utterly. And it created civilisational space for Russia's ideologies to argue that while they would never be a superpower as the USSR had one been, Russia represented a pole in the multipolar world that could never be refashioned by Western advice and censure.

Shutting down these spaces could force Russia to the negotiating table to end the war, but it was no longer within the writ of the West to adopt a stance on a matter of global importance and then to ignore divergent Chinese or Indian responses. Even if the G7 group of nations that comprises the West plus Japan were united in the cause of punishing Russia for its invasion, the G20 – which is a far more globally representative group of nations including India, China and Indonesia – was split. For these countries, punishing Russia and arming Ukraine were far less important than peace talks and, depending on how the war progresses, the pressure on all parties to bring the fighting to an end will one day mount.

For now, it is a depressing spectacle, as the Russians tear into Ukraine and, at a certain level, get away with it. For how long, we will see – and those in the wider world who did not take a strong governmental stand against Russia's aggression will have many years to wonder whether their failure to do so will have opened the gateways to wars of aggression elsewhere, by other predatory powers with the military might and the historical grievances to justify it.

China may covet this. The war in Ukraine has irrevocably changed the debate over conquests elsewhere, for instance around China's future threat to Taiwan, which it sees not as a sovereign country but as a rogue province that must be reunited with the mainland. The lessons that China draws from the Ukraine invasion will be an important matter itself.

We are now getting very far away from Ukraine, but for a country that so many people around the world knew very little about before 2022, and may not even have been able to place on a map, Ukraine has become more important than anyone could have dared to predict.

HOPE

To answer the question of how the situation in Ukraine came to this, some look to geopolitical abstraction, and the principle of Russian imperial autocracy pitted against Ukrainian oligarchic democracy. They might see prescience in the writings of the 1970s-era US National Security Advisor, Polish-born Zbigniew Brzezinski. His book *The Grand Chessboard* (1997) explained that 'without Ukraine, Russia ceases to be a Eurasian empire. Russia without Ukraine can still strive for imperial status, but it would then become a predominantly Asian imperial state,' while also warning that 'Ukraine's loss of independence would have immediate consequences for central Europe, transforming Poland into the geopolitical pivot on the eastern frontier of a united Europe.'[9]

The metaphor of a chessboard serves the kings and queens of geopolitics as they move their knights, bishops and rooks into action, but it is always a nightmare for the pawns.

Which is why others might look to ending the cycle of loss and ruin of this war as the undertaking of greatest moral imperative. Perhaps not all routes to peace are equally just or desirable, but there is no ideal way out of the mess created by Putin's invasion. Nor should there be any avoidance of the fact that, for many years, Ukraine was a grand chessboard for the vanities and ambitions of all manner of outsiders.

Hope, however, will one day spring again in Ukraine. Its blue skies will continue to abut its yellow fields when the fighting stops, its borders are secured and its people can heal.

NOTES

INTRODUCTION

1 Volodymyr Zelensky as he answered questions at the Munich Security Conference, 19 February 2022 (28:45). Other quotes are from his preceding speech. Translated and uploaded by Deutsche Welle News on 20 February 2022: https://www.youtube.com/watch?v=IVAExDHaKcc

2 President of Russia, 'Address by the President of the Russian Federation', 21 February 2022. http://en.kremlin.ru/events/president/news/67828

3 Nicholas Ostler, *Empires of the Word: A Language History of the World* (London: Harper Perennial, 2006), pp. 421–44.

4 Volodymyr Zelensky, 'Zelensky's Last-Ditch Plea for Peace', *Foreign Policy*, 23 February 2022. https://foreignpolicy.com/2022/02/23/zelenskys-desperate-plea-for-peace/

5 President of Russia, 'Address by the President of the Russian Federation', 24 February 2022. http://en.kremlin.ru/events/president/news/67843

6 Quoted in Adam Hochschild, *To End All Wars: A Story of Protest and Patriotism in the First World War* (London: Pan Macmillan, 2011), p. xv.

7 'Biden Says the US Will Defend "Every Inch" of NATO Territory', Bloomberg, 24 February 2022. https://www.bloomberg.com/news/videos/2022-02-24/u-s-will-defend-every-inch-of-nato-territory-biden-video

CHAPTER 1: ASHES OF EMPIRES

1 'Transcript: Vladimir Putin "doesn't believe he can afford to lose" – William Burns, CIA director', *Financial Times*, 9 May 2022. https://www.ft.com/content/bd87fafd-1f9c-4dcd-af64-940cf9495ce5

2 Vladimir Putin, 'On the Historical Unity of Russians and Ukrainians', kremlin.ru, 12 July 2021. http://en.kremlin.ru/events/president/news/66181

3 Fiona Hill and Clifford Gaddy, *Mr. Putin: Operative in the Kremlin* (Washington DC: Brookings, 2013).

4 Vladimir Medinsky, *Myths About Russia*, translated by Christopher Culver (London: Glagoslav Publications, 2015).

5 Serhii Plokhii, *Chernobyl: History of a Tragedy* (London: Penguin, 2018).

6 Samir Puri, *The Great Imperial Hangover: How Empires Have Shaped the World* (London: Atlantic Books, 2020), pp. 1–21.

7 Andrew Wilson, *The Ukrainians: An Unexpected Nation* (New Haven and London: Yale University Press, 2015). Preface to the fourth edition, pp. xi–xiv.

8 Michael W. Doyle, *Empires* (New York: Cornell University Press, 1986), p. 45.

9 Alexander Motyl, *Imperial Ends: The Decay, Collapse and Revival of Empires* (New York: Columbia University Press, 2001), p. 4.

10 Vladimir Balakhonov, 'Sokhranenie imperii ili samosokhranenie na puti natsional'nogo suvereniteta – glavnaya natsional'naya problema russkogo naroda segodnia' Russkaya mysl', 23 June 1989, p. 7. Quoted in Domitilla Sagramoso, *Russian Imperialism Revisited: From Disengagement to Hegemony* (Oxon: Routledge, 2020), pp. 1–2.

11 Serhii Plokhii, *Unmaking Imperial Russia: Mykhailo Hrushevsky and the Writing of Ukrainian History* (Toronto: University of Toronto Press, 2005), pp. 166–212 and 252–63.

12 David Rieff Sontag, *In Praise of Forgetting* (New Haven and London: Yale University Press, 2016), pp. 79, 106.

13   Anne Applebaum, *Red Famine: Stalin's War on Ukraine* (London: Penguin Random House UK, 2018), pp. 357–58.
14   Samuel Charap and Timothy J. Colton, *Everyone Loses: The Ukraine Crisis and the Ruinous Contest for Post-Soviet Eurasia*, IISS Adelphi Book 460 (Oxon: Routledge, 2017), p. 53.
15   V. O. Kluchevsky, *A History of Russia*, translated by C. J. Hogarth (London: Dent, 1931), p. 209. Quoted in Sagramoso, *Russian Imperialism Revisited* (2020), p. 1.
16   General Annenkov as quoted in Dominic Lieven, *Empire: The Russian Empire and its Rivals* (New Haven: Yale University Press, 2002), p. 279.
17   Serhii Plokhii, *Lost Kingdom: A History of Russian Nationalism from Ivan the Great to Vladimir Putin* (London: Penguin Random House, 2018).
18   Plokhii, *Lost Kingdom* (2018).
19   Lieven, *Empire* (2002), pp. 259–561.
20   Putin, 'On the Historical Unity of Russians and Ukrainians' (2021).
21   Serhii Plokhii, *The Gates of Europe: A History of Ukraine* (London: Penguin, 2015), pp. 97, 103, 119.
22   Vasil Klyuchevsky, *Peter the Great*, translated by Liliana Archibald (New York: St Martin's Press, 1969), p. 57.
23   Lieven, *Empire* (2002), p. 268.
24   Vladimir Putin, 'Address by the President of the Russian Federation', kremlin.ru, 21 February 2022. http://en.kremlin.ru/events/president/news/67828
25   John O'Loughlin, Gerard Toal and Vladimir Kolosov, 'The Rise and Fall of "Novorossiya": Examining Support for a Separatist Geopolitical Imaginary in South-East Ukraine', *Post Soviet Affairs* (Vol. 32, No. 2, 2017), pp. 124–44.
26   Paul Bushkovitch, 'The Ukraine in Russian Culture 1790–1860: The Evidence of the Journals', *Jahrbücher für Geschichte Osteuropas*, Neue Folge (Bd. 39, H. 3, 1991), pp. 339–63.
27   Lieven, *Empire* (2002), p. 278.
28   Hochschild, *To End All Wars* (2011), pp. 114–17.
29   Robert Service, *Lenin: A Biography* (London: Pan Books, 2010), p. 342.
30   Lieven, *Empire* (2002), pp. 60, 287.
31   Service, *Lenin* (2010), pp. 385–6, 402.
32   Service, *Lenin* (2010), p. 407.
33   Plokhii, *The Gates of Europe* (2015), pp. 245–51.
34   Richard Overy, *Why the Allies Won* (London: Pimlico, 1996), p. 2.
35   Interview with author, February 2022. Interviewee was a resident of the Donetsk Oblast and chose to remain anonymous.
36   Ryszard Kapuściński, *Imperium* (New York: Vintage Books, 1994), p. 278.
37   Anna Matveeva, *Through Times of Trouble: Conflict in South-Eastern Ukraine Explained from Within* (Washington DC: Lexington, 2017), p. 26.
38   Terry Martin, *The Affirmative Action Empire* (Ithaca: Cornell University Press, 2001), p. 18.
39   Catherine Belton, *Putin's People: How the KGB Took Back Russia and Then Took on the West* (London: William Collins, 2020), pp. 268–9.
40   Motyl, *Imperial Ends* (2001), pp. 89–90.
41   Dugin as translated and quoted in Marlene Laruelle, *Russian Eurasianism: An Ideology of Empire* (Maryland: Johns Hopkins University Press, 2012), pp. 85–97.
42   'Alexander Dugin speaking on the Ukraine conflict', 4 March 2022. https://www.youtube.com/watch?v=NXNlNsOXqsM
43   'Alexander Dugin speaking on the Ukraine conflict' (2022).
44   Samuel Huntington, *The Clash of Civilizations and the Remaking of the World Order* (London: Simon & Schuster, 1997), pp. 164–5.
45   Anna Matveeva, *Through Times of Trouble* (2017), p. 26.
46   Norman Davies, *Vanished Kingdoms: The History of Half-Forgotten Europe* (London: Penguin, 2012), pp. 449–76; Lieven, *Empire* (2002), p. 280.
47   Timothy Snyder, *The Reconstruction of Nation: Poland, Ukraine, Lithuania, Belarus, 1569–1999* (New Haven: Yale University Press, 2003), p. 11.

CHAPTER 2: INDEPENDENCE AT LAST

1   Paul D'Anieri, *Ukraine and Russia: From Civilised Divorce to Uncivil War* (Cambridge: Cambridge University Press, 2019).

2 Hélène Carrère D'Encausse, *The End of the Soviet Empire: The Triumph of the Nations* (New York: Harper Collins, 1993), pp. 244–5.

3 Mary E. Sarotte, *Not One Inch: America, Russia and the Making of Post-Cold War Stalemate* (New Haven: Yale University Press, 2021), p. 129.

4 Lukianenko quoted in Plokhii, *The Gates of Europe* (2015), pp. 319–20.

5 Plokhii, *The Gates of Europe* (2015), p. 322.

6 Carrère d'Encausse, *The End of the Soviet Empire* (1993), p. 254.

7 Anders Åslund, *How Ukraine Became a Market Economy and Democracy* (Washington DC: Peterson Institute for International Economics, 2009), pp. 66–7.

8 Kravchuk quoted in Carrère d'Encausse, *The End of the Soviet Empire* (1993), p. 255.

9 Kravchuk quoted in Åslund, *How Ukraine Became a Market Economy* (2009), p. 34. See also Plokhii, *The Gates of Europe* (2015), pp. 316–18.

10 D'Anieri, *Ukraine and Russia* (2019), p. 41.

11 Charap and Colton, *Everyone Loses* (2017), pp. 57–8; Sagramoso, *Russian Imperialism Revisited* (2020).

12 Sarotte, *Not One Inch* (2021), p. 15.

13 Gorbachev quoted in D'Anieri, *Ukraine and Russia* (2019), p. 61.

14 Sarotte, *Not One Inch* (2021), pp. 55, 68.

15 Sarotte, *Not One Inch* (2021), pp. 159–60.

16 Maria Rost Rublee, 'Ukraine – a fantasy counterfactual', *Survival* (April–May 2015). https://www.iiss.org/blogs/survival-blog/2022/03/from-the-archive-ukraine-a-fantasy-counterfactual

17 President of Russia press release, 'Acting President Vladimir Putin and Ukrainian President Leonid Kuchma visited Sevastopol', 18 April 2000. http://en.kremlin.ru/events/president/news/37618

18 Helene Cooper, Eric Schmitt and Julian E. Barnes, 'U.S. Intelligence Helped Ukraine Strike Russian Flagship, Officials Say', *New York Times*, 5 May 2022. https://www.nytimes.com/2022/05/05/us/politics/moskva-russia-ship-ukraine-us.html

19 Translation: 'Treaty on Friendship and Cooperation and Partnership between Ukraine and the Russian Federation'. https://treaties.un.org/doc/Publication/UNTS/Volume%203007/v3007.pdf

20 'Charter on a Distinctive Partnership between the North Atlantic Treaty Organization and Ukraine', *nato. int*, 9 July 1997. https://www.nato.int/cps/en/natohq/official_texts_25457.htm

21 Åslund, *How Ukraine Became a Market Economy* (2009), p. 45.

22 Ministry of Statistics, Ukraine, reproduced in Åslund, *How Ukraine Became a Market Economy* (2009), p. 49.

23 'Ukraine's Leonid Kuchma "implicated" in Gongadze death', BBC News, 20 February 2013. https://www.bbc.com/news/world-europe-21525593

24 Åslund, *How Ukraine Became a Market Economy* (2009), p. 180.

25 D'Anieri, *Ukraine and Russia* (2019), p. 118.

26 Serhy Yekelchyk, *Ukraine: What Everyone Needs to Know*, 2nd edition (Oxford: Oxford University Press, 2020), pp. 4–5.

27 Charap and Colton, *Everyone Loses* (2017), pp. 67, 71.

28 'Secretary of State Madeleine K. Albright, Prepared statement before the Senate Armed Services Committee: NATO Enlargement; Washington, D.C., April 23, 1997'. https://1997-2001.state.gov/statements/970423.html

29 'Talbott speech on NATO enlargement at Atlantic Council', 20 May 1997. https://www.mtholyoke.edu/acad/intrel/strbnato.htm

30 Sarotte, *Not One Inch* (2021), pp. 1–3, 15, 174–96, 209.

31 Charap and Colton, *Everyone Loses* (2017), p. 49.

32 D'Anieri, *Ukraine and Russia* (2019), p. 3.

CHAPTER 3: PUTIN SEES ORANGE

1 US State Department Cable, 'U.S.-EU DISCUSS RUSSIA, UKRAINE, MOLDOVA, BELARUS. 2004 March 19, 09:31. UKRAINE: OCTOBER ELECTIONS WATERSHED', released by Wikileaks.

2 Belton, *Putin's People* (2020), pp. 268–9.

3 Marlene Laruelle, *In the Name of the Nation: Nationalism and politics in Russia* (New York: Palgrave Macmillan, 2009), pp. 119, 141.

4 Belton, *Putin's People* (2020), p. 269.

5 Åslund, *How Ukraine Became a Market Economy* (2009), p. 185.

6 Åslund, *How Ukraine Became a Market Economy* (2009), p. 189.

7 Åslund, *How Ukraine Became a Market Economy* (2009), p. 179, quotes Demes and Forbig 2006.

8   Michael McFaul, 'Ukraine Imports Democracy: External Influences on the Orange Revolution', *International Security* (Fall 2007, Vol. 32, No. 2)

9   McFaul, *International Security* (2007), pp. 45–83.

10   Ian Traynor, 'US campaign behind the turmoil in Kiev', *The Guardian*, 26 November 2004. https://www.theguardian.com/world/2004/nov/26/ukraine.usa

11   McFaul, *International Security* (2007), p. 72.

12   McFaul, *International Security* (2007), pp. 63–4.

13   Åslund, *How Ukraine Became a Market Economy* (2009), p. 195.

14   Åslund, *How Ukraine Became a Market Economy* (2009), p. 194; Adrian Karatnycky, 'Ukraine's Orange Revolution', *Foreign Affairs* (Vol. 84, No. 2, March–April 2005), pp. 35–52.

15   Samir Puri, 'Ukraine; election observation matters', *Trust and Verify* (No. 118, January–February 2005). https://www.files.ethz.ch/isn/121569/TV118.pdf

16   McFaul, *International Security* (2007), p. 55.

17   D'Anieri, *Ukraine and Russia* (2019), p. 133.

18   Donnacha Ó Beacháin and Abel Polese, 'What Happened to the Colour Revolutions? Authoritarian Responses from Former Soviet Spaces', *Journal of International and Area Studies* (Vol. 17, No. 2, December 2010), pp. 31–51.

19   Ó Beacháin and Polese, 'What Happened to the Colour Revolutions?' (2010), p. 39.

20   US State Department cable, 'UKRAINE: PRESS COVERAGE OF THE GAS DISPUTE WITH RUSSIA 2005 December 23, 10:56', released by Wikileaks.

21   Belton, *Putin's People* (2020), pp. 330–39.

22   Interview with Donbas resident, op. cit.

23   *RGRU*, 'Tymoshenko wants to surround the east of Ukraine with barbed wire' quote in 'Тимошенко хочет окружить восток Украины колючей проволокой', 30 December 2004. https://rg.ru/2004/12/30/yanukovitch.html. See also *Pravda*, 'Тимошенко пришла на эфир в форме "Шахтера" и сказала, что просила повеситься как мама', 29 December 2004. https://www.pravda.com.ua/rus/news/2004/12/29/4384458/

24   The Kremlin, 'Press Conference Following Russian-Ukrainian Talks', 24 January 2005. http://en.kremlin.ru/events/president/transcripts/22795
     The Kremlin, 'President Vladimir Putin met with Ukrainian President Viktor Yushchenko', 24 January 2005. http://en.kremlin.ru/events/president/news/32637

25   '2005 Vladimir Poutine "L'Ukraine pourrait avoir des problèmes, je le dis franchement" | Archive', 25 February 2022. https://www.youtube.com/watch?v=SW-fqQIlMGk

CHAPTER 4: NATO'S FATEFUL OFFER

1   US State Department cable, 'UKRAINE: DNSA CROUCH'S NATO-THEMED DINNER INCLUDES A SPICY SERVING OF RADA COALITION TALK 2006 April 26, 08:27', released by Wikileaks.

2   Sarotte, *Not One Inch* (2021), p. 5.

3   US State Department cable, 'UKRAINE: BILATERAL COORDINATION GROUP TALKS: NATO, IRAQ, KOSOVO, TRANSNISTRIA, BELARUS 2006 January 26, 08:12', released by Wikileaks.

4   US State Department cable, 'UKRAINE ON THE ROAD TO NATO: A STATUS REPORT. 2006 February 15, 13:36', released by Wikileaks.

5   US State Department cable, 'UKRAINE: YUSHCHENKO DISCUSSES ENERGY, RUSSIA, DEFENSE REFORM, DOMESTIC POLITICS 2006 January 25, 15:07', released by Wikileaks.

6   US State Department cable, 'UKRAINE: NATO REFERENDUM ON HOLD AFTER CONSTITUTIONAL COURT APPEAL 2007 January 29, 15:46', released by Wikileaks.

7   US State Department cable, 'UKRAINE: DAS KRAMER DISCUSSES NATO/SECURITY ISSUES IN UKRAINE 2007 March 22', released by Wikileaks.

8   Vladimir Putin, 'Speech and the Following Discussion at the Munich Conference on Security Policy', 10 February 2007. http://en.kremlin.ru/events/president/transcripts/24034

9   US State Department cable, 'NATO-UKRAINE COUNCIL MARKS TENTH ANNIVERSARY JULY 9 2007 July 11', released by Wikileaks.

10   US State Department cable, 'DUMA DEPUTY RYZHKOV ON HIS FUTURE WITHOUT A PARTY, KOSOVO, NATO EXPANSION, PUTIN. 2007 October 12, 08:36', released by Wikileaks.

11   US State Department cable, 'RUSSIA-UKRAINE: NATO AND HOLODOMOR 2008 April 3', released by Wikileaks.

12   US State Department cable, 'RUSSIA-UKRAINE: NATO AND HOLODOMOR 2008 April 3', released by Wikileaks.

13   'Oliver Stone on how the US misunderstands Putin', 16 June 2017. https://www.youtube.com/watch?v=eiuplgzbCC4

14 Robert D. Kaplan, *In Europe's Shadow: Two Cold Wars and a Thirty-Year Journey Through Romania and Beyond* (New York: Random House, 2016).

15 Samir Puri, 'Romania: Black Sea Security and NATO's South-Eastern Frontline', written for the Sasakawa Peace Foundation project, 'Goals and Tactics of Lesser Allies: NATO Summit Warsaw and Implication for Japan-U S. Alliance'. https://www.spf.org/projects/upload/Romania%2C%20Black%20Sea%20Security%20 and%20NATO%E2%80%99s%20South-Eastern%20Frontline%20%28Puri%29.pdf

16 'NATO Bucharest Summit Declaration', 3 April 2008. https://www.nato.int/cps/en/natolive/official_texts_8443.htm

17 US State Department cable, 'ITALY AND NATO ENLARGEMENT: MFA NATO DESK CONCERNED ABOUT DELAYING MEMBERSHIP PERSPECTIVE FOR ALBANIA, MACEDONIA AND CROATIA UNTIL 2008 2005 September 23', released by Wikileaks.

18 US State Department cable, 'NATO-UKRAINE AMBASSADORIAL APRIL 30: LAUNCHING INTENSIFIED ENGAGEMENT 2008 May 6', released by Wikileaks.

19 Paul Gallis, Congressional Research Service Report RS22847, 'The NATO Summit at Bucharest, 2008', 5 May 2008. See also: Paul D'Anieri, *Ukraine and Russia* (2019), pp. 162–3, 166.

20 US State Department cable, 'NATO-UKRAINE AMBASSADORIAL MARCH 5: PREPARING FOR THE NUC SUMMIT 2008 March 10', released by Wikileaks.

21 US State Department cable, 'NATO-UKRAINE AMBASSADORIAL APRIL 30: LAUNCHING INTENSIFIED ENGAGEMENT 2008 May 6', released by Wikileaks.

22 Steven Erlanger, 'Ally, Member or Partner? NATO's Long Dilemma over Ukraine', *New York Times*, 8 December 2021. https://www.nytimes.com/2021/12/08/world/europe/nato-ukraine-russia-dilemma.html

23 Paul Gallis, Congressional Research Service Report RL34415, 'Enlargement Issues at NATO's Bucharest Summit', 18 April 2008. https://wikileaks.org/wiki/CRS:_Enlargement_Issues_at_NATO%27s_Bucharest_Summit,_April_18,_2008

24 Archived online: https://georgewbush-whitehouse.archives.gov/infocus/nato/photoessay3/12.html

25 US State Department cable, 'UKRAINE, MAP, AND THE GEORGIA-RUSSIA CONFLICT 2008 August 14', released by Wikileaks.

26 Philip Oltermann, 'No regrets over handling of Vladimir Putin, says Angela Merkel', *The Guardian*, 7 June 2022. https://www.theguardian.com/world/2022/jun/07/no-regrets-over-handling-of-vladimir-putin-says-angela-merkel

27 AFP, 'Merkel Defends 2008 Decision to Block Ukraine from NATO', *Kyiv Post*, 4 April 2022. https://www.kyivpost.com/ukraine-politics/merkel-defends-2008-decision-to-block-ukraine-from-nato.html

28 Charap and Colton, *Everyone Loses* (2017), p. 92.

29 International Crisis Group, 'Georgia and Russia: Why and How to Save Normalisation', 26 October 2020. https://www.crisisgroup.org/europe-central-asia/caucasus/georgia/b90-georgia-and-russia-why-and-how-save-normalisation

30 US State Department cable, 'UKRAINE: GOVERNMENT CONDEMNS RUSSIAN RECOGNITION OF SOUTH OSSETIA AND ABKHAZIA 2008 August 28', released by Wikileaks.

31 Translated letter in US State Department cable, 'UKRAINE: GOVERNMENT CONDEMNS RUSSIAN RECOGNITION OF SOUTH OSSETIA AND ABKHAZIA 2008 August 28', released by Wikileaks.

32 US State Department cable, 'UKRAINE: IMPACT OF GEORGIA CRISIS ON DOMESTIC POLITICS 2008 August 12', released by Wikileaks.

33 US State Department cable, 'TFGG01: EFFECTS OF RUSSIA-GEORGIA CONFLICT ON GOR RELATIONS WITH UKRAINE 2008 August 14', released by Wikileaks.

34 US State Department cable, 'TFGG01: EFFECTS OF RUSSIA-GEORGIA CONFLICT ON GOR RELATIONS WITH UKRAINE 2008 August 14', released by Wikileaks.

35 US State Department cable, 'UKRAINE: IMPACT OF GEORGIA CRISIS ON DOMESTIC POLITICS 2008 August 12', released by Wikileaks.

36 US State Department cable, 'UKRAINE: IMPACT OF GEORGIA CRISIS ON DOMESTIC POLITICS 2008 August 12', released by Wikileaks.

37 Dick Cheney, 'Vice President's Remarks at the Ambrosetti Forum', 6 September 2008. https://georgewbush-whitehouse.archives.gov/news/releases/2008/09/20080906-1.html

38 US State Department cable, 'RUSSIAN-UKRAINIAN RELATIONS MONOPOLIZED BY UKRAINE'S NATO BID 2008 May 30', released by Wikileaks.

39 Translation: 'Treaty on Friendship and Cooperation and Partnership between Ukraine and the Russian Federation': https://treaties.un.org/doc/Publication/UNTS/Volume%20300/v3007.pdf

40 Michael E. O'Hanlon, *Beyond NATO: A New Security Architecture for Eastern Europe* (Washington DC: Brookings Institution Press, 2017).

41 US State Department cable, 'UKRAINE, MAP, AND THE GEORGIA-RUSSIA CONFLICT 2008 August 14', released by Wikileaks.

CHAPTER 5: YANUKOVYCH, VIKTOR AND LOSER

1 Special Counsel Robert S. Mueller, III, 'Report On The Investigation Into Russian Interference In The 2016 Presidential Election' (Volume I of II, March 2019). https://www.justice.gov/archives/sco/file/1373816/download
2 D'Anieri, *Ukraine and Russia* (2019), p. 128.
3 Franklin Foer, 'Paul Manafort, American Hustler', *The Atlantic*, March 2018. https://www.theatlantic.com/magazine/archive/2018/03/paul-manafort-american-hustler/550925/
4 Volodymur Kulyk, 'The End of Euro-Romanticism in Ukraine', SWP Comments, December 2009. https://www.files.ethz.ch/isn/117384/2009_zzz_E.pdf
5 US State Department cable, 'UKRAINE: NATO, RUSSIAN LANGUAGE ISSUES ENTER ELECTION FRAY 2007 September 19', released by Wikileaks.
6 'OSCE/ODIHR Election Observation Mission Final Report', Warsaw, 28 April 2010. Results in 'ANNEX 2 – TURNOUT AND RESULTS BY REGION'.
7 Светлана Дорош, '"Донбасский узел": как заселяли шахтерский край', BBC News Ukrainian, 4 July 2016. https://www.bbc.com/ukrainian/ukraine_in_russian/2016/07/160704_ru_s_donbass_migration_ussr
8 Interview with Donbas resident, op. cit.
9 Anna Reid, *Borderland: A Journey Through the History of Ukraine* (London: Weidenfeld & Nicolson, 2015). Chapter 3 focuses on the Donbas.
10 Åslund, *How Ukraine Became a Market Economy* (2009), pp. 6, 55, 82. Data quoted from the European Bank for Reconstruction and Development.
11 Ukraine's rich list came from the magazine *Novoye Vremya* (*New Times*) and was translated by Thaisa Semanova, 'Wealth of 100 richest Ukrainians highest since 2014', *Kyiv Post*. https://www.kyivpost.com/ukraine-politics/wealth-of-100-richest-ukrainians-highest-since-2014.html
12 'Corruption Perceptions Index — Ukraine 2021'. https://www.transparency.org/en/cpi/2021/index/ukr
13 John Lough, 'Ukraine's system of crony capitalism: The challenge of dismantling "systema"', Chatham House, July 2021. https://www.chathamhouse.org/sites/default/files/2021-07/2021-07-01-ukraine-crony-capitalism-lough.pdf
14 John Lough, 'Ukraine's system of crony capitalism' (2021).
15 'Global Organised Crime Index – Ukraine'. https://ocindex.net/country/ukraine
16 Francis Fukuyama, *Political Order and Political Decay* (London: Profile Books, 2014). Chapter 5, 'Corruption'.
17 Belton, *Putin's People* (2020), p. 249.
18 'Medvedev attacks Ukraine leadership', *Financial Times*, 11 August 2009. https://www.ft.com/content/533af6fe-866b-11de-9e8e-00144feabdc0
19 'Viktor Yanukovych, President of Ukraine, Speech made to the Assembly, 27 April 2010', Council of Europe Parliamentary Assembly. assembly.coe.int/nw/xml/Speeches/Speech-XML2HTML-EN.asp?SpeechID=252
20 Peter Kennedy and Christos Kassimeris, *Exploring the Cultural, Ideological and Economic Legacies of Euro 2012* (Oxon: Routledge, 2014), p. 4.
21 D'Anieri, *Ukraine and Russia* (2019), pp. 150–52, 196.
22 'A Conversation with Štefan Füle Transcript, The Brookings Institution, November 29, 2010'. https://www.brookings.edu/wp-content/uploads/2012/04/1129_eastern_partnership_transcript.pdf
23 'EU's New Eastern Partnership Draws Ire From Russia', Deutsche Welle, 21 March 2009. https://www.dw.com/en/eus-new-eastern-partnership-draws-ire-from-russia/a-4116554
24 D'Anieri, *Ukraine and Russia* (2019), p. 174.
25 Charap and Colton, *Everyone Loses* (2017), pp. 96–7.
26 D'Anieri, *Ukraine and Russia* (2019), p. 197.
27 Charap and Colton, *Everyone Loses* (2017), pp. 114–23.
28 'Füle Says Brussels Regrets Kyiv's Decision', Radio Free Europe, 28 November 2013. https://www.rferl.org/a/eu-ukraine-fule/25183010.html
29 'New EU Eastern Partnership seen leaving out Russia', Reuters, 1 September 2008. https://www.reuters.com/article/us-georgia-ossetia-eu-partnership-idUSL137059420080901
30 Carl Bildt, 'Speech at the Summit on the Future of Europe', 22 September 2014. https://www.government.se/49b729/contentassets/9bbda6b81b16402bbab82aa0c02c2e16/speeches-2010-2014---carl-bildt
31 Meeting of the Valdai International Discussion Club', 19 September 2013. http://en.kremlin.ru/events/president/news/19243

32 'On the number and composition of the population of Ukraine according to the results of the All-Ukrainian census of 2001', State Statistics Committee of Ukraine. http://2001.ukrcensus.gov.ua/results/general/nationality/

33 Mustafa Nayyem interview on CNN: 'Protestors object to govt. rejecting trade deal with EU', 4 December 2014. https://www.youtube.com/watch?v=1UvdVpwDfdE

34 'Nuland-Pyatt leaked phone conversation _COMPLETE with SUBTITLES', 30 April 2014. https://www.youtube.com/watch?v=WV9J6sxCs5k

35 Transcript of the call: 'Ukraine crisis: Transcript of leaked Nuland-Pyatt call', BBC News, 7 February 2014. https://www.bbc.com/news/world-europe-26079957. Recording: Марионетки Майдана, 'https://www.youtube.com/watch?v=MSxaa-67yGM#t=89

36 'Heavenly Hundred', Maidan Museum. https://www.maidanmuseum.org/en/node/348

37 Jean-Jacques Rousseau, *The Social Contract* (London: Penguin Great Ideas series, 2004), p. 93.

CHAPTER 6: THE INTELLIGENCE OFFICER'S WAR

1 OSCE, 'Deployment of an OSCE Special Monitoring Mission to Ukraine', 21 March 2014.

2 Olga Oliker et al., *Security Sector Reform in Ukraine* (California: RAND Corporation, 2016), p. 48.

3 Alexander Salenko, 'Legal Aspects of the Dissolution of the Soviet Union in 1991 and Its Implications for the Reunification of Crimea with Russia in 2014', 2015. https://www.zaoerv.de/75_2015/75_2015_1_a_141_166.pdf

4 'Address by President of the Russian Federation', 18 March 2014. http://en.kremlin.ru/events/president/news/20603

5 Anna Doglov, 'Russia's Igor Strelkov: I Am Responsible for War in East Ukraine', *Moscow Times*, 21 November 2014. https://www.themoscowtimes.com/2014/11/21/russias-igor-strelkov-i-am-responsible-for-war-in-eastern-ukraine-a41598

6 Oleg Kashin, 'The Most Dangerous Man in Ukraine Is an Obsessive War Reenactor Playing Now with Real Weapons', *New Republic*, 23 July 2014. https://newrepublic.com/article/118813/igor-strelkov-russian-war-reenactor-fights-real-war-ukraine

7 Belton, *Putin's People* (2020), pp. 418–27.

8 Eur-Lex. 'COUNCIL IMPLEMENTING REGULATION (EU) No 826/2014 of 30 July 2014'. https://eur-lex.europa.eu/legal-content/EN/TXT/?uri=CELEX%3A32014R0826

9 'Ukraine crisis: Dozens killed in Odessa fire amid clashes', BBC News, 3 May 2014. https://www.bbc.com/news/world-europe-27259620. 'Ukraine's turmoil: chaos out of order', *The Economist*, 3 May 2014, pp. 31–2. 'The war in Ukraine (2): closing in', *The Economist*, 2 August 2014, p. 26.

10 Doglov, 'Russia's Igor Strelkov' (2014).

11 Olha Kashpor, *War: Journalism from the front line* (Kyiv: Osnovy Publishing, 2015), pp. 18–38 for eyewitness accounts.

12 Alexander Zhuchkovsky, *85 Days in Slavyansk*, translated by Peter Nimitz (independently published, 27 April 2022).

13 DPR leader quoted in International Crisis Group, 'Russia and the Separatists in Eastern Ukraine Crisis Group Europe and Central Asia Briefing (No. 79, 5 February 2016), p. 10.

14 Shaun Walker, *The Long Hangover: Putin's New Russia and the Ghosts of the Past* (Oxon: Oxford University Press, 2017), p. 220.

15 Adda B. Bozeman, *Strategic Intelligence and Statecraft* (Nebraska: University of Nebraska Press, 1992), p. 12.

16 'Crash MH17, 17 July 2014'. https://www.onderzoeksraad.nl/en/page/3546/crash-mh17-17-july-2014

17 'Crash MH17, 17 July 2014'. https://www.onderzoeksraad.nl/en/page/3546/crash-mh17-17-july-2014

18 'MH17: Four charged with shooting down plane over Ukraine', BBC News, 19 June 2019. https://www.bbc.com/news/world-europe-48691488

19 Kashpor, *War* (2015), pp. 98–102.

20 Quoted in International Crisis Group, 'Eastern Ukraine: A Dangerous Winter Crisis Group Europe', 18 December 2014. https://d2071andvipowj.cloudfront.net/eastern-ukraine-a-dangerous-winter.pdf

21 Kashpor, *War* (2015), pp. 30, 132–9.

22 Defence Intelligence of the Ministry of Defence of Ukraine, 'Film about the defenders of Donetsk airport was showed on Ukrainian screens. May 11, 2015'. https://gur.gov.ua/en/content/na-ukrainski-ekrany-vyishov-film-pro-zakhysnykiv-donetskoho-aeroportu.html

23 Kashpor, *War* (2015), pp. 116, 184–6.

24 Zelensky, translated and uploaded by Deutsche Welle News on 20 February 2022. https://www.youtube.com/watch?v=IVAExDHaKcc

25 'Protocol on the results of consultations of the Trilateral Contact Group, signed in Minsk', OSCE, 5

September 2014; 'Ukraine deal with pro-Russian rebels at Minsk talks', BBC News, 20 September 2014. https://www.bbc.com/news/world-europe-29290246

26 'Ukraine Conflict: battle rages ahead of Minsk talks', BBC News, 10 February 2015. https://www.bbc.com/news/world-europe-31357588

27 International Crisis Group, 'The Ukraine Crisis: Risks of Renewed Military Conflict after Minsk II', 1 April 2015. https://d2071andvipowj.cloudfront.net/b73-the-ukraine-crisis-risks-of-renewed-military-conflict-after-minsk-ii.pdf

28 OSCE SMM, 'Latest from the OSCE SMM based on information received as of 21 April, 18:00', 22 April 2015; 'Latest from the OSCE SMM based on information received as of 9 May, 18:00', 9 May 2015.

29 Shaun Walker, 'Dill with it: Russia's obsession with the spindly herb menace', *The Guardian*, 10 August 2015. https://www.theguardian.com/world/2015/aug/10/dill-russia-herb-pizza-sushi-soup-hummus-food-ruin

30 Matveeva, *Through Times of Trouble* (2017), p. 27.

31 Jim Acosta, 'US, other powers kick Russia out of G8', CNN, 25 March 2014. https://edition.cnn.com/2014/03/24/politics/obama-europe-trip/index.html

32 D'Anieri, *Ukraine and Russia* (2019), pp. 245, 252, 263.

CHAPTER 7: HOME FRONTS AND FRONT LINES

1 I returned to the Donetsk region to contribute to the following report: 'Ukraine: A peacebuilding agenda to bridge the divide', Peaceful Change Initiative Policy Briefing, January 2017. https://peacefulchange.org/wp-content/uploads/2021/01/16_ukraine_policy_brief_final_for_print_2.pdf

2 Korrespondent.net, 3 August 2016. https://ua.korrespondent.net/ukraine/3726408-sprava-tornado-scho-slid-znaty-pro-novyi-skandal

3 Figures from the Government of Ukraine, UN Human Rights Monitoring Mission and the IISS, as presented in *Armed Conflict Survey 2019*, p. 147.

4 Oliker et al., *Security Sector Reform in Ukraine* (2016).

5 Anna Babinets and Vlad Lavrov, 'Ukraine's President offshores revisited: Swiss trust and millions moved out of Ukraine', Organised Crime and Corruption Project, OCCRP, 20 May 2016. https://www.occrp.org/en/panamapapers/ukraines-president-offshores-revisited-swiss-trust-and-millions-moved-out-of-ukraine/

6 gov.ua, State Sites of Ukraine, 'About the Ministry'. https://minre.gov.ua/en/rubric/about-ministry.

7 'Ukrainian National Guardsman Killed at Protest Outside Parliament', Radio Free Europe, 31 August 2015. https://www.rferl.org/a/ukraine-decentralisation-bill-protests/27218087.html

8 'Ukraine: The Line', International Crisis Group, 18 July 2016, p. 10. https://d2071andvipowj.cloudfront.net/ukraine-the-line.pdf

9 Mueller, 'Report On the Investigation Into Russian Interference In The 2016 Presidential Election' (2019), pp. 125, 140. See also: Megan Twohey and Scott Shanel, 'A back-channel plan for Ukraine and Russia, courtesy of Trump associates', *New York Times*, 19 February 2017. https://www.nytimes.com/2017/02/19/us/politics/donald-trump-ukraine-russia.html

10 President of Russia, 'Vladimir Putin addressed the eighth meeting of Russian Federation ambassadors & permanent envoys at the Russian Foreign Ministry', 30 June 2016. http://en.kremlin.ru/events/president/news/52298

11 'Russia guarantor of Ukraine settlement, not party fulfilling deal – Kremlin', *Sputnik News*, 13 February 2015. https://sputniknews.com/20150213/1018209668.html. 'Ukraine: The Line', International Crisis Group, pp. 9–10.

12 'OSCE Mission to Ukraine to Augment Monitoring Capacity', Ukraine Crisis Media Centre, 13 October 2014.

13 'The Delegation of the Republic of Moldova to the Joint Control Commission'. Government of the Republic of Moldova, 2022. https://gov.md/en/content/delegation-republic-moldova-joint-control-commission

14 President Petro Poroshenko, speech to Verkhovna Rada, Kyiv, 14 April 2016.

15 Author interview with Donbas resident, op. cit.

16 Details on the crossing system for the Donbas front line are included as part of my research for the NGO report 'Ukraine: A peacebuilding agenda to bridge the divide', Peaceful Change Initiative Policy Briefing, January 2017.

17 'Ukraine conflict: Poroshenko calls for UN peacekeepers', BBC News, 19 February 2015. https://www.bbc.co.uk/news/world-europe-31527414

18 'Report of the Eastern Ukraine Forum "Reconstruction through Dialogue"', 13–14 May 2015, Kramatorsk', OSCE Project Coordinator in Ukraine.

19 UN Comtrade, 'International Trade Statistics Database'. https://dit-trade-vis.azurewebsites.net/?reporter=804&partner=643&type=C&commodity=TOTAL&year=1998&flow=2

20 'Press Release: IMF Approves Stand-by Credit and Second STF Drawing for Ukraine', 7 April 1995. https://www.imf.org/en/News/Articles/2015/09/14/01/49/pr9519
Press Release: IMF Approves a Stand-By Credit for Ukraine, 10 May 1996. https://www.imf.org/en/News/Articles/2015/09/14/01/49/pr9624
'Press Release: IMF Approves Stand-By for Ukraine', 25 August 1997. https://www.imf.org/en/News/Articles/2015/09/14/01/49/pr9739
'Press Release: IMF Approves Three-Year Extended Fund Facility for Ukraine', 4 September 1998. https://www.imf.org/en/News/Articles/2015/09/14/01/49/pr9838
'Press Release: IMF Approves 12-Month Stand-By Arrangement for Ukraine', 29 March 2004. https://www.imf.org/en/News/Articles/2015/09/14/01/49/pr0462
'Press Release: IMF Approves US$16.4 Billion Stand-By Arrangement for Ukraine', 5 November 2008. https://www.imf.org/en/News/Articles/2015/09/14/01/49/pr08271
'Press Release: IMF Executive Board Approves US$15.15 Billion Stand-By Arrangement for Ukraine', 28 July 2010. https://www.imf.org/en/News/Articles/2015/09/14/01/49/pr10305
'Press Release: IMF Executive Board Approves 2-Year US$17.01 Billion Stand-By Arrangement for Ukraine', US$3.19 Billion for immediate Disbursement, 30 April 2014. https://www.imf.org/en/News/Articles/2015/09/14/01/49/pr14189
'Press Release: IMF Executive Board Approves 4-Year US$17.5 Billion Extended Fund Facility for Ukraine, US$5 Billion for Immediate Disbursement', 22 March 2015. https://www.imf.org/en/News/Articles/2015/09/14/01/49/pr15107
'Press Release: MF Executive Board Approves 14-month US$3.9 Billion Stand-By Arrangement for Ukraine, 4 Billion for Immediate Disbursement', 18 December 2018. https://www.imf.org/en/News/Articles/2018/12/18/pr18483-ukraine-imf-executive-board-approves-14-month-stand-by-arrangement
'Press Release: IMF Executive Board Approves 18-month US$5 Billion Stand-By Arrangement for Ukraine', 9 June 2020. https://www.imf.org/en/News/Articles/2020/06/09/pr20239-ukraine-imf-executive-board-approves-18-month-us-5-billion-stand-by-arrangement
'Press Release: IMF Executive Board Approves US$ 1.4 Billion in Emergency Financing Support to Ukraine', 9 March 2022. https://www.imf.org/en/News/Articles/2022/03/09/pr2269-ukraine-imf-executive-board-approves-usd-billion-in-emergency-financing-support-to-ukraine
21 Congressional Research Service, 'U.S. Security Assistance to Ukraine', 24 June 2022. https://crsreports.congress.gov/product/pdf/IF/IF12040
22 Valentyna Romanova and Andreas Umland, 'Ukraine's Decentralisation Reforms Since 2014 Initial Achievements and Future Challenges', Chatham House, September 2019. https://www.chathamhouse.org/sites/default/files/2019-09-24-UkraineDecentralization.pdf
23 John Lough and Vladimir Dubrovskiy, 'Are Ukraine's Anti-corruption Reforms Working?', Chatham House, November 2018. https://www.chathamhouse.org/sites/default/files/2021-04/2018-11-19-are-ukraine-anticorruption-reforms-working-lough.pdf
24 Carl Von Clausewitz, *On War*, translated by Michael Howard and Peter Paret (New Jersey: Princeton University Press, 2008), p. 86.
25 Clausewitz, *On War* (2008), p. 182.
26 'Syria Chemical Attack: what we know', BBC News, 24 September 2013. https://www.bbc.com/news/world-middle-east-39500947
27 'Russia's Valery Gergiev conducts concert in Palmyra ruins', BBC News, 5 May 2016. https://www.bbc.com/news/world-middle-east-36211449

CHAPTER 8: ZELENSKY'S DESTINY

1 Robyn Dixon and Natalie Gryvnyak, 'Ukraine's Zelensky wants to end a war in the east. His problem: No one agrees how to do it', *Washington Post*, 19 March 2020. https://www.washingtonpost.com/world/europe/ukraines-zelensky-wants-to-end-a-war-in-the-east-his-problem-no-one-agrees-how-to-do-it/2020/03/19/ae653cbc-6399-11ea-8a8e-5c5336b32760_story.html
2 'Read Trump's phone conversation with Volodymyr Zelensky', CNN, 26 September 2019. https://edition.cnn.com/2019/09/25/politics/donald-trump-ukraine-transcript-call/index.html
3 'John McCain at the base of regiment "Dnipro-1" V.2.0', 2015. https://www.youtube.com/watch?v=yVUMjapUEoE
4 'John McCain: "Ashamed of my country" over Ukraine response', 23 February 2015. https://www.youtube.com/watch?v=wBvFsrG92n0
5 'Ukraine's Zelensky calls for direct talks with Russia "to end war"', *France24*, 1 December 2021. https://www.france24.com/en/europe/20211201-ukraine-s-zelensky-calls-for-direct-talks-with-russia-to-end-war

6   Special Monitoring Mission to Ukraine, 'January–March 2021 Trends and Observations', Organization for Security and Co-operation in Europe, 5 May 2021. https://www.osce.org/special-monitoring-mission-to-ukraine

7   Alvydas Medalinskas, 'Kremlin TV Chief: Russia Must Annex East Ukraine', Atlantic Council, 9 February 2021. https://www.atlanticcouncil.org/blogs/ukrainealert/kremlin-tv-chief-russia-must-annex-east-ukraine/

8   Mike Eckel, 'In First Interview Since Departure, Russia's Former "Gray Cardinal" Questions Existence Of Ukraine', Radio Free Europe, 26 February 2020. https://www.rferl.org/a/in-first-interview-since-departure-russia-s-former-gray-cardinal-questions-existence-of-ukraine/30456301.html

9   'Putin's interview to TASS: Putin says Russia, Ukraine torn apart to prevent major rival from emerging', TASS, 21 February 2020. https://tass.com/politics/1122727?utm_source=rferl.org&utm_medium=referral&utm_campaign=rferl.org&utm_referrer=rferl.org

10 Dimitri Medvedev, 'Why contacts with the current Ukrainian leadership are meaningless: Five short polemical theses', Kommersant, 11 October 2021. https://www.kommersant.ru/doc/5028300

11 'Readout of President Biden's Video Call with President Vladimir Putin of Russia', 7 December 2021. https://www.whitehouse.gov/briefing-room/statements-releases/2021/12/07/readout-of-president-bidens-video-call-with-president-vladimir-putin-of-russia/

12 'Press release on Russian draft documents on legal security guarantees from the United States and NATO', 17 December 2021. https://www.mid.ru/en/foreign_policy/news/1790809/

13 US State Department Cable; 'RUSSIA-UKRAINE: NATO AND HOLODOMOR 2008 April 3 – BURNS', released by Wikileaks.

14 'Blinken announces US has delivered written responses to Russia over Ukraine crisis', CNN, 27 January 2022. https://edition.cnn.com/2022/01/26/politics/us-russia-ukraine/index.html

15 'Ukraine crisis: Biden warns Russia may invade next month', BBC News, 28 January 2022. https://www.bbc.com/news/world-europe-60164537

16 'Zelensky in Munich demands security guarantees, calls for pre-emptive sanctions against Russia', Kyiv Independent, 19 February 2022. https://kyivindependent.com/national/zelensky-in-munich-demands-security-guarantees-calls-for-preemptive-sanctions-against-russia

17 'Joint Statement of the Russian Federation and the People's Republic of China on the International Relations Entering a New Era and the Global Sustainable Development', Russian Government, 4 February 2022. http://en.kremlin.ru/supplement/5770

18 'Zelensky's full speech at Munich Security Conference', Kyiv Independent, 19 February 2022. https://kyivindependent.com/national/zelenskys-full-speech-at-munich-security-conference/

19 'Biden says Zelensky, Ukraine "didn't want to hear" U.S. warnings of invasion', Washington Post, 11 June 2022. https://www.washingtonpost.com/politics/2022/06/11/biden-zelensky-russia-invasion-warnings-putin/

20 Alexander Zhuchkovsky, 29 April 2022. https://vk.com/juchkovsky

21 'Relations with Ukraine. Last updated 15 June 2022', NATO [this page has since been removed and was accessed by the author in March 2022]. https://www.nato.int/cps/en/natohq/topics_37750.htm

22 'CONSTITUTION OF UKRAINE Adopted at the Fifth Session of the Verkhovna Rada of Ukraine on June 28, 1996 Amended by the Laws of Ukraine No. 2222-IV dated December 8, 2004, No. 2952-VI dated February 1, 2011, No. 586-VII dated September 19, 2013, No. 742-VII dated February 21, 2014, No. 1401-VIII dated June 2, 2016, No. 2680-VIII dated February 7, 2019'. https://www.refworld.org/pdfid/44a280124.pdf

23 'Defence Department Announces $125M for Ukraine', United States Department of Defence, 1 March 2021. https://www.defense.gov/News/Releases/Release/Article/2519445/defense-department-announces-125m-for-ukraine/

24 Michael Walzer, Just and Unjust Wars: A Moral Argument with Historical Illustrations (New York: Basic Books, 2006), pp. 58, 72, 108.

25 Samantha Berkhead and Pjotr Sauer, 'Russia Issues Demands to Limit NATO's Influence in Post-Soviet Space, Eastern Europe', Moscow Times, 20 December 2021. https://www.themoscowtimes.com/2021/12/17/russia-issues-demands-to-limit-natos-influence-in-post-soviet-space-eastern-europe-a75857

26 Tweeted by Ned Price, State Department Spokesman, 2:13 a.m., 21 February 2022: https://twitter.com/StateDeptSpox/status/1495461649683202051

27 Robert Hunter, 'The Ukraine Crisis: Why and What Now?', Survival, 4 February 2022, pp. 16, 20.

28 Rodric Braithwaite, 'The Ukraine Crisis: Why and What Now?', Survival, 4 February 2022, p. 41.

29 Zaheena Rasheed, Ali Harb, Umut Uras and Federica Marsi, 'Russia-Ukraine latest updates: Raid hits Mariupol theatre', Al Jazeera, 15 March 2022. https://www.aljazeera.com/news/2022/3/15/biden-approves-billions-in-historic-aid-to-ukraine-liveblog

30 Ken Booth, Strategy and Ethnocentrism (New York: Routledge, 1979).

CHAPTER 9: WAR OF CONQUEST

1 Simon Shuster, 'Inside Zelensky's world', *Time*, 28 April 2022. https://time.com/6171277/volodymyr-zelensky-interview-ukraine-war/

2 Glen Kessler, 'Zelensky's famous quote of 'need ammo, not a ride' not easily confirmed', *Washington Post*, 6 March 2022. https://www.washingtonpost.com/politics/2022/03/06/zelenskys-famous-quote-need-ammo-not-ride-not-easily-confirmed/

3 @ZelenskyyUa, 5:54 p.m., 24 February 2022. https://twitter.com/ZelenskyyUa/status/1496785547594924032

4 @Vitaliy_Klychko, 4:26 p.m., 26 February 2022. https://twitter.com/Vitaliy_Klychko/status/1497488342002323461

5 @Klitschko, 11:29 and 11.34 p.m., 24 February 2022. https://twitter.com/Klitschko/status/1496869988917182470 with italics added for emphasis in the quotation only.

6 Mason Clark, George Barros, Kateryna Stepanenko, 'Russian Offensive Campaign Assessment', Institute for the Study of War, 16 March 2022. https://www.understandingwar.org/backgrounder/russian-offensive-campaign-assessment-march-16

7 World Bank, 'Cities in Europe and Central Asia: Ukraine'. Data ending in 2014. https://documents1.worldbank.org/curated/en/294341511956937400/pdf/121735-BRI-P154478-PUBLIC-Ukraine-Snapshot-Print.pdf

8 @Vitaly_Klychko, 4:34 p.m., 18 March 2022. https://twitter.com/Vitaliy_Klychko/status/1504738035765813248

9 Mark Urban, 'The heavy losses of an elite Russian regiment in Ukraine', BBC News, 2 April 2022. https://www.bbc.com/news/world-europe-60946340

10 'U.S. plane brings Javelin missiles and launchers to Ukraine', Reuters, 25 January 2022. https://www.reuters.com/world/europe/us-plane-brings-military-equipment-munitions-ukraine-2022-01-25/

11 'Ukraine to produce Turkish armed drones: Minister', Al Jazeera, 7 October 2021. https://www.aljazeera.com/news/2021/10/7/ukraine-to-produce-turkish-armed-drones-minister

12 'Russian airborne troops land in Ukraine Kharkiv, clashes erupt', Al Jazeera, 2 March 2022. https://www.aljazeera.com/news/2022/3/2/russian-airborne-troops-land-in-ukraines-second-city-kharkiv

13 Jeremy Bowen, 'Ukraine war: Kyiv terrain will slow Russian troops, say Ukraine generals', BBC News, 15 March 2022. https://www.bbc.com/news/world-europe-60745493

14 Gil Hoffman, 'Kyiv's mayor learns from the IDF how to defend Ukraine', *Jerusalem Post*, 11 March 2022. https://www.jpost.com/international/article-700968

15 Dan Sabbagh, 'As Russia tries to focus its offensive, Ukraine seeks to scattergun', *The Guardian*, 28 March 2022. https://www.theguardian.com/world/2022/mar/28/as-russia-tries-to-focus-its-offensive-ukraine-seeks-to-scattergun

16 'Top Russian general claims military efforts now centred on eastern part of Ukraine', CNN, 25 March 2022. https://edition.cnn.com/europe/live-news/ukraine-russia-putin-news-03-25-22/h_c643e508161e80821fff786bbbfbc16e

17 Douglas Barrie and Nick Childs, 'The *Moskva* incident and its wider implications', IISS, https://www.iiss.org/blogs/military-balance/2022/04/the-moskva-incident-and-its-wider-implications

18 Hew Strachan, 'The lost meaning of strategy', *Survival* (Vol. 47, No. 3, 2005), pp. 33–5.

19 Luttwak: 'The entire realm of strategy is pervaded by a paradoxical logic very different from the ordinary "linear" logic by which we live in all other spheres of life.' Edward Luttwak, *Strategy: The Logic of War and Peace, Second Edition* (Cambridge, Mass.: The Belknap Press of Harvard University Press, 2001).

20 Freedman: 'By and large, strategy comes into play where there is actual or potential conflict, when interests collide … Strategy is also frequently presented as a duel, a clash of two opposing wills.' Lawrence Freedman, *Strategy: A History* (Oxford: Oxford University Press, 2013).

21 Colin S. Gray, 'Why strategy is difficult' in Thomas G. Mahnken and Joseph A. Maiolo (eds), *Strategic Studies: A Reader, Second Edition* (London and New York: Routledge, 2014), pp. 40–48.

22 Helene Cooper and Eric Schmitt, 'Russia's War Lacks a Battlefield Commander, U.S. Officials Say', *New York Times*, 31 March 2022. https://www.nytimes.com/2022/03/31/us/politics/russia-military-ukraine.html

23 Larisa Brown, 'Senior Russian commanders fired for military failures', *The Times*, 19 May 2022. Citing a report issued by the UK Ministry of Defence's Defence Intelligence Staff. https://www.thetimes.co.uk/article/fleet-commander-may-be-under-arrest-after-moskva-sinking-8ss25rgg2

24 'Russia has said that the bodies of 152 Ukrainian soldiers were found in Azovstal. They promise to hand them over to Ukraine', BBC News Ukrainian, 31 May 2022. https://www.bbc.com/ukrainian/news-61643297

25 Niccolò Machiavelli, *The Prince* (London: Penguin Great Ideas series, 2005), pp. 21, 40.

26 Martin Van Creveld, *Technology and War: From 2000 B.C. to the Present* (New York: The Free Press, a division of Simon & Schuster Inc., 1991), p. 266.

27 Samir Puri, *Fighting and Negotiating with Armed Groups*, IISS Adelphi Book 459 (Oxon: Routledge, 2016). See section entitled 'Russia: playing politics and war to quell Chechnya's rebellion'.

28 Samir Puri, 'Russia could still salvage victory in Ukraine', *Wall Street Journal*, 30 March 2022. https://www.

wsj.com/articles/putin-salvage-victory-in-ukraine-russia-invasion-takeover-war-division-destabilize-turkey-peace-ceasefire-negotiations-talks-donbas-crimea-nato-us-security-guarantees-11648674411

29 'ICC sends 42-member team to probe alleged war crimes in Ukraine', Al Jazeera, 17 May 2022. https://www.aljazeera.com/news/2022/5/17/icc-sends-largest-ever-investigative-team-to-war-torn-ukraine

30 Jake Tapper, 'Top international prosecutor speaks to CNN after visiting Bucha', CNN, 14 April 2022. https://edition.cnn.com/videos/world/2022/04/14/karim-khan-international-war-crimes-prosecutor-ukraine-sot-lead-vpx.cnn

31 Sarah Rainsford, 'Russian soldier pleads guilty in first war crimes trial of Ukraine conflict', BBC News, 18 May 2022. https://www.bbc.com/news/world-europe-61496428

32 Clive Myrie, 'Ukraine war: BBC interview with Russian ambassador to the UK', BBC News, 29 May 2022. https://www.bbc.com/news/av/world-europe-61623278

33 Caroline Davis, 'Ukraine war: Resistance to Russian rouble in Kherson', BBC News, 1 May 2022. https://www.bbc.com/news/world-europe-61286505

34 Laurence Peter, 'Ukraine says giant Zaporizhzhia nuclear plant can't supply Russia', BBC News, 20 May 2022. https://www.bbc.com/news/world-europe-61524376

35 'Russian-Ukrainian talks to be continued online on March 14 — Kremlin spokesman', TASS, 14 March 2022. https://tass.com/politics/1421507

36 'Russia Sees "Progress" at Conflict Talks With Ukraine', Moscow Times, 13 March 2022. https://www.themoscowtimes.com/2022/03/13/russia-sees-progress-at-conflict-talks-with-ukraine-a76901

37 'Ukraine official says Russia talks are very difficult, sees room for compromise', Reuters, 15 March 2022. https://www.reuters.com/article/us-ukraine-crisis-negotiations-compromis-idAFKCN2LC2G4

38 'Lavrov: Russia doesn't plan to attack other countries', Euronews, 10 March 2022. https://www.euronews.com/2022/03/10/lavrov-russia-doesn-t-plan-to-attack-other-countries-and-did-not-attack-ukraine

39 'Kremlin says Russian military operation to stop "in any moment" if Kiev meets conditions', TASS, 7 March 2022. https://tass.com/politics/1418257?utm_source=google.com&utm_medium=organic&utm_campaign=google.com&utm_referrer=google.com

40 Simon Shuster, 'Inside Zelensky's world' (2022).

CHAPTER 10: ROAD TO RUIN

1 Civilian casualties in Ukraine 14 April 2014 to 31 December 2021. United Nations Human Right Office of the High Commissioner, United Nations, 'Conflict-related civilian casualties in Ukraine, 27 January 2022', p. 3. https://ukraine.un.org/sites/default/files/2022-02/Conflict-related%20civilian%20casualties%20as%20of%2031%20December%202021%20%28rev%2027%20January%202022%29%20corr%20EN_0.pdf

2 UN High Commissioner for Human Rights, 'Ukraine: civilian casualty update 12 July 2022'. https://www.ohchr.org/en/news/2022/07/ukraine-civilian-casualty-update-12-july-2022

3 'Latest from OSCE Special Monitoring Mission (SMM) to Ukraine based on information received as of 18:00 (Kyiv time), 11 February 2015', OSCE, 12 February 2015. https://www.osce.org/ukraine-smm/140271

4 'Ukraine bid to join EU will take decades says Macron', BBC News, 10 May 2022. https://www.bbc.co.uk/news/world-europe-61383632

5 Jennifer Rankin, '"Ukraine's future is in the EU": Zelensky welcomes granting of candidate status', The Guardian, 23 June 2022. https://www.theguardian.com/world/2022/jun/23/eu-leaders-ukraine-candidate-status-russian-attack

6 Ekaterina Grobman, 'Russians more often talk about supporting the special operation', Vedomosti, 28 June 2022. https://www.vedomosti.ru/society/articles/2022/06/28/928943-rossiyane-podderzhke-spetsoperatsii?utm_campaign=newspaper_29_6_2022&utm_medium=email&utm_source=vedomosti

7 'Opening speech by NATO Secretary General Jens Stoltenberg at the High-Level Dialogue on Climate and Security, NATO Public Forum', 28 June 2022. https://www.nato.int/cps/en/natohq/opinions_197168.htm

8 Dan Murtaugh and Debjit Chakraborty, 'China and India Funnel $24 Billion to Putin in Energy Spree', Bloomberg UK, 6 July 2022. https://www.bloomberg.com/news/articles/2022-07-06/china-and-india-funnel-24-billion-to-putin-with-energy-spree

9 Zbigniew Brzezinski, The Grand Chessboard: American Primacy and its Geostrategic Imperatives (New York: Basic Books, 1997).

ACKNOWLEDGEMENTS

As strange as it sounds, I never wanted to write this book but felt compelled to do so after watching from afar the tragedy of Russia's invasion. I had reams of unpublished personal notes and diaries to draw on from my work in Ukraine, and I wrote this book to help me make sense of the background behind the unfolding catastrophe. I hope it helps others to do the same. The advance payment I received for this book has been donated to charities responding to Ukraine's humanitarian crisis.

Rapidity was the key to writing this book and I thank Darryl Samaraweera at Artellus and Olivia Beattie at Biteback for believing that it could be done. Ryan Norman at Biteback provided first-rate editorial input, working at pace to match our ambitious timetable. Gratitude is also due to those involved in typesetting, proofreading, cover design and publicity.

Over many years, my Ukrainian friends and colleagues taught me more about their country than I would ever have gleaned from arriving at Boryspil and remaining with my outsider assumptions. A big thanks goes to Svetlana Chastinakova, whom I worked with as a translator in the first Donbas war in 2014–15, and who in 2022, having escaped under immense difficulty from the jaws of Russia's invasion, generously answered my call to assist me with this book.

Further back in time, I thank James Blair and Tim Baines for getting me involved in election monitoring in 2004.

How do you read a madman's mind? Teach me the art of war. Copious amounts of *Senjutsu* was consumed during the marathon writing process, essential to keeping going during the monastic days of authorship.

Which is why the warmest thanks of all go to the A-Team, Anna and little Asmi, who only arrived in 2022, and who generously accepted my long mental absences over several intense months of writing. I thank them profoundly. May Asmi never witness what so many have been forced to see this year. *Finis belli.*

INDEX